Headlines All My Life

This photograph was taken by BARON in 1954 as a fiftieth birthday
gift; it also celebrated my twenty-first anniversary as an editor.

ARTHUR CHRISTIANSEN

Headlines All My Life

HEINEMANN

LONDON   MELBOURNE   TORONTO

William Heinemann Ltd

LONDON   MELBOURNE   TORONTO

CAPE TOWN   AUCKLAND

THE HAGUE

First published 1961

© Arthur Christiansen 1961

Printed in Great Britain
by The Windmill Press Ltd
Kingswood, Surrey

To the Wives of Newspapermen Everywhere

Contents

Illustrations

ix

Foreword

A newspaper editor is three people.

He is a behind-the-scenes observer of great men and great events, who often knows as much about the nation's business as the men who conduct it and who can, directly or indirectly, wield great power through his newspaper.

Next, he is a dedicated technician for whom the blank columns of tomorrow's newspaper are an ever-renewed challenge and excitement.

Finally, he is an ordinary man, with his average share of success and failure, remembering events great and small with the random selection of fallible human memory.

Any of these three men can write a book. I thought that in my case the last should be first, because on my retirement from Fleet Street my memories were so personal and so pleasurable that they took priority over the other aspects of my career.

It may be that one day characters One and Two will write their autobiographies too; but for the moment, set down in affection and enthusiasm, here is my purely personal story. After all, on the newspaper I edited for nearly twenty-five years we always went for the human angle first.

1 . . . The Fleet Street Story

One foggy January afternoon in 1949 I travelled from London to Derby where Arsenal were playing Derby County in the Football Association Cup. I am a Soccer fan and an Arsenal supporter, and made the journey eagerly despite the fact that fog threatened to postpone the match. At Euston Station Sir Bracewell Smith, the blunt and jovial chairman of Arsenal, had chided me about some criticism in the *Daily Express* directed at Tom Whitaker, the Arsenal manager. 'You shouldn't be so rough on Tom,' he said.

'Write to me at my office,' I retorted. 'I'm here as a football fan, not as an editor.'

But when hours and hours later the train crawled into Derby and I walked through its sad streets to the County ground, I realised that there was no escape for me. I was an editor. I could not shed my load just because it was Saturday afternoon. The people who lived behind those clean lace curtains in row after row of identical boxes were newspaper readers, and every word that appeared in at any rate *my* newspaper must be clear and comprehensible to them, must be interesting to them, must encourage them to break away from littleness, stimulate their ambition, help them to want to build a better land.

When I got back to Fleet Street I put my views on record in one of the staff bulletins, pinned up as usual in the glass box in the Big

1

Room, where the reporters and sub-editors work side by side. The bulletin this day was headed: REMEMBER THE PEOPLE IN THE BACK STREETS OF DERBY.

Some time later my wife and I were in Rhyl. We left the car to walk along the sunny promenade crowded with people from Liverpool and Manchester and other even less salubrious Lancashire towns. Their flat, sallow northern faces, their Sunday-best clothes, their curious capacity for enjoying themselves without displaying any sign of emotion, moved me – people in the mass always do. I saw them all as a challenge. It was my job to interest them in everything that was happening, to make the arrival of the *Daily Express* each morning an event, to show them the world outside Bolton and Bacup, to fire them with the ambition to travel, to give them the courage and confidence to overcome the drabness of their lives, and to show them *how* to overcome it.

When I returned to London I dictated another bulletin. In it I described a composite Englishman and I called him THE MAN ON THE RHYL PROMENADE.

Everyone pulled my leg, for people in Fleet Street pretend to be just as unimpressionable as the people who live in Derby or take their holidays in Rhyl. When I went on to the 'stone' which is where a newspaper is assembled into type, even the printers chaffed me about the people in the back streets of Derby and on Rhyl Promenade. But the mood took hold. Headlines, writing, thinking, phrasing, lay-out, recipes, fashion, all came under the ruthless test of whether they would be comprehensible to the people of Derby and Rhyl. I sent Anne Edwards, the Women's Editor, almost direct from the Paris fashion shows to spend a week in Wigan. My purpose was twofold: to give her a glimpse of Wigan's newspaper requirements, and to tell the rest of our four million readers what went on in that town beloved of music-hall comedians. (The visit made such an impression on Miss Edwards that after my retirement from the editorship she addressed herself to the people in the back-streets of Wigan when writing an article on the Royal Family.)

You may, of course, say 'What a fuss about a phrase!' But ideas are invariably simple. It is the drive that goes into carrying them out that counts, and to me it has always been the ordinary people, the human story, the news behind the news, that has served to throw the important events into relief. This was the guiding principle throughout my years in journalism. News not only written *about* but written *for* those Great Unknowns of this country, the readers of the so-called 'popular' newspapers.

When I retired from the editorship of the *Daily Express*, the staff presented me with two photographs. One showed the mean streets of Derby taken from the roof-tops, the other showed Rhyl Promenade on a wet day.

I sprang from such a place myself. For Derby, read Wallasey in Cheshire, where I was born; for Rhyl, read Douglas, Isle of Man, where with my mother I spent the first holiday I ever had when I was about fourteen years old. My father could not come with us; there were then no holidays with pay for manual workers and he had to work through our week's holiday in Douglas. He could only afford a day excursion from Liverpool to bring us home. My parents knew what it was like to scrape and strive and sacrifice for the sake of their children. They epitomised the people of Derby and Rhyl.

When Beverley Baxter left the editor's chair vacant in the *Daily Express* building after ten distinguished years of office he had said, 'The trouble with you, Chris, is that you reduce journalism to a formula. Everybody is expected to write your way. You don't allow anybody to be himself. The result is glossy and brilliant, but it's soulless. It's no good.'

I admit that I did try to impose my will on all and sundry. In the thirties I dictated boxing stories to that master of the ring newscraft, Trevor Wignall. In the forties I encouraged Alan Moorehead, the greatest correspondent of the Second World War, to look for detail, to describe the flowers that grew in the desert, oblivious of man, while the big battles raged. In the fifties I put dozens of people who are household names through the wringer and moulded them my way. Throughout the years I bullied the critics, like James Agate, Daniel George, John Pudney, Paul Holt, Jonah Barrington, Leonard Mosley, John Barber, Nancy Spain, into telling the news even though they aired their views. Some were amenable, some were not. For those who were not the association with the paper came to an end quickly enough – the incorrigible

Agate being the shining exception.

'Take it away and re-write it this way,' I would say. 'What do you think the reader will understand by this sentence? What's the readable angle? Do it this way, make it exciting.' Thus it was that with strong language, laughter and a strong-willed arrogance, the *Daily Express* came out.

Fleet Street is to me a street of dreaming spires. The only spire in it, seen from the Editor's room at the *Express* office, ennobles St Bride's Church – the Germans failed to knock it down in the 1940 blitz – but to me the Street is all spires and all beauty. Nowhere else in the world does its like exist. In New York they publish their newspapers just anywhere, and so they do in Paris, in Tokio, and in every other capital. In London, newspaper people have gathered together to create their own village. They have their own pubs, their own clubs, their own language, in which words like spike and pica and ems and ens and nuts and indents and splashes and clocks, all have special meanings that outsiders would not understand.

When I retired I was asked to write about my beloved Fleet Street. So here it is – an entirely personal story that is in no sense a history of a newspaper, a proprietor, or an era. You will have to come the whole journey from Wallasey with me, because it was there that the foundations were laid.

2 . . . Boy, Wash the Steps!

My grandfather was Danish. Lord Beaverbrook, in what he calls 'high good humour', used sometimes to introduce me to his guests, particularly if they were farmers, as 'Mr Christiansen the foreigner who edits my chief newspaper'. My reputation as a Dane-baiter pursued me even into retirement, for when I visited Copenhagen in 1959 an interview published in *Berlingske Tidende* was headed: DENMARK'S UNFRIEND NO. 1 IN BRITISH PRESS.

'Unfriend' is a fine word (it means, I was told, something just short of 'Public Enemy') but after describing my 'light-waved poet's locks', the interviewer wrote: 'So sympathetic is the effect of this charming gentleman that you can hardly believe him responsible for the bad things his newspaper has been writing about Denmark through the years.'

The Danes blamed Lord Beaverbrook for the anti-Danish agricultural policies of the *Daily Express*, but they were puzzled that a man with a name like mine should act as devil's advocate. Every so often Count Reventlow, the Danish Ambassador in London, would invite me to lunch at the Embassy and sometime after the entrée I knew he would say, 'If you did not buy our bacon we could not buy your coal.' Always these words were accompanied by a weary but patient smile, as though I were the black sheep of the family who might yet be saved from perdition.

When I went to Denmark for the first time in 1938, armed with the family album to search for the origin of the Christiansen species, a reporter boarded the train at the seaport of Esbjerg and interviewed me as we sped to Copenhagen. Photographers flashlighted us at the family birthplace, Middelfart, which means Middletown, and is half-way on the journey across Denmark. Ivan Opffer, one of Denmark's top artists, sketched me for the front page of *Politiken*. The headlines banked high.

The Danes publicised the search for my forbears so vigorously that no less than seventeen hundred Christiansens claimed relationship before two days of my visit had passed, and when the claimants were reduced to five families I was much relieved.

The man in charge of the search was yet another Christiansen – Einar Christiansen, a former London correspondent of *Politiken*. He sent me a photograph of a vast crowd in a Copenhagen square which bore the caption:

The scene last night as thousands of people named Christiansen besieged the offices of *Politiken* claiming relationship with Arthur Christiansen, chief editor of Lord Beaverbrook, the arch-enemy of Danish agriculture.

The photograph had in fact been taken on the return of Danish athletes chosen to represent their country at the Olympic Games in Los Angeles!

Like all families, the Christiansens had had their ups and downs, and had become scattered through distance, family disputes, and so on. Cousin Andrea was a frail widow who seemed to have been born to trouble. Uncle Christian had spent his entire working life on the Danish State Railways. Uncle Rasmus was, at seventy-two, a towering red-headed ex-sailor who fell for my wife so heavily that it was clear he must in his day have had 'a girl in every port'. Another uncle was a third generation leaseholder of an eel fishery at a heavenly inland lake between Middelfart and Odense, the birthplace of Hans Andersen. And finally Great Aunt Jo Jacobsen had married one of the Carlsberg brewery Jacobsens, whose millions have enriched Danish culture, and endowed museums, art galleries, universities and many other forms of artistic life in Copenhagen.

Whatever family schisms existed, they were all dropped on my arrival, and under the guidance of Einar Christiansen, my wife and I toured from relative to relative. The Union Jack flew proudly in the garden of every home we visited. Tables were decorated with red and white flowers, the national colours of Denmark. Ducks were killed and roasted for the occasion. Toasts were drunk in schnapps and claret. Speeches of considerable length were made which taxed Einar's powers as an interpreter. If I had been Hans Andersen reincarnated, I could not have been more affectionately received.

Fru Jo Jacobsen was clearly the leader of the family. She recalled that at one time the family were known as the 'Engels', or the English, and she thought that the mixture of the bloods of the two nations accounted for our individualistic personalities. She was a strikingly handsome woman in her early fifties when we met. She had long since divorced her husband (a habit not uncommon in Denmark) and was an authoress of distinction – the only other link with any form of journalism that I could trace in my family. She took us to visit her son Carl, a farmer in Jutland, where we stayed for a week studying on the spot the efficiencies of Danish farming. Then I returned to England to resume the direction of Lord Beaverbrook's campaign to tie up the home market for the British farmer. I was not in the least sorry to be a quarter Danish. Nor, for that matter, to be three-quarters English.

Before this time I had not been particularly interested in Niels Christiansen, my father's father, a strong powerfully-built Dane who had died of lockjaw before I was born in 1904. He had led my father the harsh life that seems to have typified the Victorian attitude to children, and my father had left home young to become a shipwright rather than stay in the grocery business set up by my grandfather when he retired from the sea in the 1870s. A pity this, for whereas there were at one time three Christiansen grocery shops – surely the makings of a modern 'chain' – my father's chosen trade was always the victim of boom and slump in world trade. When I was first conscious of the power of money, my father was glad to earn an occasional extra eight shillings on his day off for pulling a ship in at the Birkenhead Docks to augment his wages of thirty-eight shillings a week.

But I was not conscious of the fact that these were hard times. My elder sister Dorothy and I were happy with, first, our Saturday ha'penny, then our Saturday penny, pocket money. We were by no means the poorest of the residents in Evelyn Road, Seacombe, a street of privet-hedged, six-roomed terraced houses, occupied by ship's officers, clerks, master-tailors and post office officials. Dorothy took piano lessons at a guinea a quarter from the best music teacher in the district. I was taught the piano by my Uncle Sam, a schoolmaster who lived with us, occupying the front parlour and the back bedroom. The rent of the house was less than ten shillings a week, and while there was nothing to spare for such luxuries as that much coveted bicycle that every boy dreams about, we lived well enough.

As far back as I can remember I was going to be 'an author'. When at the age of eight I fell into two feet of water in the boating lake at Wallasey Central Park, my mother, carrying me home wringing wet, proclaimed to anyone who would listen that one day the incident would be featured in my reminiscences – at least this is what she told me when I announced my intention of writing this book, and I am delighted to oblige her.

Physically my mother and I are as alike as two peas, with thin lips (although we both laugh easily) broad foreheads and *retroussé* noses which happily have broadened and bent a bit as we have grown older. Mentally we are even more alike, for whereas my father was the shyest and most retiring of men, my mother and I have a tendency to 'show off', given the right audience. Our minds never settle for long on any one subject – a shrewd Fleet Street character once flatteringly described me as 'ambi-mental'. We do not retain knowledge readily – 'in one ear and out of the other' is the appropriate *cliché* – but we are constantly moved to 'improve' ourselves. I think that when I produced the *Daily Express* I had my mother almost as much in mind as my proprietor.

I suppose that I started preparing to be an editor at the age of twelve when I won one of the sixteen annual scholarships awarded to the local Grammar School among Wallasey's brightest four hundred boys, and met Eric Edwards, a classmate whose father was

Sports Editor of the *Liverpool Echo*.

Even then I was completely consumed by and entirely enamoured of newspapers. We took the Manchester *Daily Dispatch* at home, but I often bought a copy of a London paper, either the *Daily Chronicle* or the *Daily News*, which seemed to me to have the Fleet Street touch. (None of these newspapers exists under its old title today.) I haunted the Wallasey Public Library and read its surprisingly extensive range of books on the technique of journalism, some of them American. I inveigled my mother into subscribing to a postal course in short story writing on hire purchase – ten shillings and sixpence a lesson for twenty-four lessons instead of a lump sum of ten guineas, which we could not have found – and only gave it up when the third lesson seemed no more instructive than some of the three-and-sixpenny textbooks published by Newnes and C. Arthur Pearson.

But to meet the real live son of a real live journalist – and a sports editor at that! – was more than a stroke of luck, it was an act of providence. I imposed my friendship on the amiable Eric Edwards until he finally invited me to his home. By now it was 1917, when the First World War fortunes of the British were at their lowest. I was still personally mourning Kitchener's death and had his photograph on the bedroom wall over my bed. We were eating black bread; seed potatoes at the week-end were a luxury. Butter was unknown; a margarine called 'Brito' did instead. But the Edwards family shared their rations with me and I ate them shamelessly and regularly while awaiting the return of the great man himself from his labours at the *Echo* office.

Ernest Edwards, who for thirty years wrote a sports column under the pseudonym 'Bee', was the inspiration of my journalism. He was a big-hearted, squarely-built Midlander with a weather-tanned ruddy face, acquired no doubt in the exposed Press boxes of those days, for when I was a boy I never saw him drink, nor take more than a small Scotch when I myself had learned what it was to drink in Fleet Street. He exuded confidence. He had a broad, generous lower lip, and smiled and smiled with it. He was adored by his family – his wife, his two sons, his daughter, a dependent relative, and Ike, his dog. He had such a sense of family that he imparted it to me too, and I have tried always to induce his sense of family around my own hearth – when the newspaper permitted me to be there.

Ernest Edwards made me one of his family when he saw how desperately I wanted to become a journalist. He took me to the Claremont Road Wesleyan Church – my first return to Church since I had screamed with fear at the age of four because I understood the preacher to say that the Christian*sens* were to be thrown to the lions – and made me take down the sermons in shorthand. He read and criticised my articles – and even published one in 1918 (fee: one guinea) entitled 'Get Off the Field'. It was a plea to allotment holders to allow the playing fields to revert to their pre-war use so that returning soldiers could play soccer, a plea that caused a vast correspondence in which I was described as a 'muddied oaf' and a 'flannelled fool'.

These activities occupied more of my time than my lessons. I found that I had enough talent to sit in the first half-dozen in a class of thirty without straining too hard, so I became editor and author simultaneously. Throughout my schooldays, I produced a class magazine modelled on the most famous boys' magazines of those days. I wrote the short stories, based on Billy Bunter. I wrote the Boy Scout news, although I was never a Scout. I wrote a feature called 'The Editor's Chat'. I reported the school and class sporting occasions and wrote that A. Christiansen played well – I was the school goalkeeper at fifteen – when I did so. I laid out the magazine in columns so that even in handwriting it looked a professional job. I wrote the headlines and drew the illustrations. And finally I stitched the whole thing together on my mother's sewing machine and 'sold' it for current copies of *The Magnet*, *The Gem*, the *Union Jack Library* and Amalgamated Press bloodcurdlers of such ferocity that they would send a tingle of dismay down the spines of the TV-crazed parents of today.

In my 'spare' time I contributed half-crown paragraphs to a feature called 'Echoes of the Day' in the *Liverpool Echo*, and ambitiously bombarded the Sunday papers with articles. Once I was wildly excited to receive a letter signed 'J. Meares, Northern Editor', on *Sunday Chronicle* notepaper. It said: 'I am sorry we can't make use of your article "A Schoolboy replies to Robert Blatchford" as we have commissioned an article on the same subject by His Honour Judge Parry.'

To me and to my mother and father, this meant that if Judge Parry had not been writing, my article would have been published, especially as the article was about corporal punishment, which I (liable to be on the receiving end) favoured, while Blatchford, the Socialist sage, opposed it.

These replies to Robert Blatchford were a weekly occurrence and were written before I went to church on Sunday nights. Out of his overtime my father had been able to buy a piano – people buy TV sets now, but a piano was the thing then – and I used it as a desk. Every Monday morning my article was posted to the *Sunday Chronicle*. Every Thursday morning the article came back, with a printed rejection slip, save for that one occasion when Jimmy Meares – I gave him a job on the *Sunday Express* years later – wrote personally. Only once did I lose my patience. On that occasion I returned the article by the next post, demanding that the editor should send it to Mr Blatchford so that he could be aware of my views.

I did not hear from Mr Blatchford.

I had one other personal letter from an editor while I was still at school. It was to the effect that a serial story which I had written with an eye to publication in *Chums*, dealing with buried treasure in the South Seas, could not be published because Frank H. Shaw, whose writing everyone of my age or older will remember with affection, had just completed one on a similar theme. I took this letter to school with me every day, and when I was bored or baffled, which was frequently, took it out of my wallet and read it. I was caught one day at this day-dreaming by the chemistry master, W. A. Kynaston, and hauled from my bunsen-burner. 'Kynnie' confiscated my precious letter and stood there reading it. Suddenly his eyes blazed and his Edwardian moustaches bristled. 'Boys,' he exploded, stopping all activity, 'Chrissie here has very nearly had a serial accepted by *Chums*!'

But I wish that I had worked harder at school. When the time came to leave I did not attempt to enter for my School Leaving Certificate, then known as the Oxford and Cambridge Locals, because I would have failed in one of the basic subjects, mathematics. Of maths I knew nothing and cared less.

I could not wait to leave the Grammar School and did so soon
after my sixteenth birthday in 1920. Ernest Edwards got me an
interview with the editor of the *Liverpool Echo*, Ernest Hope Prince,
who, if he had accepted offers to go to Fleet Street, would undoubtedly have wrecked my subsequent career by himself becoming
Editor of the *Daily Express*.

Prince was a dandy with a cravat, spats, and hair dramatically
parted so wide in the middle that the parting might have been the
estuary of a river, preferably, of course, the Mersey. He saw me in a
cubby-hole that served for his office and our interview was punc-
tuated by printers and sub-editors arriving with proofs and page-
pulls.

The room stank of ink and cigarette smoke, but to me it was a
romantic boudoir. We got down immediately to what Northerners
call brass tacks. It was no good my thinking, said Prince, that I
could join a paper like the *Echo* straight from school and start half-
way up the ladder as a useful reporter. I would have to get a job
on a smaller paper altogether, a weekly, or something like that.
What good would I be to the *Echo*? On the other hand if he offered
me a job scrubbing the office steps I would be a fool not to take it,
because it was difficult to get a job of any kind in a newspaper office,
and if scrubbing the steps was the only way in, then scrub the steps
and like it, my boy. If you were going to become a journalist,
nothing would stop you. Nothing had stopped him. He had not
had to scrub the steps of the *Manchester Evening Chronicle* office,
but he would willingly have done so and that was his advice to me.
So get yourself a job, any kind of a job in a newspaper office, my
boy, and good luck and good day.

Many years later I heard Sir William Haley, the editor of *The
Times*, describe how he got his first job on that august journal – as
a £3-a-week shorthand telephonist taking down reporters' copy. To
reach the eminence of editorship, Haley went by way of the
Manchester Evening News and the B.B.C., but first he had got his
foot in the door of *The Times*.

I have since harangued hundreds of young fellows as Ernest
Hope Prince harangued me, and so no doubt has Haley. But at that
time it was a crushing blow that the great and mighty *Liverpool
Echo* did not want me, even to wash its front door step.

3 . . . Brother Blatchley Began It

The *Wallasey and Wirral Chronicle* office was at the dirty end of Borough Road, Seacombe. It was a good thing it was not press day when I called looking for a job, or I would have first started looking for the bomb, for on press days the whole rickety soot-stained building went into convulsions and gave the impression that at any moment it would disappear heavenwards. These tremors were caused by the starting up of the flatbed Wharfedale press, which had to be hand-fed with sheets of cut paper, and was so old that it protested in every nut and bolt as each copy of the *Chronicle* was completed.

It was said of the *Wallasey Chronicle*'s Wharfedale that it shook so much that the editor of the rival paper two hundred yards away felt the tremors and said 'Ah, the *Chronicle*'s gone to press – now let's get a scoop or two'. But I do not suppose the yarn to be true, for it was well known that, if the *Chronicle* was to be on sale on Saturday morning, printing had to start at 4 o'clock on Friday afternoon. The Wharfedale ran at a maximum speed of four hundred copies an hour. To print four thousand copies took ten hours (by comparison with the modern rotary press speed of fifty thousand an hour).

When I visited Wallasey after the 1939–45 war, a new press had been installed. But the old Wharfedale was still there. So was

Thomas Brown, the frugal manager. He obviously loved the Wharfedale, which had done so much for so many years – and for so few readers – and had preserved it in a corner of the machine shop as a museum piece. It was shown all the affection that could be lavished on a faithful servant. Which it was, as faithful after its fashion as 'Old Brown' himself.

When I opened the front door on that first day in July 1920, a bell jingled as if I had entered a draper's shop. I went up to the counter made of varnished wood and handed over a letter of introduction from Ernest Edwards to a downcast grey-headed man. He was what we now call the Advertisement Manager, but in 1920 he was known as 'The Canvasser'. He was paid £2 a week and one per cent commission, which could not have brought in more than an extra five or six shillings a week.

A minute after the letter passed, the editor was at the counter – a man with a rust-coloured head of hair, a rust-coloured moustache, a cherry-red nose, and such a cherry-red chin that he might have been suffering from a boil on it. In his mouth was a clay pipe. He was in his shirt-sleeves, his waistcoat was open, though joined by a gold watch-chain, and his suit was of blue serge. As with Sports Editor Edwards, I never saw him in any other kind of clothing.

'This note,' said the clay pipe (for the lips hardly moved), 'it comes from a man Ah disli-ike very mooch, but Ah moost not hold that against you –' (I will not try to keep up this attempt to imitate his Northern accent, because I have always loathed dialect spelling in books and newspapers).

Thereupon, without getting past the counter, I was hired: three years as an apprentice – fifteen shillings a week the first year, twenty-five shillings the second, and thirty-five shillings the third. The terms were translated into a six-line letter signed by 'Thos. Brown, Manager', and that was that; I was on my way to becoming a journalist. It was a big moment. All sense of humiliation at having to start work on a local weekly, instead of the mighty *Liverpool Echo* to which I aspired, disappeared. The fact that I had failed to impress Ernest Hope Prince, the editor of the *Echo*, into giving me a job was no longer important. I was on a paper. ON A PAPER! I had begun to be what I had set out to be, a newspaperman, a reporter. I WAS a newspaperman! I WAS a reporter! And I had just passed my sixteenth birthday.

My first assignment was to gather the facts about the death of a local churchman. The parlour blinds were drawn as the widow gave me the age of her late husband and details of his work. I felt more embarrassed than she, and reporting seemed to me to be a distasteful job. I went on to report the funeral and my story appeared in an issue of August 1920. It was long, thanks to the list of mourners and wreaths, and it began:

> The death occurred on Friday last of Mr W. E. Blatchley, for many years a leader of the Seacombe Brotherhood and Pleasant Sunday Afternoon Association which is attached to the Seacombe Congregational Church. Mr Blatchley was sixty-three years of age . . .

This was topped with the headlines:

BROTHER BLATCHLEY

WILLING WORKER FOR P. S. A.

These headlines were typical of the editor's technique. E. G. (Ted) Wilkinson believed in alliteration. Most of his headlines were alliterative. Thus any suicide in the district of Seacombe, no matter what the circumstances, was blazoned forth as

SORDID SEACOMBE
SUICIDE

The annual dinner of the Wallasey Conservative Club was headed annually CONVIVIAL CONSERVATIVES. The Magazine Bowling Club's hot-pot supper was always headlined MERRY MAGS. If Wilkinson could write a headline on a Poulton church meeting PROUD POULTON PARISHIONERS, his day was made. He wrote the headline WALLASEY WANT on an article I wrote demanding the formation of a professional football club in the district – a demand that led to the formation of New Brighton F.C., once in the Football League. Wilkinson judged the success of every issue this way: if it was full of alliterative headlines it was good; if not, then it was bad.

The reporters' room at the *Wallasey Chronicle* office was fifteen feet by ten and furnished with two tables covered in old newspaper and surrounded by four wooden chairs. There was a mantelpiece on which sat a pot of paste and the Wallasey Street Directory, our only book of reference. The floor was covered with rotting linoleum and the floral paper on the walls was peeling.

This was not journalism as I had romantically imagined it, but it was a romantic period of my life. The Chief Reporter (now a newspaperman in America) was Harold Butcher, an Essex man with a high-pitched voice. The two others were William Fraser, who disliked his first name and rechristened himself W. Gilbert Fraser (he came to Fleet Street later, on one of Benn Brothers' trade papers) and a ginger-headed learner six or seven years older than myself who signed his name Thos. P. Tiplady, and whose shorthand was worse than mine.

Harold Butcher tried hard to transform me. I wanted to become a sports editor. He wanted me to study literature. I ran the sports pages. He organised reading classes for me. He fixed trips to Liverpool when opera took over at the Shakespeare theatre. And I was always assigned to cover the meetings of the local Poetry Society in the belief that they would improve my mind.

But none of this changed me. I remained stubbornly determined to be a sports editor and rejoiced that no one else on the staff was interested in sport. By way of expressing my hero-worship for Ernest Edwards, who, as I have said, called himself 'Bee', I initialled my sports reports 'A.B.C.' (the B for 'Bee'); and I increased the sale of the *Wallasey Chronicle* from its normal 3,800 copies a week to a record 4,200 copies, which was a ten per cent increase – equal to putting on more than 400,000 to the *Daily Express* today.

This was all done with only half-a-crown – but quite a sum for the manager of the *Wallasey Chronicle* to invest. Over seven months of the football season it represented an outlay of £3 10s 0d which is a lot when you appreciate that the total profit, including the jobbing printing side, was about £100 a year, out of which a ten per cent dividend had to be paid on a capital of £1,000. Nevertheless Mr Brown agreed that my scheme could be tried for a month to see how it worked. The scheme was – to award half a crown a week to the football secretary who, in my opinion, wrote the best report of his team's Saturday match.

The response to this, my first journalistic promotion idea, was tremendous. The *Chronicle* found itself having to devote two pages to amateur soccer reports, instead of one page, and the circulation grew week by week until the cricket season started. (Cricket has never sold newspapers with anything like the certainty of soccer.)

But the life of a learner in journalism is tough. He is inexperienced and he makes mistakes. I made an enormous mistake when I was trusted with the coverage of the local police court. I confused a respectable boarding-house in Wallasey with a brothel by recording the street number 73 as 37 in my report of a case. Thus the brothel-keeper was spared publicity, while the poor boarding-house keeper, who was a perfectly respectable widow, found that people were pointing at her in the street.

She called at the office to complain. I saw her and was fool enough to slip a correction into the next issue of the paper without the knowledge of the editor. I tucked it away at the end of a column of brief items called 'Local News' (although why it was so called is a mystery, as all the news in the paper was local).

That week-end passed and Monday came without any comment on my blunder from Editor Wilkinson or any other member of the staff. For my evening assignment I went to the Tivoli Theatre, New Brighton, where Gracie Fields, an unknown youngster in her twenties, was the star in a show called *Mr Tower of London*. I gave her a magnificent write-up and all thoughts of the brothel case vanished from my mind.

But on Tuesday the widow called again. My subterfuge had been so successful that not only had the paragraph escaped the editor, but it had escaped her too.

I saw her at the counter and pointed the paragraph out. Her comment was that if *she* had been unable to find it, then it could not have had much effect in retrieving either her own reputation or that of her boarding-house. So there was nothing for it but to own up and bring the editor into the case.

Ted Wilkinson's rust-coloured hair and cherry-red nose turned a deeper colour as I confessed. In front of the staff he declared that I was a bloody little fool and not only a bloody little fool but a deceitful little fool too. But for the fact that I had been an apprentice for only a month, if it had been any of the senior reporters, it would have been a case of sacking without notice. He had not known that I had been left to cover the police courts on my own, and Butcher, the Chief Reporter, had bloody well better see that the diary was properly marked in future so that another reporter was at the police court to ensure that the paper was not let down again. And if there were a libel action I might have to be fired in any case.

With that, he stormed out and wrote an apology which got top-of-the-column treatment in the next issue. It was not alliteratively headlined. It just said:

MRS BLANK – AN APOLOGY

Ted Wilkinson was a figure of immense dignity. He had to do a spot of reporting himself, as we four members of the general staff constituted the entire force at his disposal; but if he had been the editor of *The Times*, he could not have been more awesome.

Years later I learned that his salary was £4 10s 0d a week – just half-a-crown more than the National Union of Journalists' minimum scale in the twenties for towns the size of Wallasey, 100,000 population or less. But Wilkinson held his head high in the community and was much respected.

He wrote few leading articles on local matters. As a rule, he thundered away on national issues with high Tory gusto – we marvelled at his grasp of affairs as we revised the proofs of his leading article. This was always delivered to the printers on Thursday afternoon at 4 p.m. just twenty-four hours before the entire paper went to press. It was always in Ted's own handwriting, thick and round, with a 4B pencil, and it was one of those old-fashioned pieces that ran to a column-and-a-quarter in one solid paragraph.

Eventually he went on holiday and his secret was discovered. The leader was provided by Tory Central Office, but he concealed

the fact by copying it out rather than appear to his staff in the role
of party hack.

Ted died, I hope without knowing that we knew. It would have
been a dreadful blow to his pride.

I was making more than the salary of the editor in my second
year at the *Wallasey Chronicle*. There are many ways in which a
local newspaperman can add to his regular income. One way is to
contribute copy to national newspapers. For this he is paid by the
line – hence this copy is called linage. One Wallasey journalist was
making £3,000 a year out of his linage for the national newspapers
when I was appointed editor of the *Daily Express* at £5,000 a year.

It was my role as the junior in the office linage pool to carry copy
across the Mersey by ferry boat each night to the Liverpool offices
of the *Daily Mail*. Thus I met for the first time a couple of – to me
– giants of the newspaper world, Northcliffe men; one a copper-
head named Campbell, the other a snapdragon named Airey. Both
were chronically bad-tempered and much harassed. I could do
nothing right. Night after night I was sworn at for being either too
early or too late. Neither read the copy; it was just the sight of me
that maddened them. Once Campbell actually took a kick at me.

Many years later, when Campbell was an old man, I was guest of
honour at the Liverpool Press Club. I had long since appreciated
the pressure under which Campbell and Airey had worked (I did
in fact become Airey's editor on the *Daily Express* in Manchester
in 1933). When I told Campbell what a terrifying figure he had been
to me as a lad, he blushed and mumbled his apologies.

By my third year as an apprentice I had become prolific. I wrote
short stories, special articles, and even poems. I edited the Children's
Corner as 'Aunt Clara'; I ran the sports section; and I was even
trying my hand at displaying the paper in modern style.

This typographical experiment was made in face of the hostility
of Clay, the head printer, who believed that all news stories should
run to their natural length up and down the columns, and that
where one item of news finished the next should begin.

Clay was an artist in this technique, and made up the main pages
of the paper himself so that the first story turned to the top of

column two by about three inches. Thereupon he would select
another long story that would turn into column three by about six
inches – and so across the page. The big headlines got deeper and
deeper down until the middle column was reached, when they
would start going upwards again. The result was a triumphant V
of headline type on the main page that resembled Churchill's
victory sign.

I have never met the equal of Clay at this form of newspaper
make-up, possibly because no other Head Printer thought much of
it. When one day I suggested it was wrong, he hissed, 'What do you
think this is, sonny, *Comic Cuts*?'

But that day I took my first step in technical journalism. I told
Clay that what was good enough for the *Liverpool Echo* ought to
be good enough for the *Wallasey Chronicle*. He showed surprising
meekness. Soon I was allowed to select the splash story for the
week, and arrange the news in order of importance rather than of
length.

When I left the *Wallasey Chronicle* after three and a half years,
Ted Wilkinson made the traditional presentation speech (I was
given a pipe) and said with pride that it was his lot to train people
for other newspapers and that very few people had left the *Chronicle*
office without bettering themselves. He gave a list of people who
over the years had gone to bigger newspapers, some even to Fleet
Street.

All this training of men Wilkinson did for four pounds ten shillings a week. Local newspaper editors are the salt of the earth, even
if the good things of the table are so often denied to them.

4 . . . Our Man in Bootle

I loved London from the moment I arrived at Euston Station in 1924 to visit the Empire Exhibition at Wembley. But it was not Wembley that I loved, it was Fleet Street.

I went to the Great Exhibition twice during my week's stay. I went to Fleet Street every day from a seven-and-sixpence bed-and-breakfast Bloomsbury hotel. In a way the Street was a disappointment, for the only newspaper offices I could see were those with provincial headquarters. I found the offices of the Liverpool papers. I found the offices of the Irish papers, the Scottish papers, the Welsh papers, the Midlands papers, the overseas papers – but never a sign of Lord Northcliffe's *Daily Mail* office, or of the *Daily News*, or the *Daily Express* (which was almost unknown in the North at that time). And when I did find them tucked away in the alleys around Bouverie Street and Shoe Lane, I was too awed to do more than gape.

The *Daily Express* office faced in black glass is now in Fleet Street on the site of the old Sausage Shop, at which half a pint of bitter, two pork sausages, mashed potatoes and fried onions cost one shilling and three ha'pence, the food all on display in the window. Nowadays, a Sausage Shop 'veteran', I still stand on the corner of Fleet Street and Shoe Lane almost as awed as I was when I gaped as a twenty-year-old in 1924. If I had known then as much

21   c

as I know now about what happens inside a Metropolitan newspaper office, I doubt whether I would ever have had the courage to
invade Fleet Street at all, for I have never got over the feeling that
I am not really a good craftsman and that the next twenty-four
hours will find me out. The bouncy, self-confident exterior that I
developed was a façade, a hide that grew on me like an elephant
skin. In those days it did not exist. I was worried like most adoles-
cents by spots on my chin and by the fact that I blushed like a girl
even when asking questions on the telephone (which scared me).

I stood on the pavement in Fleet Street gaping at the passing
throng of Londoners and wondering who were the journalists. For
how could I tell which was which? I did not drink, and it therefore
did not occur to me to go into Ye Olde Cheshire Cheese where I
might have been able actually to stand next to Jimmy Dunn, who
wrote the *Daily Mail*'s Human Stories from the Courts under the
nom-de-plume of R. E. Corder, or Stanley Bishop, the legendary
chief reporter of the *Daily Express*, or some other great man of the
day.

Instead, I imagined that everyone who walked in Fleet Street
during that magic week was a journalist. They were all gods who
walked on air. They were all unattainable. This was no place for a
Wallasey boy in his third year as a reporter on the *Wallasey
Chronicle*. It seemed to me that I had better get right back home
and set my sights on a more modest target than a London newspaper, then or ever.

But I have always been lucky. Instead of my going to Fleet Street,
Fleet Street came to me. When I returned home, I began applying
for jobs on provincial evening papers in other parts of the country.
I also answered an advertisement for a job on Kipling's old paper,
the *Civil and Military Gazette* at Lahore, and for one in Singapore.

Finally I did not cross the Indian Ocean but the River Mersey to
join the Liverpool *Evening Express* and *Daily Courier* as their
Bootle correspondent, Bootle being the enormous area once owned
by the Earl of Derby that straggles down to the Liverpool Docks
via some of the most appalling slums in the Western Hemisphere.
The job was no great plum or glittering prize. The pay was
£3 10s 0d a week – I was knocking up a fiver in Wallasey from
my linage activities – and as a district man I was responsible, seven

days a week, for anything and everything that was worth reporting
in the Bootle area. The hours were arduous and the pay was low.

Just the same, Fate was taking a hand, for one Sunday night not
long after I had joined the *Courier* I heard for the first time the
voice of a man who was to play a big part in my career. 'Who the
hell are you?' I was asked as I came into head office in Victoria
Street from police and fire station calls in my district.

The voice belonged to T. A. Innes and he was the new man from
Fleet Street about whom rumours had been spreading. Newspaper
staffs are gifted with a Sixth Sense – I once *thought* of sacking a
reporter and was told an hour or two later that I had already done
so – and long before Fred Burchill, son of the Big Boss Alfred
Burchill, imported his bus load of London 'celebrities', the tom-
toms had been beating out the news.

The Burchills had decided to transform the ailing and failing
Daily Courier into 'the National Newspaper of the North'. Fred
Burchill daringly purchased the rights to reproduce the news
services of the *Daily Express* simultaneously in the *Courier* (which
did not matter to the *Express* in those days, as it did not circulate
much this far from London) while at the same time impudently
tempting four members of the *Express* staff to come back with him
for the purpose of putting Metropolitan zip into provincial
journalism.

Innes was the biggest catch. He was a 'splash' sub-editor, and
he was appointed Managing Editor, which meant that he had
charge of the entire production, subject only to a veto retained by
Alfred Burchill as Editor-in-Chief.

Next, there was a cherubic character named John Heather, the
Night Editor, who wore an eye shade and looked as though he had
stepped out of the railroad cable office in a Hollywood movie.
Then there were two star reporters, H. W. Seaman and Harold
Sanders, who were glad to escape from Fleet Street after they had
sent a moving description of a mass migration to America of some
hundreds of Hebridean islanders that did not in fact take place
(don't ask me how such things can happen; sometimes they just
do so). The other London recruits included a talented young man
named Anthony Praga, and a toothy young cartoonist who signed
himself 'Lee' – the same 'Lee' who has for years been drawing

'London Laughs' for the London *Evening News*. Withal a formidable crew to hit a town like Liverpool.

On the night that I first heard Innes roar at me with the voice of
a ship's captain mastering a gale-force storm, a national railways
strike threatened. I had a story about a Bootle dock labourer who
had hatcheted his wife and two children (it was headlined BOOTLE
LABOURER'S STRANGE CONDUCT in the rival *Daily Post*) but
that, it seemed, could wait.

I introduced myself by saying 'Christiansen of Bootle', as though
I were as famous as Nanook of the North. Innes asked with judicial
severity where the hell Bootle was. I told him, and he told me to
get to Lime Street railway station to cover the threatened strike. I
said that Lime Street station, being in the centre of the city, was
not in my district. He said what the hell did that matter, and a
further flood of invective drove me down the corridor, into the
street, and all the way to Lime Street, from which place such news
as I gathered failed to 'make' the following day's issue.

We were not used to such language in Liverpool, but we were to
hear plenty of it in the next year. It was not that Innes, a squat,
handsome, horn-rimmed, firm-heeled man in his early thirties,
was an ignorant bully; in his quieter moments or in his cups, the
richness of his mind would show itself as he spouted Greek heroic
verse or yards of Burns. But as a newspaper editor he behaved as
though he were in charge of a sinking ship that had to be brought
safely to harbour, or as a pirate in charge of a boarding party. He
blasphemed and he roared and he bludgeoned. He seemed incapable of saying a kind word. His praise was limited to a resigned
grunt which seemed to indicate that although one's work was not
very good, it would have to do. It was the kind of attitude that I
was to find when I went to Fleet Street, but it was quite unusual in
the gentler waters of the provinces.

It was not very long before Innes's emphatic personality was
stamped on the entire paper. Sir Archibald Salvidge, the much-
feared brewer and Tory caucus boss of the City Council, quarrelled
with Alfred Burchill, his lifelong friend, over the new *Daily Courier*,
with its news on the front page and its piping-hot methods. The
paper crusaded against Salvidge. In fact it crusaded about practically everybody and everything. When we could not get all-night

trams to the suburb of Wavertree where Innes lived, the Tramways Manager was pilloried; every mention of the poor fellow's name was followed by the letters A.M.I.E.E., which were sneeringly explained to mean that he was a fee-paying Associate Member of the Institute of Electrical Engineers and that his tram-drivers should use the letters N.A.M.W. after their names to signify they were fee-paying members of the National Association of Municipal Workers. We went to war with Emanuel Shinwell, then secretary of the Garment Workers Union, and christened him 'Shinwell the Tailor' long before the phrase reached the National Press. We refused to allow the trees in a Bootle street to be cut down, and plastered every one that had been condemned with posters saying WOODMAN – SPARE THIS TREE. Small local scandals were featured; I hit the front page three days running when I unearthed the story of a woman who had been refused adequate out-patient treatment at Bootle Hospital owing to the blundering of an officious hall porter.

News angled to attract women was new to the provincial Press. I was assigned the task of producing a woman's story a day for months on end. One of my contacts on this 'beat' was Fred Marquis, the General Manager of Lewis's, the biggest store in the City, but even that bright spark, who became Lord Woolton, war-time Food Minister and post-war architect of Tory revival, eventually ran out of ideas. So did I.

The headlines – for those days – were as strident as the positioning of the news. A sub-editor who claimed to have worked on the *Chicago Tribune* wrote the headline JAPAN CEASES TO BE A FIRST CLASS POWER on a Japanese earthquake story; fortunately Innes got back from having a couple of quick Scotches in Christensen's Bar (nothing to do with my family, worse luck) to kill this classic exaggeration before the first edition went to press. But it was typical of the mood that beset us all.

In the reporters' room even the linage pool, from which we all augmented our incomes by sending messages to the National Press, was neglected in our frenzy to outdo each other. I do not suppose there has been a provincial training ground for newspapermen like it before – or maybe since.

I was an indifferent reporter. I hated this side of newspaper work. I hated calling at the homes of the bereaved in train disasters and

the like to collect pictures of the victims – although I always found
people helpful and friendly and was often invited in for a cup of tea.
I hated pushing people around as reporters must sometimes do,
and I viewed with equal dislike pushing a crook around as I did an
honest business man. I was frightened of tipping eye-witnesses in
case I gave them too much or distressed them by giving them
nothing at all. I hated being in the 'ring' of shorthand reporters that
evening newspapers employ for the purpose of getting important
speeches quickly to the printer; once during an election I was so
showered on the Press table with the champagne-soaked saliva of
F. E. Smith, the first Earl of Birkenhead, that I panicked and got
on to my notebook less than one hundred words out of about a
thousand uttered during my three-minute 'take'.

What is left of my cuttings book from those days bears testimony
to a degree of successful publication, but those old cuttings bring
memories of fright, nausea, hot embarrassment, and near-failure.
One day I was sent to Warrington to investigate reports that the
Celanese company had established a new factory for the purpose
of manufacturing artificial silk – big news in Lancashire, the county
of cotton. When I reached the gates of the factory I made so little
impression on the timekeeper that he refused even to send my
visiting card in to the manager. His orders, he said, were to keep
people out. It was typical of my approach to life in those days that
I was completely nonplussed. Fearfully, I walked round the
enormous walls of the factory. They yielded nothing by way of fact
or inspiration. As the midday buzzer went, hundred of girls poured
through the gates, but I did not have the wit or the guts to talk to
any of them. I went into a dingy 'good pull-up for car men' café
for a sausage-and-mash lunch and got talking to the proprietor.
He said that there was some new-fangled process going on at the
factory and that as far as he knew even the girls at the machines
hadn't the faintest idea what they were doing.

This aroused the glimmerings of news sense in my addled mind
and I went back to the factory when the buzzer blew at 1 o'clock
to call the girls back. Again I was ejected by the gate-man.

Then I got on to the telephone to the *Evening Express* and put
over three hundred words on how I had been twice thrown out of
a 'hush-hush' factory that was making artificial silk and how the

hundreds of girls employed at the factory were quite unaware of the potentialities of this great new rival to cotton. I described my walk round the walls of the factory and concluded with a sentence about the security regulations that made the place seem like Walton Jail.

Few editors can resist a piece of news in which the word 'secret' occurs. If the phrase 'hush-hush' also appears, then all normal sense of news values disappears. Newspapers love to blow the gaff. The sure way not to get publicity is to seek it. The sure way to hit the headlines is to try to avoid them. Thus it was that the *Evening Express* that night and the *Daily Courier* the next day ran these headlines:

NEW INDUSTRY FOR SOUTH-WEST LANCASHIRE
GIRLS WORK AT HUSH-HUSH FACTORY
OUR MAN THROWN OUT

When I got back to Liverpool, the News Editor was so inflamed by my coup that he was telephoning the Celanese head office to protest against my treatment. The reporters clapped me on the back; if I had been a drinking man there would have been a cele-bration in Christensen's Bar. By this time I had forgotten how nearly I had failed, and I accepted the congratulations as to the manner born. I stayed around the office so late that I found myself sitting at the piano of the Press Club, a small port and lemon at my side, playing 'In Cellar Cool I'm Drinking' for Chris Davies, the late duty reporter of the *Daily Post*, whose voice was finely mellowed for such a song, as were those of most of the veteran Liverpool journalists still around at 3 o'clock in the morning.

I called on the father and mother of a girl I knew when she had been stabbed by her jealous lover. I was out all night on the Lytham train disaster when fourteen people were killed. I got a clean scoop for the *Courier* on a ship breaking her back on a Mersey sandbank, thanks to the know-how of my shipwright father. I was made News Editor for a day during an influenza epidemic when I was twenty. I was mistaken for a constituent by Vesta Tilley, the famous male

impersonator, and treated to a great big kiss on behalf of her
husband Sir Walter de Frece, M.P., who was seeking the favours
of the citizens of Blackpool at the time. I braved the wrath of Tom
Innes and got another ten shillings a week, bringing my wages up
to £4.

'I help keep my mother,' I said in justifying the impertinence of
my application.

'Who cares about that?' snarled Innes. 'We'll give you more if
you're worth more.'

I was glad I got it, because it was 1924, and things were bad on
Merseyside. Not as bad as they were going to become, but bad,
with Cammell Lairds and Graysons having less and less for men like
my father to do.

The *Daily Courier* was feeling the draught, too. It failed to
establish itself as 'the National Newspaper of the North', or for
that matter as even a successful rival to the *Daily Post*, published
as the *Echo*'s morning stable companion. National newspaper
technique does not go down well in provincial journalism. Local
newspapers have a duty to be journals of local record and it is at
their peril that they neglect that responsibility in pursuit of 'bright'
coverage. It was not the fault of the Fleet Street brigade that the
Daily Courier experiment failed; many years later the *Daily
Dispatch*, Manchester, which in Sir Edward Hulton's days between
World Wars I and II was truly the National Newspaper of the
North, also died by falling between two stools.

It was a sad and disillusioned Tom Innes who disappeared from
the Liverpool scene, but when I next caught up with him he had
established himself as the Managing Editor of the then puny
Sunday Express that was giving its founder, Lord Beaverbrook, as
much trouble as the Burchills had with the *Daily Courier*. The
Sunday Express survived. The *Courier* died, unmourned, in 1929.

I caught up with Innes by the roundabout way of the sub-editors'
table of the *Liverpool Evening Express*. I was delighted to escape
from the reporters' room, and felt that at last I had found my niche
in journalism in the department responsible for typography, lay-
out and headlines.

A sub-editor is often taken by the general public for the man immediately junior to the editor. In fact he is a long way from the top. The Managing Editor, the Deputy Editor, the Associate Editor, the Night Editor, the Chief Sub-Editor, and many others with fancy titles are all senior to a sub-editor.

There are on a newspaper like the *Daily Express* thirty sub-editors, paid, according to their skill, anything from £25 a week to more than double that amount. But, despite what will seem to many people their handsome earnings, their task is to do what they are told and to shape the raw copy into printable form as it comes from the reporters and the news agencies. Often a piece of news is big enough to demand the services of six staff reporters, as well as the local correspondents and news agencies like the Press Association. As the bits and pieces come in from these sources the sub-editor must compose the coherent running narrative. It is a tough job. And the toughest of all sub-editorial jobs is on an evening paper. The speed required from a sub-editor on evening papers is almost certainly not to be equalled in any other profession. News has to be shovelled to the printer accurately and grammatically so quickly that it makes even the modern factory conveyor belt system seem like an invention that goes back to the days of Caxton.

In my first week as a sub-editor Jimmy Meares, the Chief Sub (the same Meares who had edited the northern edition of the *Sunday Chronicle*) threw me a bundle of copy within twenty minutes of edition time. 'Put a splash on that, lad,' he said, which meant the main display on the front page, with a seven-column banner headline and four decks of headlines set across two columns.

For Newton, the splash sub-editor, this would have presented no problems. But I was hot under the armpits by the time all the copy was with the printer, leaving me with only five minutes to write my headlines. I had also panicked and could not remember a single word of the story then being set into type.

I know now that it was about a little girl named Nellie Clarke who had been strangled in Birkenhead and that a bloodstained clue had been found in a dustbin. But on this day I had to be rescued by Newton. He was sitting next to me and wrote the headlines for me. He and Meares exchanged cynical winks. I had been 'blooded' all right; and I have inflicted this form of torture on countless

youngsters in my time in the belief that experience is the Great –
and Only – Teacher.

Six months later I was the 'stone' sub-editor – the 'stone' man is
the editorial representative in the printing office, who tells the
printers where to put the type in order to get the paper to press in
time. The printers on the *Evening Express* rarely failed. Between
putting pages to press every ten minutes or so, they would back
Solario to win, take snuff, air their views on women – 'They're all
the same, Mr Chris,' said Ernie Dowling, who taught me to read
type upside-down. Then in a prodigious five-minute burst the old
page of the previous edition was stripped and a new page assembled
and shot to the stereotyper's mangle just about one second before it
was due. My heart nearly stopped twenty times every afternoon,
for those were the number of pages involved in this process as one
edition succeeded another.

Only once was I late by as much as a minute – and that was how
I came to be sent to Fleet Street.

It was not my fault (or Ernie Dowling's) that the page was late.
Just the same, Fred Burchill, who had by then transferred his
affections from the *Daily Courier* to the evening paper, called me
a bloody young fool. I shouted back 'Don't bloody fool me, you're
a bloody fool yourself' and rushed off to the men's room literally in
tears.

The next day I was sent for. I thought I was going to be sacked.
Instead Burchill looked at me through his thick glasses in rather a
kindly way and said he was sorry about yesterday's 'scene' and I
was a good man and would I like to go to London as London
Editor of the *Evening Express*?

I was not yet twenty-one and could only feel flattered and excited.
There and then I signed a three-year contract; first year, seven
guineas a week, rising by a guinea a year to nine guineas. Although
I was an editor, I was at these prices not being paid the minimum
scale laid down by the National Union of Journalists, but I recalled
the words that Ernest Hope Prince, the editor of the *Echo*, had
addressed to me when I was a boy in a Grammar School cap: scrub
the office steps rather than miss a chance. So I was content.

I left Wallasey in the early summer of 1925 to the tears of my
mother, my aunt and my ten-year-old sister, who all gathered in

the front room with the Robert Blatchford piano in it, to watch from behind the lace curtains as I walked down Evelyn Road with my suitcase. No taxi-cabs in those days. A tram to Seacombe Landing Stage, a ferry boat across the Mersey, a tram to Lime Street Station, a third-class compartment to Euston, a bus to Lewisham where I had arranged digs with an old friend.

Some three hundred miles in all, and not a penny spent on porters.

5 . . . There Are No Tom-Cats

My life had now really begun. My Fleet Street life. All that had happened since I left the Wallasey Grammar School had been basic training to fit me for what was to be the advanced course leading to editorship. Were these my feelings as I stepped into the Fleet Street offices of the Liverpool *Evening Express* one fine spring morning in 1925? I should say not. I was scared.

I had never had charge of staff before and as I was not yet twenty-one years of age, I was overwhelmed by Ernie Roberts and Teddy Linger, my Cockney editorial assistants, who had to show me the ropes, as well as by the patronising pince-nez of Sammy Cox, the chief telegraph operator who was quite a noise in his trade union and seemed to spend as much time on its affairs as he did punching up the Morse tape that got the news to Liverpool.

I soon discovered that the work of a London office staff was largely clerical, with the one saving journalistic grace that urgent news had to be given priority in the wire room. The pace was hot, but it was a job of shovelling out masses of words, with none of the joys of headline-writing and marking instructions to the printer to 'set the first para across two columns in pica black followed by single-column long primer, dropping into brevier and indented both sides', which will give a specific typographical result when the newspaper is printed. I missed the smell and the bustle and the

technique of Head Office, and sought to introduce a system of re-
writing, type marking, and headline-writing, but this caused such
delays in getting the news to Liverpool that complaints began to
arrive from the editor. I was miserable at the dead end in which I
found myself.

Nor was my morale improved by an encounter with an imposing
figure dressed in a black homburg, astrakhan-collared overcoat,
and grey spats over patent-leather boots, who called at the office
one night and asked to speak to the editor.

Looking up from a pile of Exchange Telegraph Company tape
that had just been pasted up for me, I replied 'I am the editor'.

'In that case,' said Mr Astrakhan scornfully, eyeing my rolled-
up shirt-sleeves and modest frame, 'I had better get in touch with
Liverpool office direct.' (I always believed that Mr Astrakhan was
Philip Page, then a famous music critic, but he denied it, and his
kindness to me years later belied the idea that he would have
sneered at a callow youth.)

I was also lonely. Every writer from the provinces will tell you
about the loneliness of London. No one seems to care. Everyone
seems to be in a hurry. The fact that Londoners are the most talka-
tive people in the world if the provincial braces himself to speak
first is only revealed when the provincial has become a Londoner
himself; and it is then useless knowledge.

Stanley Robinson, my room-mate at a vicarage in Lewisham, was
not much help, for his job as a Parliamentary shorthand reporter
(he is now head of *The Times* Parliamentary team) kept him busy
every night, while I worked by day. My 'landlady', the wife of the
Rev. Maxwell Carnson – the Carnsons had a large vicarage and a
small stipend and had to take 'paying guests' (not 'lodgers') to
make ends meet – tried to interest me in the local tennis club, but
the idea bored me and I never went. Instead I hung around Fleet
Street and walked the West End looking in the shop windows,
eating tomatoes on toast in the A.B.C. at tea-time, or fried plaice
and chips for supper in the Coventry Street Corner House, where
in the 'twenties there was a sixteen-piece string orchestra always
grinding away. Every Friday I called on Tom Innes to inquire if
there was a chance of getting some Saturday work on the *Sunday
Express* and every Friday the great man sent a message to the hall

porter rejecting my services. I never saw him. We might never have met in the good old Liverpool days. The impression made on me by Innes's constant refusals was so indelible that I have never consciously savaged a young journalist in my life. The number that I have personally seen, or written to, must run into many hundreds.

But at that time I savaged poor Roberts. I sacked him. He was the first man I deprived of his job. It was a merciless and a mean act because Roberts did not need to be a good journalist, only a good clerk, and he was a good clerk. But I wanted a good journalist.

The vacancy caused by his departure was filled from Liverpool. An old chum of mine named Martin Healey, who had helped me on my first assignment as Bootle correspondent, grinned his way into my life once more. If you believe in a personal God – as I do although logically it seems all wrong – you will believe that the sacking of Roberts and the appointment of Healey was a providential act, for within a few weeks Healey was to break down the Iron Curtain that Innes had erected against me at the *Sunday Express* office. The debt that I owe to this cheerful Liverpool Irishman on this account is immense, for without him I might have remained for ever in obscurity.

Tom Innes and Tim Healey were drinking companions from their Liverpool days. All Tim had to do to get a Saturday job on the *Sunday Express* was to pick up the telephone and hoot a toothy greeting into the mouthpiece, 'Hello, Tom! This is Tim!' This, of course, was no way to address a Fleet Street editor, but Tim was and is the exception to all the rules, and within a few seconds I heard him say 'All right, Tom. 12 o'clock Saturday, Tom. I'll be there, Tom'. Tim was in.

Sunday papers are nowadays extravagantly staffed, but in 1926 a paper like the *Sunday Express* was brought out by four full-time editorial men, implemented on Saturdays by reporters and sub-editors from other newspapers. Nowadays as much as ten guineas can be picked up by a first-class journalist willing to sacrifice his Saturday off, but at that time the fee was two guineas for an eight-hour shift – and good pay it was because there were no fiddle-faddle deductions for P.A.Y.E., nor did many chaps declare the money on their income-tax returns.

I listened enviously to Tim Healey's account of his first day as a *Sunday Express* sub-editor. 'It's about the same as Liverpool,' he said, 'but none of the other subs are up to much. I got three Page-One stories, two black splashes inside and thirteen nibs to handle.'

I did not mind so much Tim being asked to handle thirteen 'nibs' (a contraction for News In Brief), but the thought of his being regarded as good enough to be thrown three Page-One items, and two black splashes – a four-decker headline job then fashionable – soured me. Here was I, his boss at the *Liverpool Evening Express* office, yet unable even to get a trial on a London paper.

But one day Healey had an urgent call to visit his parents in Liverpool and nominated me as his stand-in. I arrived at the Shoe Lane entrance of the *Express* offices at the stroke of midday, and sent in my name to the Chief Sub-Editor, F. W. Wilson.

Wilson had achieved notoriety in 1924 by writing a description of an interview with the Prime Minister, Stanley Baldwin, in which Lord Beaverbrook had been savagely attacked. Baldwin repudiated the interview as a fake when it was published in *The People*, then under the editorship of Hannen Swaffer, and the scandal lasted for weeks. With typical impishness Lord Beaverbrook gave Wilson a job on the *Sunday Express*. It was Wilson's last job. He was a likeable, but unreliable character, and I suspect that, whatever Baldwin's views on Beaverbrook then were, he would not have expressed them to Wilson, even if he believed that he was talking confidentially. But let it be admitted that Wilson had charm.

He threw me a mass of police court 'flimsy' – a ghastly, but quick, tissue-paper method of circulating the news that has long since gone out of date.

'Ever handled police?' he asked with a sweet smile. 'Yes,' I replied, never having handled 'police', and got down to the messy, illegible copy. As I read of a man being fined £10 for dangerous driving at Bow Street while another was sentenced to one month's imprisonment at the Mansion House on a similar charge, a thought struck me. I made these items into one yarn and wrote this headline: TWO VOICES OF THE LAW.

'Very good idea,' said Wilson. 'I'll make it a "top" on Page Five.' I was much flattered to get my first idea for a Black Splash accepted and continued my work in buoyant spirits.

But disaster was to follow, as it invariably does when you are riding high. At three p.m. the great man Innes stamped into the room. You could hear him coming before he took his place at a desk behind the sub-editors' horse-shoe table.

He began to read the proofs, neatly assembled on a spike, of news stories that had been set into type. One after another the proofs went without comment into the waste-paper basket, until suddenly came an anguished roar, a cry that only a wounded man on a battlefield could have made. And then the words, 'Wilson, who wrote this?'

Wilson rose deferentially from his seat. 'Sir,' he said, 'what?'

The proof was hurled at Wilson as though it were a paving stone. 'THIS.'

And there, marked with a dreadful cross of ink, was the head-line: TOM-CAT KILLS CHICKENS.

'Christiansen,' said Wilson.

'CHRISTIANSEN!' roared The Voice, as though we had been seeing each other every day since we worked together in Liverpool.

I went to the Editor's table.

'Don't you know,' said Innes, 'that on this newspaper there are only CATS? Not TOM-CATS or any other kind of bloody cat. Only CATS!'

'Yes, sir.'

A volley of abuse followed. If I knew, why had I written 'tom-cat'? What was my excuse? And if I did not know, what was I doing working for the *Sunday Express*?

To all this I had no answer.

And to this day I cannot see that 'tom-cat' is offensive. But the impression that lecture made on me was such that for the rest of my career I bawled at anybody who wrote the word 'tom-cat'; that, maybe, is how traditions are born.

The day wore on. I handled lots of stories and my count of publication amounted to a round score of news items, big and little. Not bad – but after the bawling out over the tom-cat I was shaken and pessimistic. At 7.30 I collected an envelope containing my fee of two guineas, but it was unimportant to me. I would have worked on this paper for no fee at all, just for the chance to learn something and to be with real Fleet Street men.

At 8 o'clock I was told I could go. I was also invited to stay. 'Can you come in every week?' Wilson asked. It remains the biggest thrill of my career, surpassing everything that has happened since in the sharp impression it made.

The circulation of the *Sunday Express* in 1926 was a modest and uncertain 300,000. But to a newspaperman it is not the sale but the soul that counts in deciding his loyalties, as I was to find now and then when, as an editor, I invited men I admired to join the mighty *Daily Express* from their own struggling sheets.

6 . . . Pity the Newspaper Wife

London was ceasing to be a lonely city. I was starting to become a Londoner even though I had not lost all my Northern accent. (I still say 'wonn' for 'one', and while it seems correct enough to my ear, I am told that Southerners say 'wun'.) I moved from the vicarage in Lewisham to share digs in a foreman-painter's house in Streatham with a former classmate who had also migrated from Wallasey. This helped considerably, despite the fact that Alec Wilson was a constructional engineer and seemed as completely preoccupied with the merits of roof sheeting as I was by the merits of the *Sunday Express*.

'You're a bore,' said Alec, 'all you can talk about is newspapers.'

'So are you,' I retorted, 'and what's more, most people would consider newspaper talk more interesting than your chatter about the corrugated iron roofs you climb over.'

But we were generally companionable enough, and played snooker at a hall in Streatham Hill once or twice a week, and every Friday paid 1s 10d to sit in the 'gods' of the old Alhambra music-hall (now the Odeon, Leicester Square).

These relaxations were all I permitted myself. The rest of my time was spent in study of the three London evening papers. Item by item, line by line I worked my way through their columns, contrasting their headlines, news angles, human interest, selection, and the dozens of personal touches that make one newspaper different from another. It must have been excellent training, and it helped to overcome the tedium of shovelling the news over the wire to Liverpool.

Tim Healey and I now sat together at the *Sunday Express* sub-editors' table. One afternoon he made a demonstration that I have never heard repeated. Standing up suddenly, he announced in a firm voice, 'I cannot conscientiously handle this copy.' Everybody stopped work as Healey said that he did not believe a word of a man-bites-dog type of news item, the details of which have been long forgotten by both of us. The chief sub-editor had handed Tim the copy, but, accustomed to every kind of newspaper experience, he merely laughed and replied 'All right, Tim; spike it'. The mutiny was over and we all got on with our work.

But once again I was indebted to Healey. The little Liverpool Irishman had taught me something that I should never have forgotten, but frequently, to my regret, did. It is that integrity springs from a sense of moral indignation. Any skilful operator can handle news and make with it what impression he wishes. But to handle news with integrity requires a sense of moral values that burns and burns and burns. Sometimes the flame may have died in me in the hustle and cynicism of Fleet Street. When it did I regretted it and sometimes recalled Healey's Mutiny.

A jovial old boy with a rich bottom lip that had been moulded into shape by many a tankard, called at the *Liverpool Express* office. He asked to borrow the agency tape on an inquest he should have been attending at Worcester. 'Missed the train,' he said cheerfully, 'but the train fare won't miss my swindle sheet.' He said that his name was Vincent Wray, and I remembered reading his articles on criminology in the *Sunday Chronicle* many years back. I was flattered to meet an old Fleet Street hand and, at his invitation, crossed the threshold of a Fleet Street pub for the first time in my life. It was an unhappy experience, for my first-ever half-pint of bitter – at the Cock Tavern – made me sick half an hour later in the presence of my colleagues.

Vincent Wray invited Tim Healey and myself to have dinner with him at his flat and it was here that I met the girl I was to marry. I

saw her reflected in a mirror as I mounted the stairs to a first-floor
flat in an old house on Streatham Hill – the site of the modern
theatre – and I 'fell' first time. My wife tells me that she was not
very impressed with me then, with my Northern bowler hat in my
hand and my Northern suit of unstylish cut. But she thought even
less of toothy Tim, and when we both invited her to go to the
movies the following night, I won.

Vincent did not turn up to his own dinner party until half an
hour after the pubs in Fleet Street had closed, but he was sober
enough to take all my money in a diabolical hour of Slippery Sam,
a card game that young men should not play with their more
experienced elders. 'You looked as though you earned about five
pounds a week and I was extremely sorry for you when Vincent
fleeced you,' said Brenda, explaining that she accepted my invitation
out of sympathy rather than liking for me.

'Brenda Shepherd (otherwise Wray)', as she is described on our
marriage lines, should have known about the habits of journalists,
but the Bohemian life led by her guardian Vincent Wray did not
teach her any lessons. She was just over eighteen years of age when
we met and she was going to be an actress; her mother was a
singer, her father was a singer, her uncle was an actor, so the stage
was in her blood. But like the majority of young actresses she was
out of work. She had just returned from a 'fit-up' tour (in which
Robert Coote, who for four years played the part of Pickering in
My Fair Lady in both New York and London, was also a struggling
beginner) and was, she said, in the language of the theatrical profession, 'resting'.

Robert Coote went on with his profession, Brenda Wray did not.
Instead we visited the theatre together with tickets sent to the
Liverpool Express office in expectation of London Letter 'puffs'.
One night we went to the old Empire theatre in Leicester Square for
Katja the Dancer, starring Ivy Tresmand and Gene Gerrard, the
next to His Majesty's Theatre for *The Student Prince* (in the interval
of which Brenda whispered to me the balcony scene from *Romeo
and Juliet*); then to *The Co-optimists* as the guests of Archie de Bear
and Davy Burnaby; next an invitation from Clifford Whitley to his
Midnight Follies at the Metropole Hotel in Northumberland
Avenue; then a glittering first night for the film *Les Misérables*,

followed by dinner for five hundred people at which we ate the oysters that had been placed on the tables long before most of the guests had sat down.

We visited the Café Royal in the days when it was all plush and Augustus John, and although sweet vermouth then was our tipple, we felt we were going places. We pulled up at the now-vanished Westminster Bridge coffee stall at one or two o'clock in the morning. It was the high life, save for the fact that when the parties were over it was a late tram-car that took us home to Streatham Hill.

We married within three months of our first meeting, on a total capital of £73, out of which we furnished a three-roomed flat in Lambert Road, Brixton. Our honeymoon was confined to the wedding day, Monday 31 May 1926, as I was by this time a full-blown member of the staff of the *Sunday Express* and Sunday papers do not call in their staffs on Mondays. On Tuesday I reported for duty and went immediately to the Managing Editor, Tom Innes, to tell him my news. He looked up at me with a puzzled expression. 'Bloody fool,' he said. Years later I reminded him of this and he was horrified at his brutality. His reaction surprised me, for although I was probably embarrassed by his explosion, I cannot recall that I resented it. In those days, Fleet Street was a tough place. I got my own way later by mockery, by joking on subjects that I was in earnest about, by gentle persuasion. But I wonder if this approach is a sound substitute for straight talk. It is doubtful.

From this time on, with the exception of high days and holidays, Brenda became a completely neglected newspaper wife. Newspaper wives are much to be pitied. They are in many ways more lonely and frustrated than the wives of sailors. A sailor's wife at least knows when her husband's ship is in port, but a newspaperman's wife rarely has any idea where her husband is. An old friend of mine on the reporting staff of the *Daily Express* turned up at my flat one morning after a night on the tiles, and telephoned his wife. 'I'm calling from Eastbourne,' he said. 'You see that story about the man who jumped off Beachy Head – they sent me down on it at midnight. Sorry I couldn't telephone you. See you later.' Some wives no doubt get wise to their menfolk but they have to be very wise indeed, for of course reporters are in fact pushed around at all sorts of odd and inconvenient hours; it is part of the thrill of news-paper business.

As for executive journalists like myself, I worked an eighteen-hour day for more than twenty years and found my newspaper completely absorbing. This remarkable woman whom I married provided the contented background for my career in Fleet Street. She says now that she knew when we were married that the news-paper came first and she was in second place. She does not know (or care, I suspect) how important she was to the *Daily Express* through all the years. I owe her much; so does Lord Beaverbrook.

7 . . . Quick! It's the Little Man

I have a vivid memory of working on a 'scab' or 'black' edition of the *Sunday Express* on 8 May 1926, when the General Strike which had paralysed all Britain for the previous five days was at its bitterest. I can recall writing 'streamer' headlines and handling masses of big news. But, such are the tricks that memory plays, when I consulted the office files I found that the paper resembled one of those circulars that is stuffed through your letter-box to advertise a sale of carpets.

My streamer headlines were not there. There were only twenty-two items in the paper altogether. It consisted of three miserable columns and was printed on one side of the sheet only. The biggest headline was only about one-quarter of an inch tall and was in single-column form (for the experts it was 14-pt Cheltenham Bold). It said:

RAILWAYMEN WISH TO RETURN

The centre column consisted of a leading article under the simple headline TO-DAY and said the Government was governing, that mob rule was failing, that food, light, power and public safety had been preserved, that Parliament and the courts were functioning and that sanity would prevail soon because of the political genius of the British people.

The remaining column was similar in size to that in Column One and was headed:

APPEAL FOR 30,000 'SPECIALS'

The rest of the paper was filled with items ranging from the announcement that Regent's Park was to be closed so that all available buses could be parked there, to the news that 'a young woman named Piobini had been found with her throat cut at Thundersley, near Southend, on Friday night'. The pubs in Liverpool had been closed at the request of the Government. There had been mass arrests in Glasgow. Fourteen hundred volunteers had been trained to man the London buses. And of course county cricket was being played as usual, with Woodfull 40 not out for the Australians against Surrey at the Oval.

There is a curious old-world style about the way in which much of this news is written. Nowadays a Night Editor, for example, would not tolerate the phrase 'a young woman named Piobini'; he would demand to know her age and her Christian name. Yet there was a tremendous to-do getting the paper out and we were very proud of it. Blumenfeld, the venerable, dignified and much-feared Editor-in-Chief, took off his black coat and wrapped a white apron round his middle to become Head Printer for the day. Sydney Long, the Works Manager, fresh from his labours on the official *British Gazette*, for which he was awarded an O.B.E., was the one and only linotype operator. The Chief Sub-Editor was assigned to the Machine Room. I was one of the two sub-editors. And in charge of the canteen were two Society lovelies, Lady Louis Mountbatten and the Hon. Mrs Richard Norton, who, I was told, were friends of the 'Little Man', as Lord Beaverbrook was then known.

I did not mind being accused of scabbing any more than did Lady Louis and Mrs Norton – Lady Louis went Left in politics many years later. I had given my situation much thought, since I had been a probationary member of the National Union of Journalists at the age of sixteen and active in the Liverpool branch in a campaign to secure votes for the under twenty-ones. But the union's attitude to the General Strike was confused; first-we-could-and-then-we-could-not about summed up instructions from our head-quarters. I was not prepared to be mucked about, so I resigned from the union – I never rejoined it – and carried on with my job. Francis Williams, nowadays the heavy-jowled television character, carried on too.

Francis, who was twenty-three years of age, came from Liver-pool to Fleet Street by the dramatic method of driving himself in a horse caravan. During the strike, he and Tom Darlow, another reporter, drove a pair of horses with a wagon of newsprint through the picket line at the entrance to Shoe Lane. I watched them from a window on the second floor where the editorial room was situated; Lord Beaverbrook watched them from the window of his flat at the top of the building, from which he directed the fortunes and policies of his newspapers. He was so delighted by what he saw that he took a personal interest in the careers of Williams and Darlow thereafter.

It seems hard on Williams that nowadays the General Strike incident is recalled with hostility from time to time in Cross Bencher's political column of the *Sunday Express* because if he had not delivered the newsprint that day there would have been no makeshift paper. But public life is a ruthless business and Williams dishes it out about Beaverbrook as lustily as Beaverbrook dishes it out about Williams. Sometimes I get fouled up in this feuding. Williams grilled me mercilessly on 'Press Conference', the B.B.C. television show; yet he wrote in the *New Statesman* in criticism of something in the *Daily Express* that 'this would not have happened in Christiansen's day'.

One of the flash-points which began the General Strike was the refusal of a mechanical union to print a leading article prepared for the *Daily Mail* (although Stanley Baldwin years later told a Press Club audience 'off the record' that he had been determined to have a show-down with Labour, no matter what the pretext). This refusal to print was regarded as interference with the traditional freedom of the Press and before many hours had passed the whole ghastly tragedy had boiled up. It seemed comically ironic to me that after-noon when Blumenfeld, the Editor-turned-Printer, kept returning copy to myself and the other sub-editor with instructions to smarten up our first paragraphs and get active verbs into our headlines.

'Blum' was always a finicky stylist. It was he who started the 'Do's and Don'ts', a manual of newspaper grammar and style. As Head Printer he nearly gummed up the works by refusing to hand out our copy to be set into type until he had approved it to the last comma and the last word. It was lucky for 'Blum' that Sydney Long was a brilliant linotype operator – he could set a column of type without a single literal and at such a fantastic speed that in his pre-managerial career he took home more money on piece rates than the star reporters or even the leader-writers.

In every respect Long was in splendid form that day. Having set the type, he assembled the pages. Having assembled the pages, he supervised the casting of the stereo-plates. Having supervised the stereo-making, he got the presses rolling. He not only overseered his departmental overseers, he bullied the great Blumenfeld into a feeling that it was easier to be an editor than to be a head printer. (I did not know then that Long would spend many years trying to induce similar feelings of inferiority in me: 'My boy, without the *mechanical departments* there would *BE* no *Daily Express*,' he used to rumble loftily through his massive jowls.)

It was, however, another figure altogether who made it a big day. As the presses began to roll and it was too late for the editorial staff to do more than wait for the first copies to arrive from the machine room – a period of expectation and apprehension that never has lost its sense of taut foreboding for me – the swing doors that led to the Composing Room opened and in walked four men. James Douglas, the white-haired, peppermint-sucking Editor; Tom Innes, the horn-rimmed Managing Editor; Fred Doidge, the smooth-talking Business Manager from New Zealand; and a little man with a large head, who seemed to me a bit lost in the crowd.

'Quick! It's the Little Man,' someone hissed. We dowsed our cigarettes and slid off the horse-shoe table.

Maxwell, the other sub-editor and a *Daily Express* man, who bore an extraordinary resemblance to Mussolini, was the first to be introduced. He reddened and seemed to have difficulty in forming the words, 'Thank you, sir,' when he shook hands with Lord Beaverbrook. When my turn came everyone seemed to have forgotten my name. I got a firm, dry handshake and a meaningful stare, but no word passed between us. I remember that stare perfectly well; I have seen it on countless occasions since. It is an all-embracing probe by the world's most inquisitive, penetrating, curious eyes. It sizes up the characters of newcomers. It diagnoses the 'what-mood-is-he-in?' attitude of his cronies and his colleagues in business. It invariably governs his conduct of the subsequent proceedings. It can reflect, too, his own moods when he wishes – his affections, his hatreds, his scorn, his delight, his good temper, his bad temper. I have experienced the lot, for the relationship between Lord Beaverbrook and myself since that day extended from the harsh realities and pressures of daily newspaper life to a friendship as close as ever that of a father and son could be.

I was a slim youth, just over twenty-one. My hair was brushed straight back but rose about two inches above my rather high brow in embarrassing, almost girlish waves. Lord Beaverbrook was a mere forty-seven, a tiny figure in a blue serge suit. In his employment I have had several 'lives', some changes of contour, and considerable development of character, but Lord Beaverbrook has for me changed little in appearance, and in character not at all. He had a little 'pot' around the middle then, and he has the same little 'pot' now. He wore blue serge suits then and he wears blue serge suits now. He wore brown shoes with his blue suits then, and he wears them now (although nowadays he occasionally goes around at home in brown open-toed sandals). He wore black trilby hats and drab black overcoats then and he does so now. He wore buttons on his shirts then, having no patience with cuff-links, and he still wears buttons now. He wore white shirts then and still does. He did not care if his collars were frayed then, nor does he now. The knot of his tie was loose and careless then and is now. Sartorially, little or nothing has changed.

As to the heart and the brain of the man, they are still as large, or larger, than life. His capacity for political intrigue, as all the world knows, was unsurpassed then; and although events have passed him by, that gift is undiminished to-day and is expressed in different ways. His capacity for re-charging the batteries that operate his frail body has changed only in one respect: in his eighties he goes to bed earlier than he did thirty years ago, and he has a nap after lunch.

This man has been such a feature of my life that I am in many ways his creation. To a great extent he formed not only my life but my character. I came to London an impressionable, newspaper-struck youth and almost at once came under his spell. Whatever likes or dislikes Lord Beaverbrook may arouse, he is one of the most dynamic personalities of our times. In his *Express* group of newspapers he was then inaugurating a new kind of journalism, a journalism of zest and drive, which discarded the stuffy pomposities of the past and strove to bring the news to the people as fresh and appetising as a loaf of new bread.

Beaverbrook used newspapers to further his own beliefs. I wanted only to use newspapers to develop and perfect the projection of news in a way that everyone could understand. No wonder that I came to admire and love Lord Beaverbrook, who trained and developed and allowed me to express my talents as few other men would have done!

But there were no clues to our future relationship that night when I first met him. The Little Man was gone within a couple of minutes. I drew my pay packet of two guineas and went off, con-cerned about nothing in the future save my forthcoming marriage.

What happened to the other young strike-breakers? Darlow died young and I have lost sight of Maxwell. Francis Williams was transferred to the Throgmorton Street office of the Beaverbrook evening newspaper, the *Evening Standard*. Here he mastered the intricacies of financial journalism under the tutelage of Lord Beaverbrook himself, until one day he spread his wings and flew off to the Socialist *Daily Herald*. As City Editor of the *Herald* he conducted immense Page One campaigns against the wickedness of capitalists like Lord Beaverbrook. It was traditional Socialist soap-box stuff and played a useful part in the *Herald*'s efforts to reach a sale of two millions a day. Williams was such a success that he was appointed editor of the paper in the late thirties. But times changed and with a drooping circulation he was regarded as being too 'political'. Editors do not always get the credit for increasing circulation, but they are always held responsible when it declines. Possibly that was why, in discussing the climax of my newspaper life in an article in the *New Statesman*, Williams wrote: 'There is no substitute for an editor.' Proprietors get the editors they deserve, and it is not altogether the fault of bad editorship that some national newspapers are in such a mess today.

Francis Williams did a spell as Mr Attlee's spokesman at Number 10 Downing Street before he returned to journalism and pioneered in television, and he wrote a magnificent history of the Press called *Dangerous Estate* in 1957. Altogether he has more than repaid to his political faith the youthful strike-breaking indiscretion of 1926.

None of the other then-unknowns came to the surface, except myself. I like to believe that James Douglas would have sent for me anyway but, for whatever reason, he did so, and invited me to join the permanent staff. Douglas was the Editor in name only. He had been brought over in 1925 from *The Star*, then London's brightest evening paper, on a fabulous contract (the like of which would have made me a rich man indeed) for it stipulated that he got a commission on increased sales. When he arrived it was discovered that he knew nothing whatsoever about the technical side of getting a paper to press and so he was diverted, most successfully, to sob-stuff article-writing. But a contract being a contract, it was Douglas who had to do the hiring and the firing, and he engaged me at a salary of £12 a week with the title of News Editor.

This was certainly something to go home and shout about. Here I was, only five years out of school and less than one year in London, signing on at the age of twenty-one as a national paper's News Editor! It did not occur to me for a moment that I was completely inexperienced to do the job, and with self-confidence I wrote to my editor in Liverpool asking him to release me from the remainder of my three years' contract with him. In a generous letter of congratulation he agreed to do so four weeks hence, 'in view of the exceptional opportunity which has presented itself'. But I started work on the *Sunday Express* the very next day, doing a double job for a month to suit the convenience of my new employers – and my own, for as my wedding day approached two salaries made life rosy. Indeed, there was only one speck of a cloud on my horizon; when my first pay cheque arrived it was for £10 instead of the promised £12. I rushed in to Doidge, the Manager, to complain. 'Son,' he said, 'we'll give you the extra £2 if you last out your month's trial.'

'But I'm not on a month's trial,' I said, utterly deflated.

'Oh yes, you are,' said Doidge. 'But you do your job well and you'll be all right.'

Moral: get a contract; have it in writing.

For the benefit of young newspapermen who read this book, let me say that my failures and frustrations have been many and from every one of them I have tried to learn. But only one fundamental thing have I learned about newspaper life: that the cards are never dealt in the same order. You have just got to keep on watching for the unexpected, for the unusual, for the new trap. It is not a profession that the unwary should enter, and looking back I am astonished that James Douglas ever gave me a job at all.

Perhaps it was because he himself was unwary. Douglas was persuaded to abandon his *Sunday Express* commission-on-sales contract just when the newspaper was starting its climb from a sale of 300,000 to to-day's 3,500,000!

8 . . . Sack Him, Said R.D.B.

If you had seen a young fellow, holding a *Sunday Express* somewhat prominently, on the top of a 16 tram from Brixton Hill to The Horns, Kennington, any Sunday morning in 1926 and for a year or two thereafter, that would have been me. The object of this exercise was to draw the attention of other passengers to the merits of the newspaper. I would open it at any interesting page and hold it high so that those sitting behind me could read if they wished, and I hoped that when they alighted they would be interested enough to make for the nearest news-stand.

The idea probably never worked even once, but I was a romantic, dedicated enthusiast. I left my copy of the paper on the seat of the tram. Often I bought six copies during Sunday morning. I mentioned the name of the paper in the pub where we gathered for a pre-lunch pale ale. Later in the day I travelled round the West End in a newspaper van with the Circulation Manager to see that the newsboys were pushing our product with vigour.

I often thought that much of this activity must have been rather childish, until one morning in the spring of 1957, when I was walking on Hampstead Heath with Lord Beaverbrook. 'There's a good sight,' he said, pointing to a man on a bench reading the *Daily Express*. 'D'ye know, in the early days, Blumenfeld and I used to walk through Hyde Park looking for women readers – there weren't many of them then. If one day we couldn't find any in Hyde Park, we'd try Regents Park the next.' He was talking of the era when the *Mail* used to advertise '*Daily Mail* – Million Sale' and the rest of the newspapers were nowhere.

Lord Beaverbrook had been playing hell with his son Max a few days previously because a newsagent's shop at the Highgate end of the Heath had had no *Daily Expresses* left at eleven o'clock in the morning. When we got to the shop I volunteered to see if the situation had been put right. It had; there were four copies on the counter and I could not resist putting up the sale by one on the principle that every little helps, even when the circulation is over four millions a day.

It is sometimes argued that the heads of great organisations should not concern themselves with detail, but Lord Beaverbrook as proprietor, and myself as editor, must be the exceptions that prove the rule. Beaverbrook's interventions into the remotest corners of his newspapers are still a daily occurrence, while I weighed myself down with so much detail that even in my hey-day I often laid out the front page myself and wrote the splash head-lines, which few editors do.

It is all a question of the way you are brought up. Tom Innes, my first editor on the *Sunday Express*, and John Gordon, my second editor, worked with the rest of us in what is called the Big Room. It seemed natural, therefore, that I should do the same when my time arrived. Changes in the habits of one's apprentice days are imposed by conditions, rarely by the exercise of native wit.

What an apprenticeship I served! In two pokey, glass-partitioned rooms on the second floor of the *Express* building (the *Sunday Express* nowadays slops over a complete floor) the entire staff of six operated; and as Innes occupied one of these rooms to himself – in which he personally laid out the feature pages – the rest of us were squashed into the other. Although I had the title of News Editor I found myself deeply involved in feature-writing. Alla Nazimova, a fabulous Russian movie star from Hollywood, was topping the bill at the London Coliseum; so we published six articles by Christiansen but signed 'Nazimova' – and how blush-ingly shy I was when I extracted her life story between perform-ances as she sat draped in an exotic kimono in her dressing-room.

Reginald Denny, the English film star who was making a hit in
Hollywood, came to the Savoy; 'Christiansen, write his life story.'
'Christiansen, see if you can get an article on "My Religion" out
of Harry Lauder – he's just back from a world tour and he might
give it to you free.' (He did in a half-hour interview in the Euston
Hotel before he left by train for Scotland.) 'Christiansen, you're a
good ghost; see if Betty Balfour [then known as the English Mary
Pickford] will play.' (She did; half a dozen free articles.) 'Christiansen, get Tallulah Bankhead to write an article on gallery girls and
what she thinks of modern youth' (the aromatic and husky-voiced
Miss Bankhead duly obliged, even though I was more obviously
scared of her than I had been of Nazimova when I called at her
lacquer-furnished house in Deanery Street, off Park Lane).

I reflect now that these early writings largely concerned people
in show business. My friends outside Fleet Street were (and still
are) also in show business. I played golf with a handsome blond
giant named Val Parnell, later to invent the idea of the Crazy Gang,
to revive variety by importing top Hollywood talent to the London
Palladium and to crown his career as managing director of Associated Television. Another golf 'regular' was a fleshy, witty young
variety agent named Henry Sherek, now an international impresario as well known in New York as he is in the West End of
London. The three of us paid weekly green fees instead of joining
a golf club, because we couldn't quite afford the annual lump sum
that membership entails!

I met a portly young film director named Alfred Hitchcock and
a handsome young cinema proprietor named Sydney Bernstein. I
did a day's work as an extra in a film for Herbert Wilcox. Perhaps
the influence of all these people developed me as a newspaper show-
man instead of the politician some of my critics think I should have
been. But keeping up with the young and confident show business
giants did not overcome my natural shyness.

I often wonder whether I spent my first ten years in Fleet Street
being scared of people. It may well be so, despite the brash exterior
which I seem to have possessed. I was scared when I was made
Chief Sub-Editor on Saturdays, which was our Press day. As Chief
Sub-Editor I was in charge of all the news pages, except for Page
One which was run jointly by the editor and the assistant editor.

E

I cannot believe that I was fitted for such a baptism of fire, and when one night in 1927 a young American named Charles Lindbergh flew the Atlantic alone, I flopped desperately in presenting the news. Innes and his assistant were out of the office when Lindbergh landed in Paris; it should have been my big moment, but I had never handled news of this magnitude before, and I was quite overwhelmed.

When newspapers – at any rate Beaverbrook's newspapers – make a botch of the news, the inquest is terrifying.

'Who was in charge?' asked R. D. Blumenfeld, the editor-in-chief. I was pointed out to him.

'Sack him,' said Blumenfeld. 'He's too good-looking to be any use.' It was as good a reason as any; my pink cheeks, curly hair and largeish sideboards could not have inspired much confidence; but I was saved by John Gordon, a lantern-jawed young Scotsman, who argued that it was ridiculous to sack the office boy when the blame lay higher up the ladder.

That was the beginning of a lifelong friendship and a profitable partnership for Beaverbrook. John, then Chief Sub-Editor of the *Daily Express*, was on loan at this time to the Sunday paper. Innes was easing himself out of journalism in favour of the movies, and Gordon was being groomed to succeed him as Editor. Pretty soon the transfer took place and the era of 'hellzapoppin' began for the *Sunday Express*.

Gordon gave me confidence. We sparked together; the bond between us was a natural, electrifying thing. Soon I was his assistant editor and my days of 'ghosting' gave place to the more satisfying work of overall newspaper construction and development.

Moreover, the contrast between Gordon and Innes was profound. Innes drank hard and liked to linger in the pubs of Fleet Street; Gordon drank nothing and, apart from a visit to the Press Club for a game of snooker, was never seen about Fleet Street. Innes growled and nothing was ever right; Gordon praised and things were almost too often right. Innes kept his own counsel on the conduct of his newspaper; Gordon talked it out to the point of indiscretion.

There are four other names associated with this period: Castlerosse, Swaffer, Gubbins and Bradburn. The first two were great stars when I met them; let me, therefore, deal with my own two discoveries, for an editor is only as good as the people he discovers. A fine editor will not succeed until he surrounds himself with a fine staff. Even the genius of Beaverbrook could not achieve the success of the *Sunday Express* until John Gordon's arrival. Lord Beaverbrook once told me, for instance, that the first week he put Beverley Baxter in charge of the *Sunday Express* (later Baxter became a very fine editor indeed of the *Daily Express*) every single major Page One headline dealt with the coal crisis, and that the paper did not recover for years from the blunder of filling its first issue, to the exclusion of all other matter, with the results of the 1919 Homes-Fit-For-Heroes General Election.

Harry Bradburn was not an important figure. There are no references to him in the annals of Fleet Street. But he was my first discovery, a natural newspaperman, and before he died in his forties he had become the Night Editor of the *Daily Express*.

Strictly speaking, Harry Bradburn had no right to be on the *Sunday Express*. A big money prize had been offered in a competition by the *Sunday Dispatch*, our chief rival. A woman, giving her address as a public house, won it. Bernard Falk, the shrewd Lancastrian editor, and one who doubted that all mankind was good and honest, felt that a pub address was suspicious. He sent an investigator to the district and established that the woman was friendly with a member of the *Dispatch* staff. The prize money was withheld. The conspirators in the *Dispatch* office took fright. Someone turned 'King's evidence' and half a dozen people were sacked. Among those fired on suspicion was Bradburn.

Many weeks later, when the scandal had died down – curiously enough, news of it had not reached me – Bradburn, a plump, unhealthy, fair-haired Yorkshireman, with a strong accent and bad teeth, asked me for a job as a week-end sub-editor. He proved to be so good that soon I gave him mid-week work as well.

His first job arose out of the trial and conviction of two men, Browne and Kennedy, for the murder of a policeman named Gutteridge. Stanley Bishop, the *Daily Express* chief reporter, had described Browne as 'the master-mind in the murder plot' and Kennedy as 'the dreamer with the eyes of a poet'.

'Bradburn,' I said, 'I wonder whether Kennedy ever really did try to write a poem.'

'Give me that cutting,' said Bradburn, 'I'll find out.'

I did not see Bradburn for the rest of the week. But on Saturday morning he came in unshaven and looking greasier and unhealthier than ever. In his hand was a scrap of paper and on the paper a six-stanza poem was scrawled out. There could be no question about it; comparison between an example of the handwriting of Kennedy and that of the poem showed that they were identical.

I reproduced the first stanza of the poem entitled 'The End of Life's Fling' in facsimile on Page One of the *Sunday Express* and the remainder on Page Three. This was the first verse:

> The dreams of our youth
> Turn to nightmares of age,
> And the fool and his folly
> Passes out with the sage.
> Life's task is completed
> With death as sin's wage,
> A crimson-hued blot
> At the end of the page.

The poem was signed 'K'.

In the office of the *Dispatch*, Bradburn's old newspaper, Bernard Falk turned his best man (it was Harold Lake, who wrote the ballad *I Hear You Calling Me*) on to every anthology in the office library to try to find the original of the poem and so expose the thing as a fake. But it was no use. Kennedy, the murderer, had written the poem in his own handwriting. There was no explanation as to how it had fallen into our hands. Nor did I dare inquire.

Years later I found out. Bradburn had cajoled an old Fleet Street hack named Charlie Miles, a jolly Welshman who might have been a Dylan Thomas judging by the amount he drank, to write the poem. Bradburn then took it to a public house used by the warders of Wandsworth Jail. He played poker with some of them all through that night, and persuaded one of them to take the poem into the condemned cell for Kennedy to copy out.

What Kennedy got out of it I do not know. Bradburn's expenses for that week were unexceptional. But maybe an item for one bottle of Scotch, 12s 6d, explained it all.

I sent Bradburn to Dover to cover the story of Mercedes Gleitz when she swam the English Channel. Bradburn disappeared for three or four weeks. We had long given up the search for him when he turned up in Blackpool, claiming to be Miss Gleitz's business manager. All was forgiven, however, and he rejoined the staff, to be sent once more to the South Coast, this time to investigate the race gangs that flourished in Brighton at that time. Instead of exposing the gangs, he brought a real-life gangster back to Fleet Street. 'Show him your razor,' said Bradburn, when I had been persuaded to meet 'Manchester Dawson' in a pub – appropriately in Gunpowder Alley. Dawson whipped out a cut-throat that had been shredded along its blade. 'Makes a nice rough cut, sir,' he leered at me, and drew it across my throat about an inch from the skin. Bradburn grinned proudly and said, 'And what do you do with a bottle?' Whereupon Dawson seized a pale ale bottle, broke it with a crash against the bar counter and thrust the jagged remnants within inches of my eyes. 'He's harmless,' said Bradburn contemptuously. 'Come on, Dawson, get out of here and get back to Brighton.' And Dawson went.

Bradburn was about my age. Yet he had served in the First World War, which ended when I was fourteen. That, he explained, was because he had faked his age and joined up as a drummer boy. By the time the British Army occupied the Rhine in 1919, Bradburn was a sergeant. He rubbed his hands with glee as he told, in the accents of his native Barnsley, prodigious stories of his adventures – he was a prodigious fellow in every way. He was always sober, as far as one could judge, yet his drinking was tremendous. He died of the stuff in the end, I imagine. It has killed better and worse men, but, for me, there was nobody quite like Bradburn.

There was no resemblance whatsoever between the character of Harry Bradburn and that of Nathaniel Gubbins, my other early 'discovery'. Bradburn's memory exists only for me and a small number of men who worked with him, but Gubbins is one of the select band of Fleet Street 'originals' whose name will live and whose like passes by but once: men such as Charles Hands, George Augustus Sala, Philip Gibbs, Hannen Swaffer, H. V. Morton, Ward Price, Strube, and Tom Webster (no modern 'immortals' in this list; only those of my boyhood and early manhood).

I met Nathaniel Gubbins (real name Norman Liefchild Gubbins) in the Cheshire Cheese. I was told that he was guaranteed only two days a week on the *Sunday Dispatch* at two guineas a day, so I offered this diffident, prematurely bald, lugubrious character a three-day guarantee, with the promise that I would push his way as much extra as I could.

Gubbins proved hard to use. The usual routine reportorial chores, such as fires and murders, not only bored him; he was just no good at them. He also hated the follow-up work. ('Here's a cutting,' says the News Editor, handing the reporter a clipping from another newspaper. 'See if you can get some fresh views on the short skirt scandal.' That is follow-up work.) His descriptive stories of big events were cynical; even on sunless days he always had 'shafts of light flooding down on the bride through the stained-glass windows' as she 'whispered her vows'. What was more, as a companion he was moody and uncommunicative. Ask him what he wanted to do, he would reply 'Nothing', and lapse into silence over a half-pint of beer or a pink gin. He hated dirty stories and said he did not listen to them at all, though he laughed in the right places.

In a burst of confession, he once told me that as a boy he had tried to commit suicide, and I could well believe that. He got me in such a gloomy state myself that it seemed inevitable I must sack him to preserve my own sanity. But opportunity finally knocked for Gubbins in November 1930, when I sent him to try for an interview with Rudyard Kipling in advance of the G.O.M.'s birthday. Kipling would not see him, but Gubbins found a roadsweeper and a hedgecutter named Lavender and Stonestreet respectively, who knew Kipling well – at any rate, Kipling nodded to them when he was out walking, and *they* knew who Kipling was. That was enough for Gubbins. He had a gift for interviewing centenarians, old people with ear trumpets, and country characters who took it out of the smart folk from Lunnon. He applied this technique to the interview with Mr Lavender and Mr Stonestreet, and although neither of them said more than a monosyllabic 'A-aah' throughout the story, it made a beautiful yarn.

On the Sunday it appeared John Gordon telephoned to ask if I knew where Gubbins was to be found. Lord Beaverbrook had read the story, as he read every word that was ever written about his old friend Kipling, and liked what he read. I found Gubbins in the Antelope, off Sloane Square, and he went off to Stornoway House, Lord Beaverbrook's town house. He was 'grilled' about his past and told the proprietor how he had actually started in Fleet Street as an office boy in the *Daily Express* library. He was asked if he would like to write a column.

His column was born the following Sunday, but until Friday lunchtime we could not think of a title. Three or four of us sat at the bar of 'The Falstaff', baffled and more than inclined to take to drink. I began to hum a popular tune, the chorus of which started:

> There ain't no sense
> Sitting on the fence
> All by yourself in the moonlight.

'That's it,' I said. 'We'll call it "Sitting on the Fence".' It was the perfect title. All that remained now was to write the perfect column.

The start was shaky. After a month Gubbins was nearly off his fence. John Gordon claims that it was he who had faith and saved it, which means that Lord Beaverbrook urged the killing of his own brain child. I claim that I was the strongest in faith, and in this Gubbins supports me. But the fact is that 'Sitting on the Fence' became established and at its peak earned its author more than £100 a week. It brought to the public such features as Sally the Cat, the Diary of a Worm, Letters to My Stomach, the Man in the Pub, the Awful Child, the Sparrow – and, in war-time, mockery of Hitler's *blitzkrieg* that must have driven the Germans frantic in their attempts to understand the mad English.

Gubbins has been compared with America's James Thurber, Robert Benchley and S. J. Perelman. But he was like none of these. He was an Original. He could label his writings proudly: ALL MY OWN WORK.

And that brings me back to my theme: an editor is no good without a good staff. I was also learning that to succeed with a newspaper an editor must know the kind of work the members of his staff can do best and have the courage and the wit to let them do it.

9 . . . Inside John Gordon

Mr Graham Greene, the novelist, recently recommended to the public the dubious virtues of the novel *Lolita*. This brought him into conflict with John Gordon, now in his seventies, and for the last few years in semi-retirement after thirty years as editor of the *Sunday Express*. Mr Greene, by way of riposte, wrote to a highbrow weekly appealing for the formation of a group to be known as 'The Friends of John Gordon', the object of which was to gather facts for a biography of this trenchant and, to some, prudish and carping controversialist. It was all good clean fun and was good publicity for both Greene and Gordon.

I could have contributed an intimate account of Gordon's early days as an editor. This Dundee-born, D. C. Thomson-trained Scot was for a long time the apple of Lord Beaverbrook's eye. He fell out of favour for a time in the early thirties but stonily stood his ground and is now back sitting on the right hand of the throne, shrewdly aiming at targets suggested by the proprietor (who does not, by the way, agree with the censorship of books).

Gordon was no intellectual. His journalistic taste was practically limited to snippets, and he abhorred anything that ran to more than half-a-column. He was a master sub-editor and could deceive the eye by breaking up a two-column story so that it fell into five or more sections of less than half-a-column each. In his

early thirties when I became his assistant editor he was even more
arrogant, self-sufficient, and dictatorial than he was later on when
success had crowned his brilliance. *His* way of life, *his* way of
journalism, was right; all others were wrong.

'Now take me,' he would say, 'I live in Croydon. My house,
which I have lived in ever since I joined the *Evening News* straight
from Dundee, costs me £50 a year and £13 rates. That's quite
enough for any man to spend on rent. Why you want to live in
the West End, Chris, beats me.

'Anybody living in Croydon can come up to the West End in
half an hour. Now take me. What do I do? I spend my Mondays
off in the West End. I go to the Plaza matinee. Then I have a good
meal. Then I'm home in Croydon before ten o'clock.'

Gordon in his early days was certainly the exception that proves
the rule. He knew only the people he wanted to know, and sought
the company of no others. The adulation of politicians, theatrical
impresarios, West End tip-off socialites, *svelte* head-waiters meant
nothing to him. He was a desk man, a chair-bound editor. He knew
what he wanted, and what he wanted was summed up frequently
by a mysterious phrase, 'the Thing'. Thus at a news conference the
staff was subjected to this kind of harangue:

'The Little Man (Beaverbrook) thinks we should use Arnold
Bennett in the Thing. What good's Bennett at a shillun' a wurrd?
But the Little Man's the capitalist millionaire proprietor, so let him
have the Thing and we'll get on with selling the Thing ourselves.'

This and other examples of outspokenness were received by us
all with hushed awe. Gordon was basically a Bolshie. He resented
those in authority and was at no pains to conceal his views. The
fact that Lord Castlerosse – if he got to the office in time for
morning conference at all – must have repeated Gordon's heresies
to Lord Beaverbrook, never succeeded, so far as I know, in curbing
Gordon's tongue.

Even more than on proprietors, Gordon took it out on managers.
He taught me that an Article of Faith in editing a newspaper was
to be at constant war with the Management. If there were too few
advertisements, whose fault was it? The inefficient Management's.
Too many? The avaricious Management's. Just right? The
wisdom of the Editor had prevailed. If the paper missed the train

delivery, whose fault? The Management, which provided such a bad mechanical set-up. If the paper caught the train? Editorial efficiency that triumphed over all obstacles.

His war against Management never ceased. 'Look at that fellow Russell,' he said of one manager. 'Brings a golf club to the office and swipes at lumps of sugar on his carpet. That's all he ever does.'

That Russell did a brilliant job advertising the life story of the actress June after her marriage to Lord Inverclyde had been dissolved, did not endear him to Gordon. The fact that Russell outbid rival Sunday papers for the life story of a woman who had been acquitted of poisoning her husband with sheep-dip earned only Gordon's grudging praise. 'Aye,' he said when the news of this coup was telephoned to him, 'that's all Managements are good for.' Surely a poor return for Russell's cunning in topping by a desperate £5 the final bid of £3,000 made by Harry Ainsworth, Editor of *The People*. It was Russell's last bid, too, if Ainsworth had only realised it, and a further £5 would have won the story for *The People*.

Gordon's defensive mechanism may have been more assumed than real, but he never let up. The Beaverbrook system has always been to work rather through the managers than the editors, editors being temperamental so-and-so's who are liable to fly off the handle.

I was in charge of the production of the news pages of the *Sunday Express* on Saturday nights. At the height of the circulation success of *All Quiet on the Western Front*, the 1914 war classic that was being serialised, the strain on the machine room resources in printing the extra copies meant getting to press especially early. Gordon had gone out for a quick supper when Russell sauntered into the editorial room. 'Where's John?' he asked. I said I did not know. 'Does he always go out without letting you know where he's gone?' asked Russell. When Gordon returned I passed on the message that Russell had been inquiring for him; that and no more. But if I had given the message as it was given to me the effect could not have been more shattering. 'That man's a spy!' Gordon hissed. 'I'll yank him off to Stornoway House for this.'

In the end, Russell left the *Sunday Express* to become a Moral Rearmer and to write a book called *All the Sinners*, of whom John

Gordon was not one of those mentioned. But by the time this happened I had left, too, so I did not find out if religion or Gordon was the real reason for Russell's departure from newspapers. All I know is that Gordon led Russell a dog's life and in consequence made the entire editorial staff very, very happy. The natural attitude of Editorial and Management towards each other is that of dog and cat; they can learn to live amicably side by side, but it takes a bit of training.

Under Gordon's editorship the *Sunday Express* expanded from its two pokey rooms to half a dozen on the fourth floor, an arid expanse that had previously stored paper reels. We were still all bunched together. The Manager was at one end. In the middle was Leslie Needham the Advertisement Manager, a bristling young ex-Army officer who, as was then the fashion, was always called 'the Captain' by his admiring staff. I was in the next room and John Gordon wound up in the extreme corner as far away as he could get from the Manager.

During the early part of the week the tiny editorial staff – Russell Stannard, the News Editor; Pat Murphy, a gay Irishman who had followed Gordon from the *Evening News*; Nat Gubbins; two other reporters; a sub-editor; and myself – saw little of John except at planning conferences. But on Friday nights the great man unbent by coming to my room and gathering us around him, like the head of a family, for reminiscence and song – yes, song. 'To be a success you've got to have the common touch,' he would say in his best Dundee. 'Now take the chappie who wrote "Who's afraid of the Big Bad Wolf?" He has the common touch. Anyone can remember the words and anyone can remember the tune.' And with that we would get the lot, words and music in a wild Highland chant until his jaw snapped ruggedly on the last note and he eyed us all as though another lesson in the art of journalism had been ingeniously delivered.

The success of *All Quiet* brought out the mood of Friday-night war-time reminiscence. Finding himself in a shell-hole in No Man's Land, John had killed the German sentry who stood between him and the British lines, by stabbing him with a sheath-knife.

'I brought the knife home with me in 1918,' he said, 'and I used it to sharpen my pencils until somebody stole it from my desk in the *Daily Express* office. I hope all you fellows have a knife on your desks to keep your pencils sharp. Clean copy sets faster and you can't write clean copy with blunt pencils.'

Again the Roving Eye swept the room to see if we had taken in the moral of the yarn. And then on to stories of Beaverbrook and Northcliffe, until suddenly he would withdraw, the lessons completed till next week.

Every afternoon – but yes, *every* afternoon another great talker descended on us. Hannen Swaffer, an untidy, cigarette-ash-stained wraith gave us two hours of his time between three and five o'clock to talk, talk, talk, about what he had said to Bernard Shaw (or Wells or Charlie Cochran) and never what Bernard Shaw (or Wells or Charlie Cochran) had said to him – it amazed me that Swaff was such a fine reporter, since I had never known him listen to anyone.

Swaff's lectures invariably began with the words 'I told him', and developed along well-worn but fascinating tracks. 'I said "why should I listen to you when I've come here to tell *you* something?' Or a story about 'the Chief' (Lord Northcliffe). 'He used to call me the Poet when I was editor of the *Dispatch*. To annoy Marlowe he used to put up notices on the *Daily Mail* board praising me. 'Once again the Poet has shown us all how to handle the news", they used to say. Pah! My secret was that I never let the Chief know what was going into the paper. When he rang up to ask what was happening I used to say "Nothing, Chief". So when he saw the headlines next morning, he got the surprise of his life. Never tell proprietors what is going to appear in their own papers.'

Swaffer had long since become a teetotaller (years later he told me that in his heavy-drinking days he was being 'prepared' for the Spiritualistic activities that came to occupy so much of his thoughts) and he was a model of reliability. His visits were time-consuming, but never boring. He was the willing victim of my developing sense of news projection. He went into the boxing ring looking like a pygmy, to be photographed alongside Primo Carnera, the outsize Italian we called the Ambling Alp when he became heavyweight champion of the world. He wrote articles for headlines I suggested, such as WHY EVERYBODY HATES ME. When his face was slapped by an American actress in the Savoy Grill, he allowed me to 'reconstruct' the scene pictorially for his page.

As far as I could judge Gordon and Swaff did not get along particularly well together at that time – their egos probably clashed. But if Gordon allowed me to run the entertainment section on my own it was just about the only section of the newspaper that escaped his vigilance.

At Gordon's suggestion in 1930 I organised an idea which started a vogue that has gone on ever since. It was a typical Gordon idea in the 'snippets' category: 'Get Cheiro (then the greatest name in the astrology business) to do a horoscope of Princess Margaret,' he said; but Cheiro was of all places in Cairo that week, which was lucky for R. H. Naylor, one of his assistants, who undertook the assignment.

Naylor and his horoscopes became a power in the land. If he said that Monday was a bad day for buying, then the buyers of more than one West End store waited for the stars to become more propitious. Gradually, of course, every paper published a horoscope and you paid your money and bought or sold from Monday to Friday according to which prophet you followed.

But that is how all those 'What the Stars Foretell' features began. In curiosity I looked up Naylor's horoscope of Princess Margaret. It says 'She will marry rather suddenly in her twenty-fourth or twenty-sixth year, as the result of an attachment of long standing. . . .' How wrong can you be!

John Gordon had immense boldness, more than I ever possessed. He once believed that he had found a cure for cancer. A writer named F. A. Mackenzie discovered that he had the disease and co-operated with Gordon in the publication of a series of articles entitled 'The Man with a Year to Live'. About this time Dr Bendien, a Dutch doctor living near Utrecht, developed a theory about the origins of cancer which promised well.

Gordon sent Mackenzie for treatment, and for a time Dr Bendien's methods seemed to be successful. Relentlessly the *Sunday Express*, under Gordon's leadership, attacked the slow-coach attitude of British researchers in refusing to investigate the Bendien

claims, until finally Dr Alfred Piney, Secretary of the Investigation
Committee of the British Empire Cancer Campaign, was forced to
visit Dr Bendien. The doctor was handed a series of test-tubes
containing malignant and non-malignant blood and asked to
diagnose them. That week-end our splash headlines announced the
result thus:

DR BENDIEN TESTED BY EMPIRE
CANCER CAMPAIGN

DIAGNOSIS 100% CORRECT

Vastly encouraged, Gordon put the paper behind Dr Bendien
with still greater fervour. He invited Dr Bendien to London and
gave him a dinner party at the Savoy Hotel, to which leading
doctors, specialists and researchers were invited. Sir Thomas
Horder and Sir John Bland-Sutton were present, the Senior
Surgeon of the Cancer Hospital accepted. Indeed, the only non-
medical people present were Gordon himself and H. G. Wells.

Alas, that week 'The Man With a Year to Live' died. It was
explained that Dr Bendien had received him as a patient when he
was beyond human aid; but gradually Dr Bendien faded from the
public view, until he, too, died, they said, heart-broken.

John Gordon taught me many things including the virtue of
loyalty to your staff. He had saved my bacon over Lindbergh's
Atlantic flight and he carried the can for an abominable mistake
that I made. A tip-off man telephoned to say that Walter Citrine
(now Lord Citrine) had been horse-whipped at an international
trade union conference in Italy which he had attended as the general
secretary of the Electricians' Union. I telephoned Citrine for an
interview and received the answer that he would neither confirm
nor deny the truth of the alleged incident. On the strength of this I
decided that the tip must be true and gave it a Page One splash.
But Monday's papers carried an interview with Citrine denying
the whole thing, and the *Sunday Express* had to apologise on the
following Sunday. In those harsh days men were sacked for less.
But thanks to Gordon's understanding compassion I survived.

Our friendship has only once been under strain – when after my appointment to the editorship of the *Daily Express*, he wrote to me attributing the increasing sales of the paper not to my editorship but to the 'free gift' circulation war then in progress. But this was in character, too. For Gordon taught his staff to hold all other papers in contempt and all other journalists too.

On Saturday nights Gordon took over the room of the editor of the *Daily Express* in order to be near the main editorial office.

'Look at this, Chris,' he said to me once showing me a note from Lord Beaverbrook to Beverley Baxter. It expressed Beaverbrook's dislike of any kind of waste thus: 'You send me a manuscript with a note attached. This note occupies one entire sheet of embossed notepaper to say "With Mr Beverley Baxter's compliments". Please instruct your secretary that I do not require compliments when communications pass between you and me.'

'Would you stand for that? I wouldn't,' said Gordon rebelliously. In those days he was always the rebel. It was the secret of his editorship. With the years he has mellowed as men do, but he is at peace with no one except Lord Beaverbrook. Every week the boy in him re-emerges in his writings and someone high and mighty catches a fourpenny one in a place where he least expects it – and the fourpenny one, as good editors from Delane to C. P. Scott knew, is the secret of successful journalism.

10 . . . The R101 Disaster

Newspaper offices are all the same when the final edition has been put to bed. The Big Room is full of stale tobacco smoke and stuffy with the generated heat of sweating sub-editors. One or two of them sit around reading page-proofs, their shirt-sleeves rolled up and their arms covered in printer's ink up to their elbows. The floor is littered with torn newspapers and the desks with bits of Press Association or Reuter copy that have escaped the piled-high spikes. An office boy moves lazily from desk to desk gathering the spikes, wrapping up their contents, and marking the bundles in blue pencil with the names of the sub-editors so that when the next day's inquests on blunders and omissions are held, the evidence of the spike can be produced quickly. No one but the boy seems to have a spark of energy left. The spluttering of the tape machines has died away as the news has dried up. Even the late-stop staff who report for duty at nine p.m. are overcome by the sense of anti-climax and sit inertly gazing at nothing.

Such was the scene as I bid everybody good night just after midnight on 5 October 1930. It had been the usual kind of Saturday – in the office by 10 a.m. to tidy up the feature pages and get the machine going; news conference with John Gordon at noon, followed by the usual desperate struggle to fill the avaricious pages for the early edition that went to press at 6 p.m.; supper break at seven o'clock with Sandy Glenday, the office lawyer, during which, as usual, he explained the mysteries of a drink of his own invention called a Blairgowrie – three single whiskies shared into two glasses and topped with a small dry ginger because a single whisky was too small at any time, and a double whisky too large while on duty; back to the office to polish up and handle the late news and to get the main edition to press by 11.45 p.m.

It was such a slack night that Gordon had left early. Time mattered little to me since I had moved to Pimlico, which was only an 11 bus ride from Fleet Street. I lingered, not in the belief that big news was about to break, but because newspapermen simply cannot bring themselves to go home. Some just sit around the office; some wander across to the Press Club to drink or play snooker, but always with the hope that a telephone call will bring them back.

On this night, as I was about to tear myself away, half a dozen of them sneaked into one corner of the Big Room, and got out the cards for a game of pontoon. 'For God's sake take care,' I said. 'No machine minders or packers in this game, or you're for it.' The Works Overseer had complained that the Saturday night editorial card game seduced his staff from their machines and it had been officially banned by the management. I turned a blind eye to the ban, because to have six journalists in the office after midnight when they are not even on duty was an insurance of incalculable value against trouble.

As you will see.

I was home and in bed by 1 a.m. The light had not been put out, because I was taking one last look through the paper and talking to my wife about the fortnight's holiday that was beginning for us on Monday morning – we were going to 'do' Brussels, Cologne, and, if the money lasted, Paris.

The telephone bell rang. It was Solomon Levy, the Late Stop. 'We've just had a flash,' he rasped. 'We think the R101 is down in flames at Beauvais in France. Thought you'd like to know. Am putting through an edition.' And with this message he hung up.

How I got back to Fleet Street in twenty minutes flat has become a legend that grows and grows. It is said that I arrived in my dressing-gown and pyjamas. It is said that I had a pair of trousers

F

over my pyjamas, but no jacket. It is said that I had my wife's handbag under my arm, having grabbed it because I had no small change in my pockets. Books by journalists have perpetuated these myths. The truth is more prosaic – it invariably is. I was fully dressed – it doesn't take a few seconds when you hurry. I did grab my wife's small change, but not her handbag. And I ran all the way down Gloucester Street, Pimlico, to Wilton Road – about a quarter of a mile – before I found a taxi. But I had recovered from even that unaccustomed exertion by the time I reached Fleet Street.

All that was visible of the pontoon school as I strode into the Big Room were little piles of money and a scattered pack of cards. Harry Bradburn, a superlative sub-editor, was in the picture library digging out some ready-made blocks of the R101, of Lord Thomson, the Air Minister, and of Sir Sefton Brancker, the Director of Civil Aviation, who were on board. Levy was in the Composing Room, stripping down the old Page One of all its superfluous type. Dennis Dunn, a reporter who had joined the pontoon school, was chattering in first-rate French to the postmaster of a village near Beauvais. The Air Ministry was being contacted by Hugh Chevins for a complete list of passengers. Billy Eales, the late duty telephonist, was sharpening his pencils.

I took over. Like an editor in an American movie, I took the risk of stopping the presses while the edition containing the big news was made ready. Special trains were hired by Reggie Back, the Night Publisher, to take parcels of papers all over the country for what is called a 'change-up' or a 'box-out' – that is, the Circulation Traveller takes back out-of-date papers and gives the newsagent supplies with the hot news. Reporters and sub-editors long since off duty were recalled. Vans were sent round for extra printers, picture process workers and other mechanical staff.

The Fleet Street drama of this tremendous disaster to the airship R101 on her triumphal voyage to India – a disaster which was to bring to an end Britain's research on this type of aviation – cannot wholly be explained by the event itself. If the crash had happened by day the disaster would have been big enough to warrant every journalistic endeavour; but there would have been time to gather the facts, to send reporters and photographers from London or from Paris, or both. But at two o'clock in the morning, time was running out on us; for it is no use printing a paper that does not reach the streets. By 2 a.m. the bulk of the newspapers printed in Fleet Street are on their way to the newsagents' shops by van, by train, even by push-bike. By 4 a.m., the last copies have been printed and there is nothing more anyone can do about it. Time was running out. . . .

Well, we made it. I wrote the headlines and did the lay-out for one, two, three editions. Bradburn wrote the narrative story as it developed. Dennis Dunn combed the whole of the Beauvais area by telephone for bits of information. Levy put the paper to bed edition by edition.

Suddenly it was dawn. I decided to have another edition at 8 a.m., a Sunday morning Special to sell on the streets of London. A machine crew stood by to plate up, while the rest of the staff went home. Bradburn rustled up bacon and eggs, a quart of milk and a gallon of tea from a Shoe Lane dairy – and a bottle of Scotch, which he drank with milk in place of tea.

I was, in fact, having this potion myself when at 9 a.m. the telephone rang. I picked it up testily, for during the past few hours it had rung many times as relatives and friends asked for news. Each time I had had to say that there was little hope, that forty-eight out of the fifty-four on board were unaccounted for, and that I did not know the identity of the six survivors. Even in the excitement of printing the news these calls had jerked my conscience. I wanted no more of them.

'*Sunday Express* News Room,' I said.

'Is that Mr Christiansen?' said a voice with a strong Canadian accent.

'Who wants him?' I asked.

'Lord Beaverbrook.'

'Yes, sir.'

It was the first time I had heard his voice since the General Strike of 1926, and his words made music. 'You have secured a wonderful feat of journalism. I am proud to be associated with a newspaper on which you work. Good-bye to you.' That was all. Before I could mumble my astonished thanks, the line went dead.

At that time we none of us knew that all this effort in the *Sunday Express* office had not been paralleled elsewhere in Fleet Street until it was far, far too late to be of much use. The *News of the*

World came out with an edition in the course of the morning; the *Sunday Chronicle*, printed in Manchester, had published a 'special'. But to all intents and purposes we had a scoop – one of the biggest scoops in the history of Sunday newspapers. The following week we all got bonuses; mine, of £50, was cabled to Cologne and enabled me to take a glimpse of the Nazi thugs then taking over in Berlin as well as of the lights of Paris, but on this Sunday morning it was the honour and the glory that mattered above all else.

Gradually the staff of the *Daily Express* began to drift in, including handsome Freddie Salusbury, who sniffed disparagingly at some phrase or other in our paper and said 'But, my dear chap, it's not accurate'.

John Gordon came in about 11 a.m. I had telephoned him at some point of the night, but he had allowed me to get on with the job on my own – years later he said in a speech at an office dinner that he had thrown the dog a bone!

His reaction to the paper that morning was fatherly. He took me on one side and advised me to go home and get some rest. 'Above all,' he said, 'don't go out with the boys. You need sleep.'

With that he left the building. I did not. I wasn't ready to go home. We went to the pub in Gunpowder Alley – all of us except the sensible Sol Levy – when it opened at 12.30. Before we parted, I said to the boys that we would meet that night in the 'Windsor Castle', opposite Victoria Station, at 8 p.m. and hold the final celebration of our triumph.

I went to bed at three o'clock in the afternoon and asked my wife to wake me at seven.

She did. I got up after four hours sleep, and dressed. My head was reeling with fatigue, but this was a sentimental journey to meet the men who had done so much for the newspaper. I walked the half-mile from my flat to the 'Windsor Castle' in the gloom of a wet Sunday night, and arrived on the stroke of eight. I ordered a drink and sat there waiting. I waited for an hour without touching it. Not a soul turned up.

So I went back to bed myself. John Gordon was right after all.

11 . . . The Sunny Side of the Street

Whatever qualities go to make an editor were being knocked into me in these early years on the *Sunday Express*. Ewart Hodgson, the ex-dramatic critic of the *Sunday Dispatch*, told Bernard Falk, his ex-editor, that if the *Dispatch* wanted a good successor when he retired, I was the man who was putting the steam behind the *Sunday Express*.

Falk was a perceptive man. 'Is that so, Hodgson?' he said dryly. 'I sometimes think, you know, that editors have something to do with the success of newspapers.'

I would have subscribed to that, for John Gordon was a magnificent editor and was bringing me out. He was living up to the precepts of E. W. ('Lusty') Scripps, the famous American publisher, who said 'Never do yourself what somebody else can do half as well', and was giving me more and more responsibility. Undoubtedly it was due to Gordon's training that when Bernard Falk did in fact retire in 1931, I was asked to go across to Carmelite House for an interview with Sir George Sutton, the grizzled managing director of Associated Newspapers which owns the *Dispatch*.

Sir George's room was furnished with a lavishness which made the *Express* rooms look like army barracks (as indeed most of them still are, reflecting the Beaverbrookian frugality). A coal fire glowed.

73

The wood panelling gleamed. The soft lights scarcely penetrated the first half-inch of the carpet. I was deeply impressed.

Sir George asked me how old I was. Twenty-six. I was very young, wasn't I? Yes, I suppose I was. Just the same, they had heard many good things about my journalism. What about the R101; had I handled that on my own? Well, yes. Where was Mr Gordon? Oh, he had gone home, and as he lived in Croydon I did not disturb him until the replate edition had gone through. How much money did I earn? £37 a week.

At this point Sir George left the room. He was away for a couple of minutes and came back with the present Lord Rothermere, then the Hon. Esmond Harmsworth. We went through the formalities again with this pleasant but monosyllabic giant. He seemed as shy of me as I was of him – an impression I retain of the man to this day. And then – how would I like to be editor of the *Sunday Dispatch*? I said I did not know. 'Esmond' said that if I accepted the job I would be paid £3,000 a year. I reeled inwardly at this, but tried to look calm and said I would like to think it over. Despite the joint efforts of Sir George and his proprietor, I escaped from the room uncommitted, promising only that if I turned the offer down I would not use it for the purpose of jacking up my salary at the *Sunday Express*.

As I walked up Bouverie Street, across Fleet Street and up Shoe Lane to the *Sunday Express* office, I was full of self-doubt. Could I take on the job of succeeding Bernard Falk, one of the wiliest of newspapermen, who had raised the sale of the *Sunday Dispatch* to a million and a half copies, then a fantastic figure for a middle-class paper?

Falk had launched the Rev. Vale Owen, the spiritualist, and I could remember the impact of his 'Do the Dead Speak?' articles when so many were mourning their own dead from the First World War. Falk had bought up Horatio Bottomley, and published his articles under the inspired title of 'I HAVE PAID BUT . . .', after his release from a seven-year sentence for swindling the public through his magazine *John Bull*. To Bottomley's revelations of life in Maidstone Jail the *Sunday Express* had replied with articles by Bernard Shaw, H. G. Wells, and Arnold Bennett, three of the greatest literary figures of this century. But Crime beat Culture

easily, even in those days when the public was not supposed to
have been corrupted by the so-called 'popular' press, and the
Sunday Express was not yet in sight of its first million.

Falk was a master journalist, full of ingenious tricks. He never
gave up. For example, when Mercedes Gleitz swam the English
Channel he got permission from the *News of the World* which had
bought her story exclusively, to quote a couple of hundred words
in the *Dispatch*, and ran it under the headline: MERCEDES GLEITZ'
OWN STORY. The *Sunday Express* could not get a word. Gordon
and I thought we were pretty hot in the pursuit of news but it had
not occurred to either of us that Sir Emsley Carr, editor of the
News of the World, would permit a two-hundred-word quote in
return for a 'plug' stating that the *full* account of Miss Gleitz' swim
was in his paper.

This piece of enterprise may not seem of much importance to lay
readers of these pages; but a newspaper's ultimate success depends
on how much news it carries. Presentation and angle can help
to make newspapers fresh and attractive but news is what they
stand or fall by. Years later I tried out Falk's idea on *The Times*
when that newspaper had the exclusive story of the conquest of
Everest; but its management did not appreciate the benefits of
editorial publicity in the four-million-a-day *Daily Express*.

The Times now takes half-page advertisements in the *Daily
Express* – at a cost of £3,000!

I returned to the *Sunday Express* office after my interview with
Sir George Sutton and went straight to John Gordon's office to
give him details of the offer. Very soon Gordon and I were summoned to Stornoway House, Lord Beaverbrook's home in Cleveland Row, overlooking the Green Park.

Although much beloved by Lord Beaverbrook and much
mourned by him when he was bombed out during the Second
World War, Stornoway House was to me a forbidding, gloomy
place – I do not suppose I noted on that first visit the wide natural
wood Adam staircase opposite the imposing double-entrance doors.
Turn right. Into an outer office, sparsely furnished, where a slim
little chap in a brown suit, 'Tich' Whelan, the secretary, said 'Just
a minute, I'll tell the Lord you're here'. (It is a peculiarity of Lord

Beaverbrook's staff, one and all and down the years, that they call
him 'the Lord'. Never his Lordship, or Lord Beaverbrook; just
'the Lord'. If you are unfamiliar with this custom, the effect can be
rather unnerving!)

Gordon and I were ushered into Lord Beaverbrook's library.
Again I was oppressed by a sense of gloom. The ceiling was high
and was not reached by the patchy lights from one or two standard
lamps scattered about. The walls were buff colour. The carpet was
drab. Two easy chairs on either side of a gigantic fireplace were
colourless, comfortable and old, and an eight-foot settee straddled
across the fireplace at the distance of an intervening rug of no
particular colour. I cannot recollect pictures on the walls, or orna-
ments on the mantelpiece to relieve the severity, although other
descriptions of this famous room insist that a portrait of Lady
Beaverbrook, who died in 1926, hung there.

It was the first time I had visited the home of a rich man – I was
depressed that wealth had not created colour and beauty. I remember this vividly, especially because with advancing years colour
and beautiful pictures have come to Lord Beaverbrook. Maybe he
was too busy then to care about his surroundings. He was always
against any display of luxury in the offices of his newspapers, and
in his own home he practised what he preached.

I have read so many accounts of the impact Lord Beaverbrook
makes on people when they first meet him that I do not know now
whether my memory is confused with that of others in describing
his physical presence – the towering forehead over the frail body
in the blue serge suit. But I am in no doubt at all about the nature
of our conversation. It was only the third time we had spoken
together, and he wanted to know who I was, where I came from,
how many in the family, what my father was, were there any other
journalists in the family, where was I educated, the names of the
newspapers I had been on. It reminded me of the oral examination
for my scholarship at the Wallasey Grammar School.

Finally we came to the point. 'I am told,' said Lord Beaverbrook,
'that you have been offered the editorship of the *Sunday Dispatch*
at a salary of three thousand pounds a year. Now that is a big job
and it is a lot of money. But I want you to know that you are
regarded by me as one of the young men on my newspapers with a

bright future. We have many young men growing up whose oppor-
tunities will come. I would naturally like you to stay on the *Express*.
Which is it to be? Are you going to stay on the sunny side of the
street, or are you going to cross to the shadows?'

I found myself stammering out that I would stay, of course I
would stay.

'Very well,' said Beaverbrook, 'then that's settled.' Turning immediately to Gordon, who had been sitting silently on the enormous
settee, he asked 'What's in next Sunday's paper?'

For twenty minutes he and Gordon discussed the leader page
article, the political notes, the latest financial theories of the Free
Trade (Manchester school, not Empire) City Editor, S. W. Alexander, and what could be done to prevent Lord Castlerosse from
writing open letters *every* week to Doris de la Vigne, his latest
girl friend, the woman he was going to marry. I seemed to have
been forgotten. My problem had been disposed of and I was going
to stay with the *Express* group.

It was 8.15 p.m. Dinner was at 8.30 – it was always, to the dot.
Lord Beaverbrook rose, and Gordon and I got to our feet too.

'Oh, Gordon' (he pronounced it Ga-arden), he said, 'put
Christiansen's salary up to three thousand a year.'

'You can't do that,' I heard myself saying. 'I promised Esmond
Harmsworth that I wouldn't use his offer for bargaining purposes.'

'Well,' said Lord Beaverbrook impatiently, 'you haven't used
the offer for bargaining purposes.'

But stubbornly I maintained that if I took the extra money it
would be an act of bad faith on my part, a betrayal of an under-
taking. More impatiently, Lord Beaverbrook said 'Let us go through
our conversation from the beginning. I told you that I would like
you to stay with the *Express*. You said that you would. We then
abandoned discussion of your situation and talked about next
Sunday's paper. Then I said to Gordon "Put Christiansen's salary
up to three thousand a year". Is that right?'

I agreed, but – (I must have been off my head).

His gigantic dome was puckered and his eyes stared harshly. We
went over the whole thing a second time. Did I, or did I not, agree
with his version of the sequence of events? Finally I had to agree
that I did.

'Very well. Gordon, put Mr Christiansen's salary up as from the first of January – back-date it to January for good measure. Good-bye to you.'

Gordon and I walked down Cleveland Row to St James's Palace. He caught a taxi; I walked across the Park to Victoria Station to catch a 24 bus into the heart of Pimlico. How was I going to break the news to my wife that my salary had been nearly doubled? – and this, in the days when income tax was 6s 6d and there was no P.A.Y.E. to take away half of what you earned before you could be extravagant with it! How was I going to tell her that at five o'clock I could have been editor of the *Sunday Dispatch* and that by eight o'clock I had agreed to stay with the *Sunday Express* as the assistant editor? The last tumultuous three hours would have to be handled with dramatic effect.

I turned my key in the door, whistled as I always did, flung myself into her arms, burying my head in her shoulder. I told her that I had been sacked.

She patted my head. What did it matter, anyway, she said, if I had been sacked? There were plenty of other newspapers where I could get a job.

I was beginning to enjoy myself. We went into the kitchen while supper was being prepared; and it was not until half-way through the meal that I told her the truth. 'Oh, well,' she said, 'I always knew that you would take the right decision.'

In my pocket that night, after I had paid the bus fare home, there was only the sum of two shillings and a few odd coppers, so we could not go out to celebrate – even at the Wilton Road spaghetti shop.

12 . . . Go North, Young Man!

In the midst of these heady successes tragedy struck at the home of my parents in Wallasey. This was no time for men who lived by the skill of their hands. There were fewer imports, fewer ships to repair, and less work for the shipwrights. The first cities to suffer were the big ports like Liverpool. The Unemployment Exchanges had long queues.

Life, it seemed to me, had always been a struggle for my shipwright father. He was known as a 'blue eye', one of the good workers who was among the first to be taken on by the charge-hand if there was anything to do. He didn't drink and he didn't smoke. He saved his money for my younger sister's music lessons and for my school books.

But an economic depression does not differentiate between the good and the bad, the useful and the useless. I went home to Wallasey one week-end, unexpected and unannounced, for the purpose of making a pleasant surprise. When I walked in, I found that all the furniture was being packed and that everything in the place had been bought by a dealer for a pitiful sum, less than my parents had paid for the upright piano on the lid of which I had written my 'Replies to Robert Blatchford' for the *Sunday Chronicle* at the age of twelve. When they were forced to sell up, my parents decided that they must not worry me with their problems. It was a

79

form of stubborn northern pride, much to be admired. I had been sending a little money home each week, but it had been spent sending my sister to school.

As the result of this unexpected visit of mine, I was able to uproot my family from the North and turn them into Londoners. My father stayed on in Liverpool for a year or so, but it was no use; he just went on making news by being a statistic in the headlines which said UNEMPLOYMENT RISES TO 2,239,301. He was the 1.

But I had no sooner settled my mother in London than I was sent back to the North. It was not to Liverpool but to Manchester that I went – and that, as any northerner will know, made it rather worse than better, for the rivalry between the citizens of these great towns will never die.

When my salary had risen suddenly, my wife and I had decided to move from Pimlico and to take a real house in St John's Wood. It was a beautiful house, with parquet floors and a double drawing-room opening on to a veranda overlooking the garden. It was of four storeys – no bother in those days, when it was possible to get domestic staff and anyway one was, heigh-ho, young. Into this enterprise my wife and I flung our not-yet-earned money. We had the place redecorated and to acquire our first close-fitted carpets we ran up big bills. We even had furniture made to our own design.

But one morning in September 1932, only a few weeks after we had settled in, the telephone bell rang as morning tea arrived at our bedside.

'Christiansen, what do you think of Manchester?'

It was the voice of Lord Beaverbrook. Since, at 8 a.m., I tend to be slow-witted, I replied that I had not thought of Manchester at all for years.

'In that case,' said Lord Beaverbrook, 'we will forget it. Good-bye to you.' And he hung up.

I turned to my wife and said, 'He asked me what I thought about Manchester. What on earth could he have meant?' She said I had better ring back and find out. So I did. I said that I had not understood the question and would Lord Beaverbrook explain its purpose to me? Yes, he would. Had I ever thought of working in Manchester?

Without hesitation I said I had never thought of working in Manchester because I never intended ever to do so, that I had worked hard in the provinces to get to Fleet Street, and having got to Fleet Street I intended to stay there.

Lord Beaverbrook, who is not a patient listener, was holding on placidly, I thought, so I added for good measure that to me a return to the North of England would be like sending a Russian to Siberia. And once more Lord Beaverbrook repeated wearily, 'In that case, we will forget it.' There was a note of finality in his voice – the resigned voice of doom.

Perplexed, I consulted my wife again. She was glad I had answered as I had, and said it would be awful if I had to go to Manchester for the paper just when we had moved into our first real home. But I was troubled and telephoned to ask if I could see Lord Beaverbrook. An appointment was fixed. As I left home I promised I would be firm, that I would refuse to go to Manchester, that in no circumstances would I waver.

But I went to Manchester just the same. The conversation went like this:

Beaverbrook: 'You know that if anything happened to the *Daily Express* there is a man who could step in as Editor and command my complete confidence and support?'

Christiansen: 'Yes, sir.'

Beaverbrook: 'Who?'

Christiansen (*not to be caught chancing his arm*): 'John Gordon, sir.'

Beaverbrook: 'Quite right. But it's not the London paper that is in trouble. How would you like to go to the Manchester office of the *Daily Express* and put it right? I started that edition in 1927 and we just can't make it go. Gordon has agreed to release you from the *Sunday Express* if you are prepared to take the job.'

Christiansen: 'What, me live in Manchester?' (*Then a slight wavering.*) 'How long for?'

Beaverbrook (*pouncing*): 'Only until you have put a hundred thousand on the sales.'

I was done for. I gave in without a struggle. No fish was ever landed so easily. What is more, I left Stornoway House with all the buoyancy of a man who has just had a tooth out and knows there will be no more pain. My wife, who was resigned to my moods, said little. For her, what was to be would be. It was only years later when I was discussing with her this tremendous transformation in my life, the first real step on the road to the editorship of the *Daily Express*, that she told me how heart-broken she was. I did not know of her unhappiness at the time, any more than I had known about my parents' misfortune until I stumbled into it. There is something about the occupation of newspapermen that makes them 'miss' the big moments in their own lives.

With Beaverbrook you have practically gone when you say you are ready to go. I was on my way before the week was out.

Just about everybody saw me off at Euston, even though my wife went home alone to weep. Some weeks later Gordon sent up a gold cigarette case to commemorate our association; the staff made me a presentation which I had to return to London to collect.

Four hours after leaving Euston I was in the Manchester office. The telephone rang. 'How are you getting on?' asked Lord Beaverbrook. I said I had just arrived. 'Good-bye to you,' he replied. On Friday I telephoned my wife. 'Come to Harrogate tomorrow and we'll spend the week-end together,' I said.

'What about your job?'

'Harrogate's in the circulation area of the Northern edition. It'll be all right.'

By midday on Saturday we were reunited among the palms and the aspidistras of the Majestic, Harrogate. We had just sat down to lunch when I was called to the telephone.

'Where are you?' asked Lord Beaverbrook. I told him.

'You will never edit the *Daily Express* Northern edition from there,' he said. 'If I were you I would learn about Manchester first.'

I stuck it out for the rest of the day, but next morning we caught a train back to Manchester. Now Manchester can be a pretty awful town at any time of the week, but that Sunday it seemed just terrible. How was I to know that within a few months I would come to admire Manchester, its ways, its people, its Great Ancoats Street,

its Sam's Chop House, its West Didsbury, its Piccadilly – as well
as its trains back to London?

My mood in approaching a new job, or a new situation, has been
the same throughout my life; gloom overwhelms me. Maybe it is
the Hamlet in my Danish blood coming out. The appointment of
a new editor to a rival newspaper – I must have experienced at least
twenty such occasions – invariably brought on one of these down-
beat moods; I always felt I would now be exposed as the incom-
petent impostor that I secretly knew myself to be.

I was more than apprehensive about Manchester, I was plain
scared. It was an unknown jungle, for although I had been born
only forty miles away I had never set foot in the place. I did not
know one single soul in or out of newspaper circles. And I had no
boss to lean on any more; this time I was the Supremo who took
the decisions, did the pushing around, and gave the leadership.

But my mood always changes at the moment for action. Surround me with people and I feel better. Before my first week was
up in the ex-corset factory from which the Manchester edition of
the *Daily Express* was produced, I had indicated the shape of
things to come by throwing a lighted match over my shoulder into
a waste-paper basket stuffed with proofs and thus setting fire to
my office. The curtains were well alight when Rowland Thornton
(now the London boss of the Motion Picture Association of
America) dashed in with a bucket of water. 'You're a fire-eater all
right,' he said. I was. Beaverbrook removed the retiring editor
within two days of my arrival so that I was forced at once to stand
on my own feet, and within a matter of weeks I appointed Thornton
Chief Sub-editor, reshuffled the executive staff and went pillaging
and raiding in all the Manchester newspaper offices for new talent.

Sir William Haley, now editor of *The Times*, was then plain
W. J. Haley, editor of the *Manchester Evening News*. He remembers
the upheaval well, and in a much valued letter to me recently
recalled 'the electrical effect your arrival from Fleet Street had on
us all'. With 'Dick' Plummer (now Sir Leslie Plummer, Socialist
M.P. for Deptford) as the new Manager, the 100,000 extra sale that
would give me the Keys to Fleet Street once more seemed to be in
the bag. Plummer had been General Manager of the Beaverbrook

London evening paper, the *Evening Standard*. Like me, he had
responded to the call of duty in leaving London for the North. He
had protested to Beaverbrook that he was 'a Metropolitan man',
but after this brief resistance had followed in my footsteps within a
few days. He tells me now that when we met he thought I was cocky,
arrogant, brash and hare-brained. For my part I thought him
cynical, supercilious, and a know-all. But soon we began to hit it off,
and liked each other so much that we rented a furnished house in
West Didsbury from which we both worked and played. Play consisted of week-end dinner parties at the Midland Hotel when our
wives came visiting; watching Manchester City's home games;
sitting up till all hours playing pontoon and solo; driving to Blackpool on Sundays; and giving imitations of visiting nabobs from
Fleet Street after they had gone home. Work consisted of trans-
forming the newspaper and making it as unlike the London edition
as human ingenuity could devise.

This was not mutiny on my part. I thought that the paper produced under the gay editorship of Beverley Baxter (now Sir Beverley
Baxter, Conservative M.P. for Wood Green) was too soft and too
Southern for the down-to-earth, hard-done-by Northerners. This
was 1933, and unemployment was still up in the millions. Lancashire was in the grip of a cotton strike against savage wage cuts.
I got a young fellow named Trevor Evans, now a director of
Beaverbrook Newspapers and the doyen of Fleet Street's industrial
correspondents, to take me on a personally conducted tour of the
stricken county. Then I cut out the South of England 'flam' from
my edition and ranged the paper on the side of the strikers. We
fought a losing battle, but when the dispute finally went to arbitra-
tion the wage cuts were considerably scaled down. And the headline on the day that master and man sat down together was warm
and human, designed to attract the widest audience. The *Manchester
Guardian* could record the straight news, but the *Express* had to
have the common touch, thus:

COTTON STRIKE ENDED OVER A 'NICE CUP OF TEA'

My London colleagues were so handsomely beaten on the night
Hitler set fire to the Reichstag in Berlin – it was in the days before

telephotos, and I had an artist paint his impression of the flames on to a photograph – that Lord Beaverbrook telephoned me to ask why the Manchester edition was so often so superior to the London edition.

Into the Saturday issue Plummer and I put an eight-page children's comic in colour. The teething troubles of this effort were so tiresome that on the first night we printed 40,000 copies upside down before the 'register' was stabilised. But eventually the Saturday comic was such a success – 27,000 increase in sales – that Jack Monk, the staff artist who now draws the Buck Ryan strip in the *Daily Mirror*, drew a sly caricature of me rushing round the office with a contents bill announcing:

FREE COPY OF THE 'DAILY EXPRESS'
GIVEN AWAY WITH EVERY COLOURED COMIC

Into the Monday issue we introduced a pull-out racing section giving the form of every horse engaged in that week's racing; this secured an extra sale of 35,000. My father, a born racing 'mug', was enlisted on this job, and single-handed kept track of the 5,000 horses in training week by week until the strain became too much for him.

Then we experimented in colour half-tone reproduction. We printed pictures of Socialist Sheffield, a weak selling area for the *Daily Express*, with the open furnace door of a steel foundry spouting a shocking red. We printed pictures of Liverpool from the air with the Mersey running down the middle, a ghastly blue. On this Lord Beaverbrook wrote:

'Let me congratulate you on your colour picture. I don't care whether you print the water in its true colour or otherwise. You show enterprise, and that is worth while.'

Work six nights a week – there were Australian Test matches that year to keep me up till 4 a.m. – and one night a week play. The sale of the paper was mounting, but my nerves were fraying. One Friday, I collapsed in my office. There was just time to get me on the London train in the hope that a week-end's rest in St John's

G

Wood would relieve the tension. Dick Plummer came to London with me, and we returned together on Monday morning. But it was no use. I was on the train for London again that evening, and before I could go back to work I had to spend two weeks in bed and another two weeks in a fishing village in Majorca. It rained all the time there and reminded me so much of Manchester that when the time came to return it was like going on a Mediterranean holiday!

A few weeks passed, and spring arrived. The office golf circle started to meet twice a week and I found myself able to play regularly. I made friends. A young fellow named Nahum (Baron the Photographer) and his twin brother Jack were a couple of sparks to laugh with. Sales showed an increase of 79,000 copies a day. I enjoyed the smell of success.

Did this mood of contentment reach the proprietor? I do not know, but with Beaverbrook, calm always precedes a storm; if life becomes tranquil, then something happens to untranquillise it.

A telephone call summoned me to London. When I arrived at Stornoway House at eleven o'clock on the dot, Lord Beaverbrook was sitting on a narrow veranda overlooking Green Park in the spring sunshine. He wasted no time in breaking the news that he wanted me to join the London staff of the *Daily Express* as Assistant Editor.

I was quite taken aback, and to gain time parried the suggestion by inquiring whether Vaughan Wilkins, who held the title of Assistant Editor, would be senior to me.

Beaverbrook: 'You will be the junior.'
Christiansen: 'In that case I would prefer to stay in Manchester. Wilkins and I do not see eye to eye.'
Beaverbrook: 'I am sorry to hear this. I hope you will change your mind. I would like you to do so.'
Christiansen (*wavering*): 'But of course I will work under Wilkins if you want me to.'

Such was the magnetism of the man that once again I gave in without a struggle; once again I left Stornoway with the buoyancy of a man leaving his dentist after a tooth extraction.

Events moved rapidly. Wilkins was told I was coming to London.

He refused to work with me and tendered his resignation. It was accepted and he left the organisation. This was wonderful for Wilkins, for he went off to the country and wrote a novel called *And so Victoria* . . . which ran into so many editions that it made him a fortune. He lived in Suffolk in great style, and wrote historical novels with unfailing regularity and much success. The cares of daily newspaper life (which had caused him to break his pipe once a week, as well as countless pencils) were forgotten. We met on the East Coast train about a year before his death in 1959. He was getting off at Colchester and invited me to do so also, in order that we could have a snifter at the George. I think he had forgiven me for forcing him out of Fleet Street!

Wilkins was not the only objector to my appointment. Beverley Baxter did not care for my arrival either, and he also resigned when Beaverbrook broke the news. This is the conversation that took place, confirmed by both Beaverbrook and by Baxter since (although from time to time Bax now denies it!):

Beaverbrook: 'I want you to know that Christiansen is coming to London as Assistant Editor of the *Daily Express*.'
Baxter: 'If that is so, then I resign as Editor.'
Beaverbrook: 'Just the same, Christiansen is coming to London as Assistant Editor.'
Baxter: 'In that case I withdraw my resignation.'

That is typical of Bax. I had been a nuisance to him during my seven months in the North: but he was cynical and gay and decided to put up with life as the Beaver wanted him to live it for a little while longer.

I joined the paper in April 1933 just after the famous black glass building had opened. A week or two later, Bax made a speech at an office dinner, welcoming the new assistant editor. He talked of it being 'the post of honour and the post of danger', and said he had seen many assistant editors come and many assistant editors go. I did not mind; it was in any case true enough.

I was rushing about in my shirt-sleeves one day when a free-lance contributor just down from Oxford asked John Rayner, the Features Editor, 'Who's that bastard in his braces?' 'You'd better watch out,' said Rayner, 'that's the new Assistant Editor.'

I don't suppose I looked like *the* Assistant Editor. I never, later, got used to looking like the Editor. I liked to work in my shirt-sleeves, and in the Big Room, with the staff all around me. For years I spent more time in the Big Room, where the news was coming in hot, than I spent in what is called the 'Editor's sanctum'. But I took the advice to heart and abandoned braces in favour of a belt. I gave up wearing striped coloured shirts and took to plain white. I wore black snap-brimmed hats and camel-hair coats. I was beginning to fancy myself as a bit of a character. . . .

13 . . . The Eaglets

An aura of omnipotence builds up around a newspaper editor. He is the king of the castle, the judge and the jury of what appears in his columns. From his decisions there is no appeal. He can be whimsical and, like Ross, the famous editor of the *New Yorker*, ask 'Which was Moby Dick, the man or the whale?', without anyone daring to question his lack of general knowledge; or he can be savage and bar the names of even the illustrious from his columns – the name of Winston Churchill was barred from the *Dundee Courier* up to the 1945 war. He can introduce new ways of spelling familiar words: on the *Express* we have always spelled 'aeroplane' 'airplane'. He can order that no article or news item shall start with the word 'the' or the letter 'a' and sack the first man to break the rule.

This atmosphere of supreme power is heady stuff.

I discovered this when I joined the *Daily Express* as the assistant editor in the spring of 1933. It was said of Beverley Baxter, my new editor, that once Lord Beaverbrook called him on the telephone and instructed him to report to Stornoway House at five o'clock. Baxter said he was sorry but at that time he had to be at 10 Downing Street to see the Prime Minister. 'I hope you don't patronise him as you patronise me, Baxter,' said the Beaver.

Baxter was delighted. He loved being omnipotent. At a staff

dinner he was the first to applaud a parody written by a reporter of
the old song *Burlington Bertie*, the lines of which ran:

> I'm Beverley Baxter,
> The Empire's wise crackster.
> At golf I'm a bit of a don.
> When I meet the Beaver
> I take my hat off,
> But at other times keep the thing on.
> I'm fair, fat and rosy,
> I never am prosy,
> And this you can safely bet on –
> I'M BAX, BAX,
> JUST YOU ASK MAX
> If I'm not his pride and his joy.
> I'm Beverley, Beverley,
> Rising so cleverly –
> BEAVERBROOK'S WHITE-HEADED BOY.

I ran hard up against Baxter. We were completely unalike. It is
the duty of the assistant editor of a newspaper to produce a paper
that his editor wants. He must get into the mind of his editor and
try not to have a mind of his own. I tried, but I did not please Bax.
He complained that I 'hardened' the news columns too much. His
journalistic flair was not mine, but I learned a lot from him about
mixing it. The art of editorship is to know when to play tough news
big and when to go for glamour – in other words not to interpret
but to combat the public mood; cheer them up when they are
depressed; depress them when they are cocky; mould them – and
carry them along in what you are doing.

The *Daily Express* was doing all this, but the going was tough.
The traditional battle between the *Mail* and the *Express* had been
bitterly fought and resolved in favour of the *Express* (my part was
only in the seven months spent in the Manchester office) but a new
competitor had emerged in the Socialist *Daily Herald* under the
guidance of Julius Salter Elias (later Lord Southwood), a printer
who knew less about journalism than the average village policeman, but who was shrewd enough to appreciate that the evangelism

of the Socialist movement could snowball a really big-sale daily for him.

Shrewd enough, too, to appreciate what many politicians forget: that a propaganda sheet will not appeal of itself, that readers require cakes and ale as well as bread and butter. Elias raided the stars of the *Daily Express*. He signed on H. V. Morton, who was at the beginning of his illustrious career as a writer of travel books, with a series called 'The Heart of London'. Elias hooked an even bigger catch in Hannen Swaffer, who was not only a passionate and sincere Socialist but a crusading newspaperman who made magnificent headlines.

He nearly landed a fish even bigger than either Morton or Swaffer – Strube, the cartoonist who immortalised The Little Man and for a quarter of a century ranked head and shoulders above all his rivals in the affections of the British public. Strube was an *Express* child. In the First World War he had sent cartoons from the trenches, and on his return had built himself into a national figure whose technique and humour was as widely copied as is that of Giles to-day. Politicians clamoured for the original cartoons in which they were featured; Strube had to bar J. H. Thomas, 'the Rt Hon. Dress Shirt', the railwayman's leader, from asking for more.

Elias thought that Strube, properly exploited, was worth a hundred-thousand sale to the *Herald* and pitched his offer accordingly; it was £10,000 a year, more than double Strube's pay cheque at the *Express*. When the news of the offer leaked out, Strube was rushed to see Lord Beaverbrook, who presented him with a new contract for £10,000 a year. Strube was much bemused, for he always insisted that he had no intention of leaving the *Express* anyway. He was also delighted. 'Thank you, George,' he said to Lord Beaverbrook as they parted – Strube called everybody, even his wife, 'George'.

'Do you think he minded my calling him "George"?' Strube asked me. 'You can call him what you like, George,' I answered, 'as long as you stay on the sunny side of the Street.'

Undaunted, Elias next raided in the *Express* executive echelons. Two first-rate News Room executives, Helsby and McBride, were recruited. Then Stanley Bishop, the Chief Reporter, who could

extract news out of a stone, let alone a susceptible barmaid, was
induced to go with one of the first-ever contracts offering a tax-free
expense account. Bishop left, he said, because he could see no future
for the paper if inexperienced whipper-snappers like Christiansen
were to be appointed to high office. Lord Beaverbrook told me to
keep the benign and twinkle-eyed Bishop if I wished, but as I took
the view that the older members of the staff were ganging up on me
I urged that he should be allowed to go his own way. (Two other
reporters also thought I was green until I spotted that both had
charged in their expenses for the hire of a motor-boat on a ship-
wreck story. They had both forged receipts from fictitious boat-
owners, so I sacked them out of hand – and neither got a job on the
Daily Herald.)

Having put the editorial side of his business into top gear, Elias
next put pressure on the politicians. Local Labour Party headquarters everywhere canvassed for the *Herald*. Ernest Bevin, one
of the movement's most powerful figures as boss of the Transport
and General Workers Union, stumped the country pleading the
paper's cause.

Then Elias organised the notorious 'free gift' war of the 'thirties,
in which everything from a twelve-volume encyclopedia to a set of
fish knives and forks was offered to newspaper subscribers. The
cost to Fleet Street before the war ended ran into several millions
of pounds. It was so ruinous that at the behest of the other proprietors Lord Beaverbrook sought to make a truce with Elias. They
met in a private room at the Savoy Hotel. Elias by this time was
ready to call the whole thing off, but not until the completion of a
printing contract for a new set of classics that was to be offered to
the public for next to nothing. This offer, he said, would have to go
on or he would lose money. Beaverbrook wanted agreement that
day, or else. . . . Drawing an imaginary sword from his side he ran
it through the heart of Julius Elias as he rasped out the words,
'Very well, Elias, it's war!' Anyone who has heard the Beaverbrookian way of using such words as 'wa-ar' will be aware of the
effect it must have had on the resolute but timid Elias.

The 'wa-ar' was won by Beaverbrook, for the *Daily Express* on
30 June of that year, 1933, announced that net sales had reached
the magical figure of 2,000,000, and a few days later published an

exact figure of 2,054,348 copies a day. On this day – 17 July, when I was within ten days of my twenty-ninth birthday – the new and familiar Page One Red Crusader design was used for the first time, the same Crusader who after the war was put in chains until the day when some government will free him by adopting the Beaverbrookian Empire Preference policies.

In this month an article was published, the fame of which still hangs around in journalistic folk-lore. It was another shot from the Beaverbrook locker in his war with Elias. The Beaver had fired several salvoes, but this was the subtlest, for of all the ways to keep a staff faithful and true, none is more effective than to make them proud of their own machine. Beverley Baxter sent for me and handed me a proof of the article, which was signed by George Malcolm Thomson, a Scot of erudite charm and political acumen, whose personal and intimate association with Lord Beaverbrook ranges over the past twenty-five years. It was headed THE YOUNG MEN WHO MAKE THEM and began boldly with the words: 'I mean the young men who make the *Express* newspapers.' This is how it went on:

... This astonishing string of newspapers, with their vast circulation and their three centres of production, is, in great measure, an achievement of youth.

One of the greatest revolutions of our time in Britain was the decision to put youth in charge of the *Express*. It was a big risk. Many shook their heads at the experiment.

But it was made by a man who likes risks for their own sake – and who is often seeing a little deeper, or quicker, when he seems to be most daring.

And there it is. The revolution is in being. In Europe, the youth are giving the Fascist salute and hailing one Caesar or another. In Britain they are producing the *Express* and hailing themselves.

These cubs are sharpening their claws on the world's news; taking on their jobs which used only to be given to men full of years and timidity; sprawling all over the delicate mechanism of the commercial side of the papers and extracting brilliant results from it; pulling the beards of statesmen more than twice their age; questioning, exploring, innovating and achieving.

Making mistakes, too, and paying the price with something between a frown and a grin. These young men have enough insight to know that Lord Beaverbrook is too busy to praise, and too fond of his newspaper and its fiery youth not to blame.

If the *Express* has faults, they are the faults of youth. They spring from enthusiasm, cocksureness and a restless urge for experiments.

The article was illustrated with photographs. Lord Beaverbrook's son Max was pictured in the muffler he wore when he received his Blue for Soccer (he was a centre-forward) at Oxford. Frank Owen the leader writer and previously the youngest M.P. (he sat as the Liberal member for Hereford at the age of twenty-three) and Dick Plummer, still isolated at this time in Manchester, were shown with toothy boyish grins. Nathaniel Gubbins and Gordon Beckles looked pensive and literary. Brian Chapman, my successor as the Manchester Editor, looked dour and grim. Dennis Dunn, my R101 disaster reporter and by this time a writer of witty news stories, looked as though he had been photographed by the Criminal Records Office. There was R. J. Thompson, the Editor of the Glasgow edition; Strube, who was described as having reached the 'great age' of 41; Owen Rowley, then in charge of classified advertising; William Barkley who, at the age of thirty-five, was Political Editor of the *Sunday Express* as well as Parliamentary reporter of the *Daily Express*; and myself, the Assistant Editor, looking pensive.

Max Aitken was the baby of us all. He was manager of the Manchester office at the age of twenty-three, and had already notched up a spell as manager of the Glasgow office. Frank Owen was the next most junior Eaglet, as we were called, at twenty-seven, and of him it was written: 'he writes with great concentration and is ill-tempered if interrupted'. Of Plummer, who was thirty-one, it was stated that his political views were at complete variance with those of the paper – 'but then he is on the business side. His views on the business side give complete satisfaction to Lord Beaverbrook. Those views must be put to the profit-and-loss test to be satisfactory to that nobleman'.

My own claims to be an Eaglet were dismissed in the middle of the article in five-and-a-half lines. It was recorded that I was twenty-nine (wrong, I was twenty-eight!) and that I was 'plump and cherubic in appearance. A humorist with a determined chin and a deceptively calm manner'.

How uplifted we all were by this accolade! Even the cautionary note with which the article ended could not diminish the haloes:

> Now, of course, there are men of mature judgement who occupy high places on the *Express*. But their part in directing its destinies need not be mentioned here. This is a record of youth.
>
> The eaglets are tumbling about in the nest, stretching their wings and opening their beaks.
>
> Near by, an older bird watches them with an amused bene-volent eye, not altogether devoid of cheerful malice. The malice springs from the fact that he is thinking what a rumpus these young birds of his are making in the world.

Naturally we who were Beaverbrook's pride and joy on that day had to put up with a fair amount of banter. It is not easy to go about your tasks in irreverent Fleet Street with the description 'Eaglet' hanging upon you. We became known by all sorts of names. We became, for example, the Eager Beavers. Many unprintable names were used, too, so there was no disposition to become swollen-headed.

And if our own colleagues had not kept us in our places, Beaver-brook would have had no hesitation in chopping down what he was building up.

Only two of the Eaglets of 1933 remain with the organisation: Max Aitken and William Barkley. Some died young; some did not live up to their early promise; some were sacked. Some became quarrelsome and resigned. I stayed for another twenty-six years, making thirty-three in all, before I handed in my cards. So help me, there was a lot of suffering, but also a lot of fun.

14 . . . Bax Hands Over His Baton

My father used to sing to us when I was young a song about a race-horse named Polly:

> Down the road away went Polly,
> With a step so jolly
> That I knew she'd win.
> Down the road, the pace was killing,
> But the mare was willing
> For a lightning spin.

Whenever I think of Fleet Street in 1933, the spirit of the song surges through my mind – 'the pace was killing'. The files of the newspaper do not help the crazy patchwork of memory – newspapermen handle so much news so quickly that its impact vanishes almost at once. Jim and Amy Mollison were flying round the world; Barbara Hutton was marrying her first Prince, a Mdivani; Sir Oswald Mosley's Blackshirts were beginning to riot – all on one typical day. The *Express* coverage looks good in the files, but I remember only the strain of it all. Perhaps neurologists can explain this paradox: I could not sleep at nights because of the noise of the traffic lumbering up Finchley Road, but I could not work in the office unless the air was filled with the noise of typewriters and telephone bells and the bawlings of sub-editors for boys to fetch them cups of tea. It was only then that the headlines came and the typography emerged and ideas were clawed out of the tobacco-smoke-laden air.

Every day at noon I arrived in time for Baxter's editorial conference with the News Editor, the Foreign Editor, the Features Editor, the Picture Editor and other day executives. Bax believed in himself completely. In rounded, honey-sweet Canadian, he dwelt on the need to regard a newspaper as an orchestra, and saw himself as Thomas Beecham. 'An editor,' he said every day in one form or another, 'must know when to bring in the brass and when to mute the strings. He must know all the music by heart – and the capabilities of his musicians.' I could not think he admired his first violin overmuch!

Morning conference was usually ended by a telephone call from Lord Beaverbrook. Baxter then went into a majestic huddle and emerged either elated or depressed. The next time we met was at five o'clock evening conference, when the day staffs and the night staffs battled it out, with Bax once again waving his baton to subdue the discordant jealousies inevitable between the two groups.

To keep up the pace – I was the first violin from midday every day until 2.30 a.m. the next day – and to use every minute profitably, I even made Michael, my nine-year-old son, read the leading articles from *The Times* to me while I shaved in my bath. (He says that his own ambition to be a journalist arose from these readings, and that after I had left for the office, he used to consult a dictionary to learn the meaning of the words he had been using; his vocabulary is now, happily, greater than mine.) I ate hurried lunches; worked thereafter till 9.30 p.m.; 'did' an occasional movie at the 10.30 showing; got back to the office at midnight for the assault on the final edition.

Life became even more arduous when Lord Beaverbrook began to telephone me regularly after morning conference with messages of criticism for Baxter which I was loath to deliver. When I protested that leading articles, leader-page features and the gossip column were all the direct preserve of the Editor, Beaverbrook replied, 'Widen your horizon. You're running the news; watch the features, too.'

Baxter did not seem to resent these developments. And anyway he never allowed me to interfere with his special preserves. If he wanted to leave the office early for a first night, a resplendent figure in evening dress, he strolled out into the Big Room and said, 'Son, see the "Dragoman" column is all right, will you?' or 'If the leader column is over-length, will you cut it for me?' But that was the limit of concession in those departments which by tradition are run personally by the Editor.

I was in Baxter's room when Strube walked in to discuss his cartoon for the next day's paper. Taking his place on a waste-paper basket – Strube never, but never, sat on a chair – he showed his ideas in 'rough' form one by one. I had not been at a cartoon conference before, so I looked over Baxter's shoulder and, when I saw a rough that I liked, I said 'That's the one'. It was Baxter's turn to be rough for a change. 'Look, son,' he said. 'You can do what you like with most of the paper, but Strube's cartoon belongs to me.' This harshness was unusual. Baxter always seemed relaxed and philosophic even when his racing trebles came unstuck, which was on many days.

Baxter liked writing, even though he had to remain anonymous in order not to anger Beaverbrook, who took the view that when an editor was writing he left himself no time for editing other people's writings! He wrote leading articles, although Frank Owen was the titular leader writer. He wrote for 'Dragoman', a gossip column, although a socialite named Sewell and a swarthy Oxford graduate named Tom Driberg were the contributors. He was as romantic about journalism as a character in Philip Gibbs's *Street of Adventure*. When the result of the trial in 1933 of the British engineers for espionage in Moscow was stuttering out on the Reuter tape machine around midnight, he arrived in the office with half a dozen guests after the theatre.

In white tie and tails, he stood aloof as I was putting an edition to press, *my* shirt tails also being almost on view, such was the haste and the pressure. Then he sat down at a reporter's table, took off his coat, rolled back his starched cuffs, and started to write. I assumed he was doing a leading article, perhaps on the big story from Moscow. But no! It was a description of the scene in the office that night. 'Put that on your front page, son,' he said, as he put on

his coat again and walked out with his bejewelled womenfolk and
their top-hatted companions. It was an embarrassment to find space
for half a column about how the *Daily Express* went to press. But
Bax was right. His story made the front page of the last edition
'different' by raising the curtain on the way the *Daily Express*
gathered and presented the news from the ends of the earth.

In April 1933, I did not have any sense that 'an epoch' was
beginning – the description given to this period by the *Yorkshire
Post* twenty-five years later. I drank regularly in the pubs with the
staff, a habit picked up in my *Sunday Express* days. Baxter was in
this respect a remote figure. He left Fleet Street by limousine every
night, saluted off the premises by his A.D.C., an ex-Guardee
named 'Jock' Selby Bradford. It was my job to stay in Fleet Street
anyway and Mrs Twomley's pub in Poppin's Court rang with
argument, anecdote and instruction. I did a lot of my best work
having the odd drink with people such as Bernard Hall, the newest
and rawest young reporter from the *Brighton Argus*, or Bobby St
John Cooper, who drew the 'Home Page Cat', or Monja Danis-
chewsky, a witty film writer who mimicked the *Express* leader-
column style and wrote articles under the name of John Nelson, or
with Frank Owen, the leader writer.

Owen and I became inseparable. Sometimes after the last edition
had gone to press we went on the town together to argue with
Calais, the London correspondent of *Paris-Soir*, on such topics as
the British being charged rent for the trenches in World War One,
or the emergence of the Popular Front, or to bandy wisecracks in
the night-clubs with the satellites of café society – once we signed
our names on the plaster caste of Peggy Hopkins Joyce, the much-
married lovely who had broken her leg ski-ing, and who became
quite a friend of ours; but mostly we drank a little and dreamed
dreams, unless some drunk like poor Robert Newton, the actor,
made a nuisance of himself, in which case he first got a warning and
then a sockeroo from Frank.

We loved each other dearly, even though we also quarrelled
bitterly. I do not know whether I taught him anything, but he
certainly taught me plenty about politics, about people, about life.
We were inseparable for weeks on end, and although it might not

have been always good for our health, it was assuredly good for our
newspaper – until one night he would turn up almost too late to
catch the edition with his leader column. We never *did* miss the
edition, but the wear and tear on the nerves were so harassing that
the explosions of our rows could be heard from my room to the Old
Bell across the street. Owen would storm out of the room shouting,
'All right, mister, get yourself another leader writer,' and slam the
door. I would roar at the top of my voice for him to come back.
Back he would come, and I would snarl, 'When I fire you, shut the
door QUIETLY behind you.' And he would go out saying, 'All right,
mister' and with a grin close the door quietly to indicate that his
temper had faded and that he knew mine had, too. Happily,
Frank's leader column was worth all the trouble.

The summer of that year wore on in this hubbub of work, late
nights and early mornings. Lord Beaverbrook went off to South
America with Lord Castlerosse and took Frank Owen with him.
Whenever he could get him, the boss had Frank around; but it was
not an easy companionship for either. Beaverbrook is the world's
most punctual man. Anyone working for him soon realises that he
need not waste his own time by being early for an appointment, or
waste the proprietor's time by being late, whereas I would not have
put it past Frank in those days to turn up promptly at 10 a.m. on a
Thursday for a date made for that time on the previous day! 'Frank
drives me frantic. Where is he now?' came a plaintive appeal to me
one day when Owen had flown to Düsseldorf where Grace, his
bride-to-be, a gorgeous American showgirl, was appearing in
cabaret.

'You'll be back by Monday, won't you?' I had said. He had
agreed. But when he turned up on Tuesday afternoon looking as
innocent as Eros, he had seemed so sure that this was in fact the
arrangement that I became convinced that my own disciplined
and organised mind had let me down.

Like the Prodigal Son, Owen was always welcomed home. When
a deep personal grief overwhelmed Owen, Beaverbrook gave him a
room at Stornoway House and fussed him like a father. And of
course the personal affection of Beaverbrook for Owen was
enhanced by professional admiration. 'He's better than Arthur

Brisbane' was the proprietor's verdict, and I endorsed the view that his leader column was at any rate as good as Brisbane's 'To-day' column that ran on the front page of the New York *Journal-American*. Owen could write, and after one of their sessions together, Owen invariably had a notebook full of stuff which would last him for weeks: ideas ranging from a leaderette on 'Why is the sea blue?' to a mighty call for Britain to disentangle herself from European commitments.

My own relations with Lord Beaverbrook were much more formal. I turned up on the dot, took my marching orders, and got out on the dot when the next appointment was due – and so it remained in all the years of work and friendship.

With Beverley Baxter the proprietor's relations seemed to fluctuate. On one of the rare occasions when Baxter and I were both at Stornoway House for dinner there was quite a scene. The beautiful Lady ('Kitty') Brownlow asked Bax, sitting next to her at the foot of the table, who had originated the well-known phrase 'Empire Free Trade' Baxter replied: 'Well as a matter of fact I did.'

'What's that I heard you say, Baxter?' came a roar from Lord Beaverbrook's end of the table. How the Beaver had heard above the hubbub of argument in which he was personally engaged can only be explained by the fact that he has always been able to listen to two separate conversations at the same time and conduct a third. Bax looked confused, like a naughty school prefect caught smoking by the Head. Lady Brownlow laughed and repeated the conversation. The Beaver's face went black and we all stopped talking, for it was generally reckoned that the phrase 'Empire Free Trade' was the spark of his own genius. The evening never quite recovered its gaiety.

As it transpired, Baxter was playing himself gently out of his job, but this I did not know when I applied for financial assistance to make a trip to the United States. (I was given £100 towards my passage – nowadays it is a commonplace to send comparatively junior executives to New York 'for the experience' at a cost of several thousands of pounds.) On my return four weeks later I found that the paper had run into trouble. By one of those freaks of bad judgement which no amount of organisation can overcome,

H

a false report of a plot to assassinate Lord Trenchard, the Metropolitan Commissioner of Police, had been published. It struck me as odd that I should be instructed to hold an 'inquest', but I got on with the job.

'This is where it hurts, Christiansen,' said Lord Beaverbrook, clutching his belly. 'This is where it hurts when the *Daily Express* is in trouble.' He rubbed his little pot with both hands and looked as miserable as a man with the colic.

Finally I recommended Baxter to sack two reporters (who got good jobs elsewhere and probably never sinned again), but I should have cleared out some of the executive staff as well, and would have done so if I could have proved what I suspected: that, it being a Friday night, and the end of the week, they were nipping out for quick ones when they should have been on the job. A little time later I caught one of them out like a light in the Features Room that I happened to enter late one night. I suspended him from duty and told him to report to me next morning. But he went to the Press Club that night and stoked up again. On the way home he rammed his car into a crossing standard and ended up in hospital.

I sacked him; but later he got a job on the New York *Daily News* – during Prohibition!

Something was wrong elsewhere. Baxter was spending less and less time in the office, and I found myself occasionally in the role of Sir Thomas Beecham at the evening news conference.

Then the explosion occurred: Baxter was leaving Fleet Street to join the Ostrer Brothers, as the £10,000 a year Public Relations Counsel to the Gaumont-British Film Company. The parting broke up the Canadian triumvirate that had made such a sensational newspaper success – Beaverbrook, Baxter and E. J. Robertson, the Toronto-born general manager. The parting was said to have been due to increasing political tension – Baxter, for example, said he was a League of Nations man while Beaverbrook abominated the League of Nations – but I have always thought that the two could have patched up their political differences if they had been so minded.

Years later Bax told me that he could not visualise the *Daily Express* continuing its success without him and that he had not regarded me as serious opposition. 'I thought I *was* the *Daily Express*,' he mused. This was a situation that in my view Beaverbrook was not prepared to tolerate, since he regarded himself as the mainspring, the driving force behind the whole concern – which he was.

Baxter's sudden departure left me temporarily in charge of the paper, but I had other problems as well. One morning, my wife got me up at seven o'clock to take her to the nursing home in Brixton where our first two children had been born. I left her there to deliver a new addition to our family and went straight to Fleet Street, catching even my secretary out by arriving so early. The day was uneventful: morning conference, evening conference, leader writers, feature writers, reporters to see and brief, a dozen phone calls from Lord Beaverbrook. A suffragan bishop called and was somewhat disconcerted when J. B. Morton, who writes the 'Beachcomber' column, crept into the room on his hands and knees barking like a dog. That was the only out-of-routine occurrence – an unusual one, of course, even for the *Express*!

At six o'clock I called the nursing home to find that two hours previously my wife had given birth to twins, a boy and a girl. Ruefully it dawned on me that I had never become a registered reader of the five popular papers which in those days paid £50,000 free insurance if you were killed in a railway smash and £50 if you became the father of twins. The size of my family had doubled, I had lost the chance of a tax-free £250 – and as the acting Editor I was too busy to get to the nursing home to see my wife.

I made the journey next morning, taking with me a sore head caused by a late celebration party at the Café Royal. Two days later I was made Editor of the *Daily Express*.

It had not occurred to me that I would get the job. I was only three months past my twenty-ninth birthday. It was only thirteen years since I had left school. It seemed to me that I was far too young and far too inexperienced for such high responsibilities.

I had heard that Lord Beaverbrook and John Gordon, the natural choice after his success as editor of the *Sunday Express*, were not hitting it off too well, but I thought that a reconciliation was inevitable. Failing this, there was Tom Clarke, the old Northcliffe News Editor and then Editor of the *News Chronicle*.

I was told later by E. J. Robertson, the long-sighted, that he advised Beaverbrook to take a chance on me; and I was told by Beaverbrook that I never had any rivals. But both of them must have had doubts about their judgement, because with me they placed George Gilliat, an elderly journalist who had been editing the *Evening Standard* for some years. It was made clear to me that Gilliat was the senior, and that while I was to run the paper, his decisions on all matters must be recognised.

This arrangement seemed fair enough. Gilliat interfered as little as possible and was such a kindly, diffident man that I had no difficulty in getting my own way. What is more, the staff seemed incapable, whether by accident or by design, of producing a good newspaper when I was not there. On my day off (one a fortnight apart from Saturdays) the paper slumped badly. Beaverbrook sent for me and delivered a homily. 'You should never cease to work,' he said.'You need not work hard, but you should work always. It is bad for a man ever to get out of the habit of work.'

I wondered what was coming, since I thought I not only worked hard but worked always. But no – why did I not work a six-day week? I need not be in my office for a great number of hours, but did I not think I should be there at least for some time on every publication day?

I agreed enthusiastically, and gave up my once-a-fortnight day off. But of course it was a fourteen-hour day that I did on that day, as every day; no nonsense about not working hard. It just did not seem possible not to.

George Gilliat was withdrawn from the scene six weeks later and went into happy retirement. I was thereafter the Editor. But nobody can give me the exact date in December 1933 because I did not receive a letter of appointment. No contract letter ever passed between Beaverbrook Newspapers and myself when I started my near quarter of a century stint as Editor. 'The date ye began?' ruminated James Hutchison, the dry so-Scottish secretary to the company, when I asked him. 'It's no' r-r-recor-rded exactly. I wasn't the secrr-etar-ry then, ye see.'

15 . . . How to Sack a Man

A year or so after I took over the editorship a telegram arrived at my house signed *Beaverbrook*. It said: *You Show Judgement and Flair of the Highest Order on your Front Page To-day.*

I was cock-a-hoop, and as it was a Saturday, my day off, we celebrated. The proprietor's praise arose from the way in which the *Express* played the news of the acquittal of an eighteen-year-old boy on a charge of murder. The case was unique. The lad had been found guilty at a provincial Assize Court trial; his counsel had failed to reverse the decision before the Appeal Court and for the first time in history a further appeal – this time successful – was made to the highest court of all, the Lords of Appeal, sitting in the House of Lords itself.

I had had a shaky start as editor. I had listened to too much advice, most of it suggesting that I should play for safety. 'Keep the size of the headlines down,' advised E. J. Robertson, and as E.J.R. was next to God I kept them down. 'Be serious,' advised the Beaver, and I tried hard. But gradually I was gaining confidence and evolving the elements of a style of my own.

I was beginning to learn, for example, that a successful newspaper must go its own way with a lofty disregard for the news selection and presentation of its rivals. Lead; don't follow. Never be a copy-cat; Fleet Street is full of dead copy-cats. But to 'play' the news of the acquitted boy my way I had first to get him to the *Daily Express* office and keep him there until the last editions of all the newspapers had gone to press.

Negotiations to buy the lad's story of his ordeal – he was old enough to hang – had been completed, but the problem was to get him to the office without our rivals either photographing him, interviewing him, or indeed kidnapping him. The Palace of West-minster was practically surrounded with reporters and chauffeur-driven limousines ticking over. As a decoy, one of our men came out of the main exit with a mackintosh over his head, and was bundled into a motor-car which made off in the direction of Putney. Most of the opposition fell for this trick and we were able to get the boy to Fleet Street without much further difficulty. But later in the day the office was besieged by reporters from other newspapers – one of them even got into the Big Room by posing as a young man from the provinces anxious to get a job on a trial. Cyril Morton (now Managing Editor of the *Sunday Dispatch*) suggested that we send cups of tea down to the less bold reporters waiting in Fleet Street, and while they were drinking it, we smuggled our hero to a hide-out in Surrey.

Our scoop remained intact, and the front page, the one that Lord Beaverbrook liked so much, was a striking affair for those days, with many pictures of the acquitted boy's facial expressions right across the top of the page, a form of presentation which had not been used before on such an intensely human news story.

Happiness is a fleeting emotion for an editor. It is also a trap. An editor who permits himself an excess of happiness because one day's issue is good is riding for a fall. I once produced three papers in succession that were scoop-laden and glittering in layout. On the fourth day I was so happy that I carelessly published a stumer about the spy Klaus Fuchs, then in prison, that still makes me shudder.

Show me a contented newspaper editor and I will show you a bad newspaper. Throughout my years of office I was brooding, carping, despairing, doleful, self-critical, snarling, suspicious, tendentious, wary – and so on, right through the dictionary. I praised extravagantly and kicked unmercifully. I was also praised and kicked in the same measure.

'You're a funny fellow,' said John Mather, one of the best re-write men I have ever met. 'You make me feel like a genius, and then you catch me out on a careless comma in my last paragraph.' (I was a demon for commas. I was so devoted to commas, the correct use of, that I encouraged Trevor Wignall and Tom Driberg, two *Express* stylists, to cable them when they were abroad at a cost – from the U.S.A. for example – of fourpence-ha'penny a comma. A message from Wignall on his meeting with Scarface Al Capone in Chicago got me into hot water with the frugal Manager, Robertson, when he calculated that two hundred cabled commas cost more than three pounds – Robbie was a devil for saving the pence.)

I pontificate thus from the experience of years, but I still had most of the profundities to master when I took over the *Daily Express* in 1933. Beverley Baxter had left behind a fine staff despite the Fleet Street poaching war. On the writing side there were people like James Agate, dramatic critic of the *Sunday Times*, who wrote the book column. On the reporting staff there were established giants like Harold Pemberton, who had been tempted from the *Daily Mail* where he had pioneered motoring news for Northcliffe. On the foreign staff there was Harry J. Greenwall, who never got over my appointment and exploded that 'Beaverbrook must have been off his head to appoint a Liverpool sports sub-editor to run his biggest newspaper'. There were also rising young giants like Sefton Delmer, the Berlin man who was making a corner in news about a man named Hitler; Pembroke Stephens, who recorded that the Germans were making U-boats all over the place in separate parts for assembly when Der Tag came (not that anyone believed him); and C. V. R. Thompson who was just beginning a twenty-year stint as New York correspondent. On the executive side the talent was just as abundant, headed by the silver-haired, scholarly, sensational News Editor known to everyone as 'J.B.' – John Berry Wilson, who eventually notched up thirty-five years in the job and, now in his eighties, still comes to Fleet Street four days a week.

Yet an editor must have his own people around him. I was very soon hiring and firing. Charles Sutton, Political Correspondent of the *Daily Mail*, became Foreign Editor; Trevor Evans joined me from the Manchester office to look after labour affairs; I hired a clutch of young reporters who could write shorthand from the Press Association, including Basil Cardew who became the Motoring Correspondent, and Morley Richards, who later did 14 years as News Editor; I poached seventeen-stone Percy Hoskins from the *Evening Standard* as my Scotland Yard man; I had already raided the *Daily Herald* for a brilliant young typographer and intellectual named John Rayner (who later brought in Osbert Lancaster to originate the famous Pocket Cartoons); I appointed Guy Eden as Political Correspondent from the *News Chronicle*. From all over the Empire talent emerged. Alan Moorehead and Noel Monks from Australia; Bob Crisp, the fast bowler, from South Africa; Geoffrey Cox from New Zealand; Howard Clegg from Canada. These men were not secured by offering them vast salaries as bait; they were all young unknowns who wanted to work for the exciting *Express*. The highest salary I paid was £30 a week – some were paid under £20.

At the same time I let some of Baxter's favoured sons out. One resignation seemed to be a real body blow, but what I did not realise then is that a newspaper can sacrifice many, many of its stars without being damaged. The institution survives the individual, even the most illustrious individual. Trevor Wignall had a fabulous reputation, in many ways deserved, and cashed in on it by throwing fits of temperament a month or two before his contracts were due for renewal. In 1930, when he had been earning £100 a week, he had used these tactics on Baxter so successfully that he secured a renewal at annual increases of £500 a year. I was next for the chopper. There were storms and threats and all the familiar prima-donna-isms. Our personal friendship was not affected and we still went to football matches on Saturdays and dined together in the Savoy Grill, but the signs of the gathering storm were clear enough and I was not surprised when Wignall announced that he would not stay unless he had another three-year contract with £500 a year increases which would have brought him up to £8,000 a year by 1935.

It seemed fantastic to me that I should have to pay up to £8,000 a year to a sports writer who was already well rewarded, and I went to Lord Beaverbrook. My experienced proprietor seemed resigned to being 'skint', but passed the buck to me: did I or did I not want Wignall? I decided to call Wignall's bluff.

'You're letting me go for a lousy junior reporter's salary,' said the little Welshman. 'You're leaving because I won't give you a lousy rise,' I replied. When the last meeting took place, I believe that Wignall thought I was going to give in. But all I said was 'Well, good-bye, Trevor'. We shook hands and he left my room.

The following day he announced in his spectacular way that he had had precisely 103 offers from other newspapers. But he never worked again for a London morning newspaper. He did the odd job for one or two Sunday papers and retired to the West Country, well breeched for money despite the fact that he was an extravagant spender and spasmodically a prodigious drinker.

I never really successfully replaced Wignall. I brought Henry Rose, the Sports Editor of the Manchester edition, to London (he was killed in the Manchester United air disaster at Munich in 1958); but that very fine newspaperman had been too long in the provinces to be quite right in London. I hired this man and that man and eventually lured over Peter Wilson, the *Daily Mirror*'s much-boosted and most brilliant 'Man they cannot gag'. But neither he, nor another brilliant, John Macadam, had quite what I pined for – the Wignall touch. Moral: a good editor should not try to repeat a success, or live in the past by trying to teach old tricks to new dogs. Journalism renews itself by new men with new ideas.

My experience of accepting resignations such as Wignall's, and sacking people, is long and varied. Summing up, I honestly believe that the task of sacking is more embarrassing for the sacker than the sackee. Most men took being fired on the chin and were disposed to blame the wicked management rather than me. There have been few squealers, possibly because I never – hand on heart – sacked anyone merely to save money. With one man who said he was going to throw himself over Blackfriars Bridge, I had to be tough and tell him that I would pay him a fiver if he gave me the time of the event so that the paper could publish a good picture. The fellow got out of journalism and made a fine success of a new career in South Africa. But mostly there would be a wry, puzzled smile, a philosophic shrug of the shoulders, a quip about the notice money paying off a few debts, a friendly handshake, and mutual expressions of goodwill and good luck.

I worked myself into a fine old lather about one of Baxter's pets, and R. D. Blumenfeld's before that. This was an extraordinary little Welshman named T. Alun Jones, who had been appointed Night News Editor, way back. As Night News Editor (the man who comes in at tea-time and assigns the reporters until 2.30 a.m. next day) Jones had become a joke. His keenness was unparalleled but his judgement was awful. He rushed madly around the office creating a great noise whenever the Thames overflowed its banks, alternatively shouting in rich Welsh tones 'Any ba-a-abies?' and 'Take a ta-a-axi, man'. Jones could not bear sending a reporter on a story unless he went by taxi; and if no babies were drowned or burned to death or in some other way made to sacrifice their lives, the news ceased to interest him.

'Any ba-a-abies?' he would hiss into the telephone to a reporter who had been despatched by taxi on a minor incident.

'No, Alun, no babies.'

'Oh damn,' Alun would say, and hang up the receiver without waiting to find out if the news had any other interest.

The man was a 'character' all right. He wore a toupee and in order to keep it in place never took his bowler hat off, even to wash his face. He brought his own food to the office, usually an enormous bone scrappily covered with ham, mutton or beef, which he gnawed like a dog-in-a-bowler. He also wore a 'dickey' over his shirt, a winged collar, and buttoned boots. He acted his way through life. He 'lived' the romantic role of Night News Editor. He loved being talked about and would do anything to make an impression. Lord Beaverbrook telephoned him one night from his country home near Leatherhead where he was entertaining Lloyd George.

'Alun,' he said, 'I have just been telling a compatriot of yours that I employ the second most famous Welshman in the world.'

'You don't mean me, my Lord?' sniggered Jones.

'Yes I do, and what's more I want you to speak to my Welsh friend here.'

'Oh damn,' said Jones (he could not help saying 'Oh damn'). 'You're pulling my leg, my Lord. You've got Mister Lloyd George with you – just a moment, my Lord.' And with that he pulled a coloured handkerchief out of his pocket to dust the seat of his chair as a mark of respect before he sat down to talk to L.G.

The sucking of teeth, the expostulatory blowing of breath, the lilting confusion of Welsh phrases, the 'Yes, sirs' and 'No, sirs' went on for minutes. Then Jones came across to me. 'What do you think, sir? The most wonderful moment of my life, sir. I have talked to Mister Lloyd George, sir. You saw, didn't you, that I cleaned and dusted my chair before I allowed myself the honour!'

Jones had to go, but I could not bring myself to swing the hatchet. For days and then for weeks I dallied, cursing myself for being a sentimental fool. The plain truth was that I was scared that the *Daily Express* really meant so much to Jones that I might well have a suicide on my hands. It took a couple of quick doubles in Poppin's Court to enable me to pluck up the courage to send for him after a fortnight of dither.

'Alun,' I said, plunging in head first, 'I am terribly, terribly sorry to tell you this, and very heart-broken . . .' Alun's beady little eyes gleamed brightly at me and I found it difficult to continue – 'but I fear that the time has come when you will have to retire.'

A torrent of Welsh accent assailed me. But it was not a torrent of imprecation. It was a gusher of gratitude. 'Sir, oh sir, this is the moment I have been waiting for. I didn't think it would come so soon. I am the luckiest man in the world, man. How much will my pension be?'

I told him it would be £3 a week (his salary was only £15) which did not seem very much to me. But to Jones it meant a return to Mold in Flintshire where he said he could live comfortably, providing I would agree to his doing linage work for other newspapers. He had obviously been dreaming of this interview for years and had all the details worked out. Within minutes what was to have been an embarrassing occasion had been transformed into a festival.

We gave Jones a pair of guns as a going-away gift and the story reached us that he used them to shoot partridge as they settled down for the night; but maybe that was just a figment of the vivid imagination of that crack-shot sporting journalist, Jimmy Wentworth Day, who had always tortured Jones by telephoning him with wildly invented blood-curdlers, the details of which were retailed to Jones

in a magnificent imitation of Jones's own unmistakable accents –
'Oh damn, it's Wentworth Day!' I often heard Jones cry out in pain.

At any rate Jones lived happily ever after. And to keep up the
romantic act that was part of his nature, he arranged for his *Daily
Express* to be posted to him each day, addressed as follows:

> T. Alun Jones, Esq.,
> Night News Editor, *Daily Express*
> Formerly News Editor, *Sunday Express*
> c/o Mold Post Office,
> Mold, Flintshire, N. Wales.

Thus he made sure until he died in 1942 that successive genera-
tions of postmistresses and postmasters at Mold would know, and
possibly be glad to tell others, about Jones, the giant of Fleet Street.

My experience with Jones did not steel or settle my nerves for the
ordeal of sacking a man. If you knew unemployment in your
father's home, the most nagging of all tortures remains for life –
insecurity. I liked to hire. I hated to fire. In twelve months I brought
to an end an old *Express* habit, which got the paper a bad name, of
having a human bonfire once a year, for the purpose of sorting out
the wheat from the chaff. I did so by reinstating ten reporters who
had been sacked by my Deputy while I was on holiday. 'Never do
that again,' I said, 'or I'll behead you, too.' From that time on the
Express became such a happy ship that there were times when I
thought I had overdone things. But the answer was in the box-office.
The circulation went on soaring after the free gift war ended, and
just about the only men who refused the invitation to join us were
those remarkable old radicals, Ian Mackay and A. J. Cummings
of the *News Chronicle*. . . .

16 . . . All in an Editor's Day

In the office which I occupied as editor of the *Daily Express* the carpet wore out two or three times in twenty-five years and the curtains were replaced once. But nothing else changed. The old-fashioned rosewood, leather-topped double desk which R. D. Blumenfeld bequeathed to Beverley Baxter was bequeathed to me in turn and then bequeathed to my successor, Edward Pickering. One day I got sick of the sight of the same old desk and ordered a new one. But I found that to buy a new desk of the same size would have cost nearly four hundred pounds and it did not seem worth while. So the old desk is still there, an inanimate but precious piece of newspaper history, that dates back long, long before Lord Beaverbrook bought the paper for £27,000 plus its bad debts.

For a medium which changes so much with the public mood, it is surprising that the method of producing a newspaper changes so little, as little in fact as Blumenfeld's desk. That great man laid down the method for the *Express* and it has been followed by the editors of the paper ever since. A day can be as dull as the Sabbath in Wales, or as exciting as Easter in Seville, but the basic routine never varies. It is the same now in its essentials as when I first sat behind that desk. At noon there is a conference in the 'editor's room with the departmental heads. What's the news? The News Editor reads his engagement book and names the reporters assigned

to the various events. Any good pictures in prospect? The Picture
Editor speaks. What's going on in the Middle East? The Foreign
Editor's turn comes. And how are the negotiations to buy the new
Agatha Christie book coming along? (Miss Christie in those days
sold her thrillers to me cheaply – for £500 – because serialisation
boosted her book sales.) Anybody got an idea for a really powerful
leading article on the Anglo-American Alliance? What did you all
think of the paper to-day? Isn't it wonderful that The Scout's tips
are coming up and how long does the Sports Editor think it will
last? How can we get more work out of that lazy genius so-and-so
and why isn't he at the morning conference anyway? Was he tight
last night, does anyone know? (Silence.) Did anybody watch TV
last night? (In 1933 the question would, of course, have been about
the radio.)

The faces of busy departmental executives look strained as the
editor launches into a reminiscence of his golden past. The staff
wonders: how are we going to get the paper out at this rate? But
they are saved by the telephone bell. It is Lord Beaverbrook calling.
He and the editor talk not about yesterday but tomorrow; *to-morrow*, the word that dies in a day, every day of the year, for a
newspaperman.

In the afternoon there is another conference, this one much more
businesslike, for tension is mounting. Night executives now have
their say about why yesterday's paper was so bad, or try to take
the credit for the fact that it was so good. And then that day's
efforts are sidetracked by a realistic discussion on what is to go
into next day's paper. The editor curses because there doesn't seem
to be much to put into any page, let alone Page One, and ends the
conference so that he can see his top brass in privacy.

Hours of intense concentration as the paper begins to take shape.
Will I talk to William Barkley, asks the Night News Editor on the
inter-com telephone system. 'My dear, my dear,' says the wise
Scot who reports Parliament. 'I've got three columns of good stuff.
How much can you take? Only two! Well there are three good
angles for the intro – which would you like?'

Ten minutes go by while Barkley thinks aloud and clarifies his
ideas; it is the nightly routine of the only reporter I have ever
known who can dictate columns of coherent copy direct from the

briefest of notes. But during those ten minutes the queue outside the office has assembled, dispersed and re-assembled. Reggie Thompson, the Assistant Editor, barges past the lot, as is his right, with a scrap of agency tape in his hand. His eyes shine with enthusiasm. 'Here it is—OIL IN THE SAHARA DESERT'[1] he says. 'Oh God, not that stumer again,' I moan. 'Give it another half-hour before we make our minds up.'

Send for the leader writer. For Pete's sake hurry, man, Beaverbrook's got to approve this lot for the first edition, can I have it in ten minutes? Miss Dale, get the Features Editor while I'm waiting. What's your headline, John? Change it; make it controversial. What about NO MORE OF THAT HELL FOR ME! That's the way to sell papers: the common touch. Be a good chap and don't argue. . . . Now get the hell out of here – the Old Man's on the phone.

Lord Beaverbrook: 'What's the news?'
Christiansen: 'Nothing fresh since we last spoke. The leader will be ready in ten minutes.'
Lord Beaverbrook: 'Keep me in touch. Watch out for Baldwin on the farmers tonight. Come in and see me at half-past ten. Good-bye to you.'

Send for the leader writer. Sorry, he's not quite ready. Anyone urgent wanting to see me? Hilde Marchant – the best woman reporter that ever worked in Fleet Street – has called four times since six o'clock. All right, let her in. 'Please can I go to Spain? No one's covering the woman's angle of the siege of Madrid.' 'All right, Hilde, go for ten days. But remember, cut out that trick of yours which makes you start as well as end sentences with prepositions.'

Hilde: 'Why should I? I write as I talk and as people talk to me.'
Christiansen: 'Don't argue. Do as you're told.'
Hilde: 'I never went to a university and neither did most of our readers. If you want that sort of prose get the *Sunday Times* Literary Critic to go to Spain and see what happens to the circulation.'

1. This 1933 forecast has at last come true, so Thompson was right.

Christiansen: 'Stop being saucy, or you won't go. And don't
forget that every soldier has a wife. Ask her what she thinks of
war. Do the troops in Madrid come home every night? What
are they using for food? How are the children standing up to
it?'

Send for the leader writer. About time this piece was ready. It's
no bloody good but it's late, so bung it across to the Old Man on
the direct wire and let's hope for the best. What about a quick one
while we're waiting? Not a chance. 'The News Editor wants you.'
What is it, J.B.? For a change the News Editor has nothing urgent
to discuss, he just wants to raise a laugh. Have I heard how Simmons, the Sports Editor, put in a call to Walsall to inquire about
the Third Division club that had been drawn at home against
Arsenal in the Football Association Cup, and had been put through
by mistake to Gurdus, our Polish correspondent in Warsaw? No,
J.B., that's good. What happened? J.B. tells his tale thus:

'Arsenal are visiting you,' said Simmons.

'Really,' said Gurdus, 'then that means war.'

'You bet,' said Simmons. 'Give me three hundred words on
your prospects.'

'Is that *all* you want?' said Gurdus. 'You'd better send Sefton
Delmer straight away.'

'What! Send Delmer for a football match?' said Simmons,
'don't be ridiculous.'

'And don't you treat our war so lightly,' said Gurdus.

That's rich, J.B. See if Driberg wants it for a Hickey paragraph;
may as well see if we can justify the cost of the phone call. Where
are the proofs of the Hickey column, anyway? Get Reggie Thompson on the inter-com. How many pages to press, Tommy? Good
God, only two! We'll never make it tonight. Eighteen pages still to
go and only an hour-and-a-half before edition time.

Get the Head Printer up. No, I'll go downstairs myself and blow
the whole Case Room to bits . . . Percy, what the hell's going on?
Why are we so late again? All right, all right, Mr Pratt, it's not
your fault; it's ours. O.K. O.K. I'll deal with Reggie Thompson.

. . . Lord Beaverbrook on the telephone for you, Chris – will you take it here, in the Big Room, or in your office?

> *Lord Beaverbrook:* 'This leading article is not quite right. I'd like to hold it till tomorrow if it's not going to make it difficult for you.'
> *Christiansen (panic-stricken):* 'Oh no, sir; that's all right.'
> *Lord Beaverbrook:* 'I suppose you have five or six columns of stock stuff you can draw on?'
> *Christiansen (lying):* 'Oh yes, of course.'

Send for the leader writer. The leader's held over, how much stock stuff have we got? NONE? Good God, what are we going to do now? Get that article on agriculture that Kenneth Pipe did last week and rewrite it to fit your column.

Have I time for a quick one before it's written? No. The lawyer wants to see me, to say that Thompson must be trying to have me sent to prison, and to prison I will certainly go, if I do not stop Thompson from publishing a criminal libel on Page One. (Stop Thompson.) Anything else? Yes, 'Prodnose' is on the warpath. Send him in. ('Prodnose' is a wise elder statesman who is my personal watchdog on everything that goes into the papers.) What is it, Harold? 'Beachcomber' has a whole paragraph in French that our readers will not be able to translate. All right, Harold, kill it, cut it out, but not if it's going to hold up the edition.

Get Thompson on the intercom. Any news of the Pope, Tommy? No, Chris, no news of the Pope. This is our favourite gag on these arid nights when, with only one hour to go before we are due to press, there is just no news at all. NO NEWS OF THE POPE would be a tremendous headline. Think of it; it could mean anything, or nothing. But for Thompson and me it means that there is another crisis, another news famine, another night of trying to persuade the readers that the world was exciting yesterday. Better get into the Big Room to deal with Page One. Better call Brenda first, though, to say I'm going to be late again and not to wait dinner for me. . . .

After one such typical night that maintained its tempo till 3 a.m. I overslept, and when Lord Beaverbrook called me on the telephone I was still at home. Three times he called before I arrived at midday. Then this dialogue took place:

'What time do you get to your office in the morning?'

'It depends on what time I finish the previous night, sir.'

'I did not ask you what time you finished. I want to know what time you come into your office in the morning.'

'It depends on what time I finish. Sometimes it's 2 a.m., sometimes it's 3 a.m. . . . .'

'I am not interested in what time you finish, only in what time you come in.'

'Well, I must repeat that it depends on . . .'

I was cut short at this point. 'Give me a time, my friend,' said Lord Beaverbrook harshly, 'and I promise you that never, never, never will I call you before that time.'

A tough nut, the Beaver; but he never called me a moment before 11.30 for the next ten years. Nor was I ever late, so I will never know whether we would have had another row if I had been.

Just the same I got a hard ride. For instance, there was an immense scene over an article which implied that Mussolini was a murderer. It was at the time when Neville Chamberlain was making a big effort to placate 'the swollen bull-frog of the Pontine Marshes'.

'Do you not see that this article is insulting and damaging to the Head of a friendly State?' Beaverbrook asked me on the telephone. I replied that I did not; the dynamite in one paragraph had escaped me.

'Then read the article again and call me back.'

I re-read the article and still missed out. So when I called Lord Beaverbrook back I stood my ground and denied that it implied that Mussolini was a murderer.

'Then read the article again and call me back,' came the voice of the Canadian growler, this time several times more menacing.

I did so and once more failed to find the offending paragraph. When I called back yet again a cyclone hit me and my temper snapped. I bellowed back, 'Leave me alone, for God's sake' and banged down the receiver.

Beaverbrook's capacity for the unexpected is always incalculable. He must have decided that he had baited me too much, for he was back on the telephone within seconds. I told my secretary to say I did not want to speak to him, but, wise girl, she refused to transmit the message, and I had to do it myself.

'Now, listen to me,' said the Beaver. 'You and I have always got to talk. Have you sent anyone to cover Ramsay MacDonald's speech tonight? It's important. Do so if you haven't. And let me tell you that far worse crises than this have happened to the *Daily Express* in the past. One day I opened my paper to find that Blumenfeld had led the front page with a stumer that the Bank of Greece had gone bankrupt. I knew that if I did not act quickly the Bank of Greece would bankrupt the *Daily Express*, so I leaped out of my bed, put on a dressing-gown and ran all the way to Leatherhead Station in my pyjamas to catch the train to London.'

'I'll be all right,' I replied uninterested by this fascinating yarn, 'but please leave me alone now.'

'No, no, no,' he said, and gave me ten more minutes of talk on the troubles of a newspaper proprietor until my spasm of wrath and grief was over and we were friends again.

But after a while I cracked under the pressure and went to see Lord Beaverbrook at Stornoway House with a real attack of the jitters. He was sympathetic. He asked me how old I was and when I told him I was thirty, he told me that he, too, had suffered from nervous exhaustion at my age (but by that age he was many times a millionaire!) and that I should not worry. Nerve storms were a weakness of youth. As I grew older I would learn to harness my energies instead of dissipating them. Age slowed men down somewhat but it brought wisdom. Now, he continued, would I like to rest from editorship until I felt fit again? If so, I could change places with the editor in Glasgow for a while. I said I would think these ideas over, but from the look in his eye it was clear that once I gave up my chair I would never get it back. So I telephoned a Harley Street friend, T. G. D. Bonar, who told me he could administer a drastic remedy if I would call on him each day 'between patients' at two minutes past three o'clock. I did so; and every day for twelve days, Bonar injected into me a preparation of strychnine, iron and arsenic. The effect was startling. My confidence came back. I returned to battle.

It must have been medicine fit only for a mule, for Bonar died soon afterwards and never again was I able to find a doctor willing to oblige me with these injections.

Beaverbrook did not inquire about my sudden recovery. Possibly he considered that by showing me the red light he had been a better doctor even than Bonar.

17 . . . Life with the Beaver

I am always asked, 'What is it like working for Beaverbrook?' Usually my questioners provide their own answer before I can get a word in edgeways. 'It must be hell.'

It is hell – and it isn't. On the days when you think it is going to be hell it isn't, and on the days when life seems serene, it turns out to be hell. During the Battle of Britain I was invited to lunch in the boardroom of *The Times*. Another guest was Sir Charles Craven, who used to be branded by the Socialists as Merchant of Death No. 1 because he was managing director of Vickers Armstrong, the giant armaments firm. We were introduced, and his handsome, bronzed face puckered in pain as Major J. J. Astor (later Lord Astor of Hever) explained that I was the youngest editor in Fleet Street and had been running Beaverbrook's top paper for seven years. 'Good God,' said Craven, 'I don't think I will live for seven days if your boss doesn't change his ways. I'm working for him at the Ministry of Aircraft Production. He called me at two o'clock this morning and at half-past eight he was on the telephone again to get a progress report. I told him that I had hardly had time to put my head on my pillow, and he didn't seem at all happy. "Neither have I," he said. "Get a move on, Charles." Does he go on like that with his newspapers?'

'You'll get used to it,' I replied. But actually I never did. No week, no day, no hour conformed to any pattern, except that the telephone constantly rang. Wherever Beaverbrook went, the telephone followed. Even when he was sunning himself on the porch of Cherkley, his country home in the Surrey Downs, there was a telephone at his side. When he went to America he telephoned for news directly the *Queen Elizabeth* cast off from Southampton. 'Where's my son Max?' he asked me. 'I expect he's quite near me in Cowes Roads on his yacht by now. Get him to call me.' When the ship got out of range for calls to England he telephoned the New York office.

Leading articles, feature ideas, news stories, gossip paragraphs, criticism and praise flooded over the telephone hour by hour. My rusty shorthand was inadequate for the task. Sometimes, if I knew what was coming, I put my secretary on to a parallel line, but even she could not get anything like a verbatim of the torrent which at its peak reaches a good 400 words a minute. That was a pity because the richness of Beaverbrook's oratory and the coherence with which he talks represents tailor-made journalism. Yet if I called him back to check a phrase it had gone from him as surely as though it were a note of music that had vanished into the air.

I write about the days before the Dictaphone and the Soundscriber; now every word can be taken down on tape and transcribed. 'Am I on the machine?' he asks with sudden caution when he is about to launch a violent diatribe; or 'Put me on the machine', when he feels a leading article welling up.

Work goes on in all circumstances. A notebook is laid on his dining-room table as though it were as essential for eating purposes as a knife and fork. 'Take this down,' he bellows excitedly, just as I am toying with the season's first asparagus. Or, 'I am going to use this in the *Daily Express*,' he says to a guest as he starts to scribble the news he has been hearing. If the guest objects then that is the end of it: the scribble is destroyed. But he will grumble, 'People shouldn't tell me news if they don't want me to print it.'

We go walking in Hyde Park and on to Knightsbridge until we come to a flower-shop. He orders roses to be sent to somebody and selects also a couple of dozen orchids all growing on one stem for my wife. This gives me time to get my notebook out in an endeavour to recall, not so much the words, but the mass of subjects we have discussed. But not for long.

'What's your address, Chris?'

'I'll write it on the envelope for you, sir.'

'No, you won't. Your wife will think *you* sent the flowers if you do. *I* want the credit.'

We walk home and suddenly he gets an attack of asthma. He has forgotten his nasal spray and by the time we are back he sounds as though he is playing the Marseillaise on his bronchial tubes.

'Bring me a drinka whisky,' he croaks to a manservant.

'It's very good for breaking up asthma,' I say sympathetically. 'I know, because it's very good for Michael Foot's.'

'If you wanta know,' says the old mischief-maker, quick-witted even in pain, 'it *causes* Michael's asthma.'

We spread all the morning newspapers on the carpet and tiptoe alongside them. 'Which d'ya like best of all to-day's front pages?' This I know to be the signal that to-day's *Express* is not popular. There is a longish story about the weather, with which subject, being a Canadian, he cannot understand our British preoccupation. One of his old political cronies from 1918 has died and has not made even a 'brief' on the front page. Some of the 'filler' paragraphs at the foot of the columns are on the trivial side. There is a murder case, which he likes, with over-prominent headlines, which he dislikes.

'Tellya what I'd have made your paper look like to-day –' he seizes a notepad and starts drawing column rules, and filling in headlines. Everything is in single-column form, and with the exception of the murder case, is news of importance: political, industrial and financial.

'What'ya think of that?'

'It wouldn't sell.'

'I agree.' And as he says it he kicks the *Daily Telegraph* right in its centre column.

This discussion of the merits of the other newspapers never ceases. 'Let's go for a motor-car ride; bring your notebook and a copy of the paper,' he said one day. From Stornoway House we travelled West until we pulled up outside a modest house in Kensington. Without any explanation he took me inside and there we were in the studio of Jacob Epstein.

Lord Beaverbrook took his place on a throne. Epstein took a
wet cloth off a lump of clay. I sat at the foot of the throne on a
wooden chair.

Said Epstein, with a sardonic grin broader if anything than
Beaverbrook's: 'Your Lordship has had his hair cut since the last
sitting.'

> *Beaverbrook:* 'Ya-as I have, and I hope I did not do wrong.
> Christiansen, do you think "Beachcomber's" column is
> funny?'
> *Christiansen:* 'It always makes *me* laugh.'
> *Beaverbrook:* 'Then read it out aloud and see if it makes *me*
> laugh.'

The Epstein head of Lord Beaverbrook was presented to him by
Isidore Ostrer, head of the film family, and has been in the main
hall of the *Daily Express* building in Fleet Street since 1934.

The unveiling of the head was the occasion of one of Lord
Beaverbrook's rare visits to the office. Long before my time, he had
given up living in a flat on the top floor of the office, and now he
came once a year at the most. His visits were supposed to catch the
staff unawares, but the management's secret service was most
efficient and the whole place was spruced up with the spit-and-
polish that usually attracts hostile Press publicity when an army
barracks gets the full treatment before a Royal visit.

Lord Beaverbrook hated untidiness in the office, although in his
own home he litters the floor with newspaper cuttings, bits of
paper and discarded manuscripts. On his occasional visits, he
rooted round even in the waste-paper baskets. 'What's this?' he
growled to the General Manager when he unearthed an empty beer
bottle and a length of electric wiring. 'Drinking *and* waste in the
office. It won't do, Robertson. Give me a report on it.'

Although he never caught his Fleet Street headquarters unawares, he succeeded once in doing so in the Manchester office.
The sturdy Lancashire commissionaire refused him admission.

'But this is Lord Beaverbrook,' said his secretary.

'Oh, aye,' said the commissionaire. 'And you can tell Lord

Beaverbrook that I'm Cecil Parkin.' (Parkin was a famous Lancashire cricketer.)

'Give Parkin a bonus to reward his vigilance in protecting my property,' said Lord Beaverbrook, who had never heard of Cecil Parkin.

He could be as penny-wise as a son-of-the-manse and as pound-foolish as a winner of the treble chance in the football pools. When I visited the Glasgow office in 1957, the local editor's secretary typed a memorandum for dispatch to Lord Beaverbrook in London. She took the view that nothing but the best was good enough for him and typed the message on double-thick cream-laid paper. 'This means trouble for us all,' I forecast to 'Sandy' Trotter, the Editor. 'Then let's have it typed again on cheaper paper,' Trotter suggested. 'No,' I said, for years soaked in the frugal approach. 'That would mean double waste; just let's see what happens.'

And sure enough, up came the rocket in the form of a message demanding to know (a) why this notepaper had been used; and (b) what stocks still existed and what other uses they were put to.

Inter-office communications must not be sent in unused envelopes in the Beaverbrook organisation; secretaries must collect old envelopes for this purpose. Nor must these communications be typed on embossed or even printed letter-head notepaper. When I told the proprietor of a local newspaper of these economy rules, he exploded that they were a waste of time. When I told Isidore Gluckstein, the benign chairman of J. Lyons and Company, an organisation far bigger than Beaverbrook's, he said that vigilance in the use of envelopes led to care in bigger expenditure and that it was not the saving of a few hundred pounds a year that mattered so much as the outlook. There must be something to this, for the gap between revenue and expenditure in the newspaper business is small.

The most recent annual figures show that the Beaverbrook group earned £26,101,328 and spent all but £1,554,515 of this sum. In round figures, paper and ink cost £9 millions, salaries £9 millions, and news services and reporting expenses £900,000. If I had had at any time a feeling of responsibility for all this expenditure I would have either shot myself or agreed to be certified. Happily the burden was on people like Robertson, the General Manager (and later

Tom Blackburn, his successor) and I was allowed to produce the
newspaper almost regardless of expense. I summed up my approach
to the financial side of editorship in the phrase: CALCULATED
EXTRAVAGANCE.

Lord Beaverbrook never looked particularly excited, happy or
even interested when I talked money, but he was a wonderful
exponent of the policy of calculated extravagance. 'Show me your
editorial salary list,' he said at least once a year (and sometimes, to
be 'different', at intervals of only a month or two). 'We mustn't
let that fellow Robertson make too much money.' With Robertson
sitting there tight-lipped but resigned, the editorial payroll would be
increased by £250 a week, spread among a dozen or so promising
youngsters.

Ben Sonnenberg, the highly sophisticated American publicist,
met Robertson some years before his retirement. 'He was a man
who *looked* as though he worked for somebody big. You see that
face all over the world,' said Sonnenberg. Robertson was the kindest
and most generous man in his personal life, but in business he had
to be hatchet-faced and to know how to wield the hatchet. He also
had to be calm and understanding in face of the Beaver's rages in
which no one was spared, including Robertson himself; yet the two
men were on very intimate terms, and the Beaver relied on Robertson as his guide and comforter.

Beaverbrook's outbursts of extravagance seemed genuinely to
upset Robertson, I suppose because he had to earn the money and
present the balance-sheet. Robertson once complained to me that
it cost a couple of shillings to airmail a copy of the *Daily Express*
to a foreign correspondent. 'Goddam it, Chris, why can't the fellow
wait for it to come by sea?' he asked, pulling his nose in a typical
gesture. On the other hand, when in the thirties I urgently needed a
bank guarantee for a loan of £3,000, Robertson went to Beaverbrook and caused the money to be given to me as a gift.

Within a few months of this act of generosity, I received a letter
from Beaverbrook which said:

> The devotion that you give to your task as Editor of the *Daily
> Express* cannot be rewarded by money . . .
> You are already well paid and your salary increases have been

many. At the same time I have no use for money in excess of my present supplies and on that account I must try to place my Editor in the same position.

Robertson has been told on the eve of my departure for a long journey to give you another £1,000 yearly salary in the New Year.

This kind of incident happened to many others as well as to myself, and at unexpected moments. 'Is Morley Richards a good man?' Beaverbrook asked me at a cocktail party he gave in a private room at the Savoy. I said he was a very good man, and my News Editor was sent for. 'How much money d'ya get, Richards?' 'Fifty pounds a week, sir.' 'Not enough. I've told Christiansen to give you another twenty.' It made no difference that Richards had been paid an extra £10 a week only three months previously.

Beaverbrook's parties to meet the staff were both fabulous and 'different'. Sometimes he invited a round hundred to 'tea' which was his way of inviting them for drinks. Sometimes he invited them for drinks and began by serving tea. Sometimes he asked the entire editorial staffs of each of his three London papers to a sit-down dinner on three successive nights.

Once he gave a reception and dance at Stornoway House. It was a gay affair and the champagne flowed. Only one incident marred the occasion: in a corner there was a complete stranger who was obviously the worse for wear. 'Who's that?' asked Beaverbrook sharply. No one could identify the fellow so instructions were given to have the gatecrasher flung out. The party continued until 1 a.m., when the liquor supplies were turned off. After much hand-shaking, and the last guest had gone, I was left with the boss. 'Godeson,' he said to his butler, 'how much did they drink?' Godeson gave the figures: sixty-three bottles of champagne; eight bottles of Scotch; and so on.

'A remarkable bunch of people,' ruminated Beaverbrook. 'So much consumed, and only one drunk.'

'My staff are always in training,' I answered.

The next morning I received a letter of resignation from the one drunk. He was in fact a junior member of the financial staff who worked in Throgmorton Street and had never been seen before by anyone in the Fleet Street head office. His letter also asked if he could have his overcoat back from the cloak-room in Stornoway House. Everybody, including Lord Beaverbrook, tried to get the young man to withdraw his resignation – we even held on to his overcoat for a day or two – but he was adamant and left the *Express* to join a firm of stockbrokers. He returned to journalism after the war, however, and is now a City Editor whom Beaverbrook Newspapers would be glad to employ.

Lord Beaverbrook was so encouraged by the behaviour of the *Daily Express* staff that he decided to repeat the success by inviting the *Sunday Express* staff to a reception and dance the following week. But the *Sunday Express* people were not in such good training as my lot. For example, Bill Taylor, the News Editor, thought his taxi-cab home had stopped when it was still travelling, and ended up in hospital. He was so ashamed of himself that he disappeared and was not heard of again until war broke out and the Germans occupied the Channel Islands, where he had repaired to convalesce from his wounds! Taylor died during the occupation, no doubt having made the enemy buy him a drink or two.

There is never a dull moment working for the Beaverbrook organisation, whether your wounds are, like Bill Taylor's, self-inflicted, or whether they are the honourable scars of battle. Every day is a new and exciting experience, and it was the Beaver's habit to make sure that no two days were alike. If he could have made the sun rise in the West, it would have delighted him, because unlike the rest of us he would have been up to see it.

18 . . . The Boss was at the Palace

The births, deaths and marriages of members of the Royal Family impose fantastic strains on newspapermen. I handled every such occasion, including the Abdication of Edward VIII and the broken romance between Princess Margaret and Group-Captain Townsend, the Queen's Equerry.

The death of King George V in January 1936 began the first of these intense periods. The first intimation that something was wrong came only ten days before the King died. It was at that time just 'a slight cold', but it meant the immediate dispatch to Sandringham of five reporters to keep a twenty-four-hour vigil. The obituary pages were brought up to date. Plates were cast on the stereotype machines every night before the normal pages of the paper went to press, since they had to bear each day's date. These plates were strategically disposed in the machine room ready to be whipped on to the presses.

On Monday, 20 January, the B.B.C. clock ticked slowly and dramatically for the last hour before midnight, the ticking broken only by the voice of Sir John (now Lord) Reith, the B.B.C. boss, repeating from time to time 'The King's life is moving peacefully to its close'. For us in Fleet Street the occasion was not only moving – and newspapermen are sometimes moved by the events they record – but professionally agonising. At ten o'clock a telephone call came from a booth in Piccadilly Circus. It was an informant to tell us that rival newspapers were on sale with the news of the King's death. We had reporters in many places to observe the behaviour of the great crowds that had gathered to await the end, but none of them had given us any indication that the *Express* had been left behind. Could it be true?

Yet another reporter was rushed to Piccadilly Circus, where there were already a couple of men as well as photographers. But before he could get there Trevor Wignall, who had good friends in Buckingham Palace, telephoned to say that the King had died soon after nine o'clock. No, he could not give me the source, nor could he vouch for its complete reliability. But, said Trevor, he was given to understand that the announcement would not be made for a little time, until various formalities had been arranged. That seemed logical, but how could I risk publication before the news was official?

In an agony of doubt I left my office and went into the Big Room. E. J. Robertson had arrived by this time. Despite his influence with Lord Beaverbrook, Robertson never sought to take a decision that belonged to the Editor. 'What are you going to do?' he asked. I said I would have to wait for first-hand news from our own sources, whether the other papers were printing or not. I said I did not believe that there were papers on sale announcing the news of the King's death, and that I did not propose to print a copy until the official announcement came out. Then I had a hunch: I gave this order: 'Plate up one machine. Print twenty thousand copies and stack them in the Publishing Office. And God help anyone if a copy gets out on the streets before I say "Go".'

It was then around 10.30 p.m. Sydney Long, the Works Manager, gave the orders and an emergency edition bearing the headlines:

DEATH OF THE KING

THE QUEEN AND THE PRINCE AT HIS BEDSIDE

was printed and stacked on one side.

Now it was a question of waiting. The first edition was due to go to press at eleven o'clock. Dare we hang on for a few minutes?

A quarter of an hour passed, then twenty minutes. 'How long can we wait, Sydney?'

'Just a few more minutes.'

'But what about the 11.40 train to Cardiff from Paddington?'

'You've missed that now, so we'll hang on for another few minutes and hire a special.'

It was agreed that we would delay till midnight. As the hour approached, a reporter came on from the Feathers Inn at Dersingham to say that if we waited 'a few minutes' (those minutes again!) he thought the end could not be long delayed. But how long? No one knew. And then at four minutes past midnight the Press Association ticked out the flash that the King was dead.

Long since, the reporter sent to Piccadilly Circus had denied the story that the other papers were on sale with the news. But the hoaxer had been, after all, my benefactor. Thanks to those twenty thousand copies which had been printed after his call, the *Express* was the only newspaper to carry the news of the death of the King in every single copy printed in Fleet Street that night. What is more, we were the first paper to reach Piccadilly Circus.

King Edward VIII was never crowned, but one day it looked as if he had narrowly escaped assassination. He was riding back to the Palace up Constitution Hill, after presenting the Colours in Hyde Park, when a man in the crowd named George MacMahon threw a revolver which landed between the King and his bodyguard.

It was a five-chambered revolver with one barrel empty, and it was this barrel that would have gone off first if the trigger had been pulled. That night sales of the evening newspapers were phenomenal, but there was still plenty of excitement left for the following morning, and my reporters went all out to get the life-history of the man who threw the gun. They collected a great deal of material. I sent for our lawyer, a wise old Lancastrian, James Critchley, and asked his view about publication. 'It will be contempt of Court,' he warned. 'You cannot give facts which may prejudice a fair trial – even if this does turn out to be an attempt on the King's life.'

I was in a predicament. Everyone was clamouring for news of MacMahon, and the background to his behaviour. We were satisfied that it had been merely a demonstration by a man with a grievance, and I believed it was in the circumstances a matter of public policy to satisfy the nation that the King's life had not been in danger.

Critchley insisted that I could not print, until along came a special late edition of the *Evening News*, containing the very stuff that I wanted for my front page. I swooped on Critchley again, and put it to him that all the morning papers would now feel themselves free to print the background story. Thus it was that I secured grudging legal consent for a Page One story on the gunman's background.

Next morning *The Times* spoke in terms of 'an attempted assassination' in a leading article; and other papers transgressed the law in varying degrees. Days went by and I began to think I had been right, that no prosecution would be launched. Then I got a telephone call from John Horwell, Chief Constable of Scotland Yard. 'Chris,' he said, 'can I come and have a cup of tea with you?' He looked embarrassed as he sat in my office, and when he asked me if my first name was Arthur, and if I was in fact the editor of the *Daily Express*, I began to suspect trouble.

Two days later a writ for contempt was served on me. The *Daily Express* and the *Evening News* had been selected for court action, and John Horwell, with all the caution of an old-fashioned cop, had just been checking up on me.

MacMahon, the gun thrower, got twelve months' jail. But the hearing of the contempt case, before Mr Justice Rigby Swift and two other judges, taught me that it is not the business of an editor to chance his arm by defying the law even when he thinks the life of the King has been in jeopardy.

Frank FitzHugh, the editor of the *Evening News*, turned up in court in morning coat, lilac waistcoat and striped trousers. He was carrying a silk topper. He was a towering figure of a man, colourful and nonchalant. He looked at me in my best lounge suit, quite a tiny fellow beside him despite my already expanding waistline. Fitz told me that he had been up once before for contempt and that I was not to worry.

His case was taken first. Sir Norman Birkett rose to apologise on FitzHugh's behalf, and in ten mellifluous minutes (it was the first time I had heard this greatest-of-all after-dinner speakers, wit,

From her family album my mother extracted this photograph of myself as a 19-year-old reporter on the *Liverpool Courier*, and *Evening Express*

Wedding Day in 1926 – and the happy couple twenty-five years later.

I love pictures of other people's families, so I present this one of my
father's parents and his brothers and sisters. My father is in the centre
of the group. My grandfather was a Dane who settled in Liverpool

Re-visiting the Wallasey Grammar School for Speech Day in 1952, the Head Boy presented me with a cigarette box carved (he said) out of my old desk. When I retired from the *Daily Express* in 1957, Fleet Street presented me with a crystal goblet, inscribed 'To Chris from Fleet Street' specially designed by the Royal College of Art

In 1930 the R101 disaster gave me my first big scoop . . . . I was assistant
editor of the *Sunday Express* and I worked like this, sleeves rolled up

In the years of my editorship the presentation of news was revolution-ised. In the early 'thirties (*Above*) make-up was formal and rigid. I sought to express the drama of events typographically.

September '38 – with the news that there was still hope of peace – see Munich Page One below – my wife and family relax at the week end.

Daily Express

WORLD'S LARGEST DAILY SALE

Thursday, September 29, 1938.   One Penny

PREMIER FLIES TODAY TO LAST-MINUTE PEACE TALK
WITH HITLER, DUCE AND DALADIER, TELLS CROWD:

"IT'S ALL RIGHT!"

HITLER POSTPONES HIS MOBILISATION

11th hour message: Now Britain, France and Italy may police Sudetenland

"TOKEN CESSION" PLAN

By GUY EDEN
Daily Express Political Correspondent

THERE IS HOPE—REAL HOPE—OF PEACE
IT CAME THROUGH THE QUIETLY SPOKEN WORDS OF THE PRIME MINISTER, MR. NEVILLE CHAMBERLAIN, IN THE DENSELY PACKED HOUSE OF COMMONS YESTERDAY, WHEN HE ANNOUNCED THAT HERR HITLER HAD AGREED TO SEE SIGNOR MUSSOLINI, M. DALADIER, THE FRENCH PREMIER, AND HIMSELF IN MUNICH TODAY.

Hitler, in a message handed to the Prime Minister as he stood at the table about to end his speech, agreed to postpone mobilisation, and to have another conference, with a view to settling the Czech quarrel. And when he flies to Munich, from Heston airport at 8.30 this

'DON'T HOARD FOOD'

"A.R.P. MUST GO ON"
—HOME SECRETARY

Spain, too

When I asked Lord Beaverbrook to autograph this photograph he sent m

refusal. 'This picture speaks for itself about our relationship,' he wrote.

We were issued with steel helmets at the outbreak of war. Managing Editor Herbert Gunn, Brian Chapman and myself posed for this picture – but feeling foolish, had stored them away by the time the Censor allowed us to print the historic news below.

Daily Express

Bear Brand STOCKINGS *A SHEER NECESSITY*

BLACK-OUT 10.2
ZERO HOUR TO-NIGHT 7.65

WORLD'S LARGEST DAILY SALE

No. 12,268 · Tuesday, September 12, 1939 · One Penny

Men in khaki lean from a train as it rumbles through a village, revealing to the world—

BRITISH TROOPS IN FRANCE

French folk run to cheer the Tommies

'TOGETHER IN MAGINOT'

From GEOFFREY COX
Daily Express Staff Reporter

PARIS. Monday.

IN A FRENCH VILLAGE THIS MORNING I WATCHED A LONG BRITISH TROOP TRAIN RUMBLE THROUGH. THE VILLAGERS RUSHED TO THE STATION AS A FEW WATCHERS ON THE PLATFORM SHOUTED "LES ANGLAIS!"

Infantrymen in khaki leaned from the carriages, waved cheerily and shouted to the French people. From the compartments at the end of the train officers saluted smilingly.

The grey-haired stationmaster turned to me, saying. "I fought beside the British at the Somme. "My son has already gone to the Maginot. He'll be with them now."

General Viscount ("Tiger") Gort, V.C., is Commander-in-Chief of the British Field Forces.

NO FLOWERS, BY REQUEST

NO flowers may be thrown at Hitler during his visits to the front, says an order from the "Fuehrer's" headquarters," quoted by the German radio yesterday afternoon. The order added: "Flowers should be handed to the troops."

U-boat sinkings: A row in the Nazi command

From SELKIRK PANTON
Daily Express Staff Reporter
COPENHAGEN, Monday.

JUST as Grand Admiral von Tirpitz, the ex-Kaiser's naval chief, clashed with his

50,000 Germans killed

IT was reported last night on the highest authority that German casualties until Saturday mid-day–after a week of war — were 50,000 killed and 170,000 wounded.

WHY THE ADVANCE STOPPED

Daily Express Military Correspondent

THE Germans have withdrawn from Warsaw, while to the south-west of the city a battle is being waged along a 16-mile front. The German

Even at parties Lord Beaverbrook and I never stopped working. In the picture below, taken at the Savoy Hotel, the first edition of the *Daily Express* had just arrived by dispatch rider from Fleet Street and I am trying to read it over the Beaver's shoulder.

Wing Commander Max Aitken, D.S.O., D.F.C., leaving Buckingham
Palace with his father after receiving Battle of Britain honours.
(*Below*) Hannen Swaffer arrives at the farewell dinner Lord Beaver-
brook gave to me in 1960. Swaff and I worked together in the '20s.

After visiting Field Marshal Montgomery's H.Q. in 1944 I sent him pictures of the German Generals Kesselring and Von Rundstedt. 'The surest way to dispose of them,' wrote Monty, 'seems to be to hang their portraits in my caravan' (*Below*).

A meeting with Earl Mountbatten at lunch during the war. (*Above*) After a visit in 1951 to S.H.A.P.E. in Versailles I prophesied to Lord Beaverbrook that if Eisenhower ran for President of the U.S.A. his sincerity would destroy Truman. (*Below*) Ike talks about N.A.T.O. problems.

In 1947, a trip to Hollywood, where my wife talks with Spencer Tracy and Adolph Menjou. Columnist Sheilah Graham is the other girl in the picture. (*Below*) A night out with some of my staff, this picture being taken in Bud Flanagan's dressing room after a Crazy Gang Show. Bud, Naughton and Gold, and Nervo and Knox are in the picture – the rest are my boys, with William Barkley in the foreground.

I worked in my shirt-sleeves to the last – and sometimes, so my staff said, looked pretty grim. But life was fun – and so was my appearance on the B.B.C. television show 'This is Your Life' in 1956. (*Below*) Eamonn Andrews presents the usual souvenir of the occasion.

advocate, and later wise judge) he pleaded for leniency for his client.

Copies of the *Evening News* were passed to the judges. They leaned over each other's shoulders as they inspected the paper. They resumed their seats. Mr Justice Rigby Swift peered down and fined FitzHugh the sum of £500 and his newspaper a similar sum. He warned FitzHugh that if he committed a similar offence in the future a more serious view would undoubtedly be taken.

Then Sir Patrick Hastings rose to address the court on my behalf. Compared with Birkett, he was a gruff little man, with no music in his voice. He made his plea by associating himself with the words 'so eloquently expressed by my learned colleague'. He spoke for a few minutes only and I rated it a poor performance.

The *Daily Express* was handed up to the judges. The offending news and headlines were ringed in red pencil. Once more the judges leaned over each other's shoulders, and it seemed for much longer than they had lingered over the *Evening News*. My account had in fact been fuller than FitzHugh's and it had been displayed with all the 'zizz' that the *Express* was then acquiring.

I was not sent to prison. I got a similar fine to FitzHugh's and the same warning. But I needed no warning by that time. I had learned my lesson, and it has stuck ever since. I have never deliberately risked my newspaper's reputation since that day.

During all this anxiety Lord Beaverbrook had sympathised with me and had uttered not one word of criticism. But when it was all over I got a sharp and angry kick in the pants. We never mentioned the matter again.

But the most dramatic of all these Royal occasions started when a cable was placed on my desk stating that the *New York Journal*'s front page headline in type one and a half inches deep read:

KING *WILL* WED WALLY

What should an editor do when he knows that the author of the news which follows this headline is William Randolph Hearst, the proprietor of the *Journal*, who had recently visited King Edward at Fort Belvedere?

K

'Within a few days,' said the *Journal*, 'Mrs Ernest Simpson of Baltimore, U.S.A., will obtain her divorce decree in England, and some eight months thereafter she will be married to Edward VIII, King of England. . . .'

The full message lay on my desk. So did a mountainous pile of sensational clippings, also from America, that had torn the conscience of British editors since the new King, obviously deeply in love, had taken Mrs Simpson on a Mediterranean cruise in the yacht *Nahlin* in 1936.

It is easy to moralise now, for the Royal Family has had another domestic crisis, that sad, sad story of Princess Margaret's love for Group-Captain Townsend, which was resolved in the full glare of publicity.

But in 1936 there was no precedent. At the time of the cruise of the *Nahlin* only one newspaper, the defunct *Sunday Referee*, published a picture of the King and Mrs Simpson seated in the yacht's dinghy. By contrast, Lord Rothermere's Sunday paper announced on Page One under the headline, WHY THERE ARE NO PICTURES OF THE KING, that 'His Majesty, like so many of his subjects, is on holiday' and that he was entitled to an 'occasional respite from public attention'.

In Monday's *Daily Express* I published a picture of the King in the dinghy, but cut out Mrs Simpson, who was sitting in the stern. I felt no spasms of conscience over this decision. The standards of the Press then in relation to intrusion into people's private affairs were much higher than they are today.

It seems to me a bad development in the journalism of the last decade that this is so, although I do feel that those who invite publicity should be resigned to being devoured by it. But the atmosphere was quite different in the thirties. The *Morning Post*, an arrogant die-hard journal of the aristocracy, spoke for all the Press when it later published a leading article saying: 'It is no part of the function of the Press to publish gossip possibly injurious to such an institution as the Monarchy. At the time . . . the friendship seemed to be a matter of private rather than of public life. It concerned the man rather than the King.'

It was for me just another busy day, with the Spanish war coverage as its chief headache, when Bishop Blunt of Bradford made the speech that began the chain of events leading to the King's Abdication. Herbert Wilcox, the film producer, was in my office that afternoon. He had called to tell me that he was going to make a movie based on the life of Queen Victoria and that his young star Anna Neagle (they were not then married) was to play the lead.

'Do you know, this is the first time it has been possible to make a film about Queen Victoria,' said Herbert. 'Thank God for King Edward! He has authorised the Lord Chamberlain to lift the ban.'

But King Edward was in the news in a bigger way, and five minutes later I had to ask Herbert to leave quickly.

Little point in my going into a day-by-day account of that exhausting marathon of news, for everybody from the ex-King and his wife to the historian of *The Times* has told the tale, and Beaverbrook has admitted his role as Censor.

My relations with Lord Beaverbrook on policy matters were as ever: his the policy, mine the paper. I knew that while Geoffrey Dawson, the editor of *The Times*, was conspiring with an advising Baldwin in Downing Street, Lord Beaverbrook was to-ing and fro-ing it to Buckingham Palace and Fort Belvedere. But sometimes I got this news in the most roundabout ways. 'Your boss has just gone in to the Palace by the back way,' was a telephone tip-off from Charlie Smith, London Manager of the American International News Service, one night. 'Bless you, Charlie,' I replied sardonically. 'Cable it to New York and then I'll be able to quote I.N.S. that the Beaver is in with the King.'

The headlines mounted in size day by day. I almost lived in the office, and so did most of the staff, except those who went hiving off in pursuit of Mrs Simpson to the South of France. The heads of departments had to cut out their supper break to cope with the rush of news; I had a ham sandwich and a nip of burgundy sent in to me from 'The Falstaff' night after night and 'dined' in the Big Room.

Lunch at Stornoway House with Lord Beaverbrook, E. J. Robertson and Frank Owen, the leader writer, was a more satisfying affair, but even there the talk was all tactics and leading articles and answering such questions as 'What is the public thinking, Chris?' I may not have formulated policy but I was regarded as having my finger on the nation's pulse, and when I reported that the people were on Baldwin's side, there was not only dismay but signs of sour disbelief. In vain I quoted, as typical of provincial Englishwomen, the view of my mother, who called Mrs Simpson 'that *woman*' with a ferocity which astonished me.

'You're falling for Geoffrey Dawson's propaganda,' growled Beaverbrook.

'My mother doesn't read *The Times*,' I retorted.

But it was no go. Beaverbrook has never been swayed by public popularity in the conduct of his newspapers, and would not be budged from his stand as a King's Man. And neither I, nor Robertson, nor Frank Owen, made the effort, so far as I can recollect, for we also, with all our training, were King's Men.

Came the night of 7 December 1936. The ham sandwich and the nip of burgundy had not yet arrived from 'The Falstaff' for my Big Room supper. Reggie Thompson, the Managing Editor, got up from his desk on my immediate left, and waddled in his portly, restless way into the news agency ticker room about ten yards away.

He was back within seconds, his eyes blazing. 'Here it is, here it is!' was all he could say. 'It' was a statement by Mrs Simpson issued through Lord Brownlow from Cannes which said: 'Mrs Simpson . . . is willing . . . to withdraw from a situation which has been rendered both unhappy and untenable.'

I was through to Beaverbrook in a flash.

'What d'ya think of it?' he asked.

'Well,' I said, 'it could be a way out for the King, if he wants a way out.'

'You are entitled to take that view – if that is your view,' Beaverbrook advised.

As I heard him hang up I wondered how much inside knowledge he had. I even wondered whether he and 'Perry' Brownlow, two very old friends, realising which way the tide was running, had concocted the message between them and had advised Mrs Simpson to issue it. Certainly the sonorous, almost Biblical, phrase 'unhappy and untenable' was typical of the Beaverbrookian style.

I went back to the Big Room and wrote a splash headline:

END OF THE CRISIS

The type was our biggest – one inch high, and the whole front page was as lavish. The rest of the paper was also transformed. Frank Owen wrote a short cautious leading article which read:

'Mrs Simpson sends a message through the newspapers to say that she would desire, if such action could solve the problem, to withdraw from the situation.

'That message can mean only one thing – that Mrs Simpson is making the renunciation.'

In Owen's racy style the leader column continued: 'Is there anything else going on? Yes, man! Spain is back to normal, with civil war raging. To-day being the day of the Immaculate Conception, . . . Franco promises the biggest mass onslaught of the war on Madrid . . . The 5,000 Germans are said to have arrived. . . .'

But not a word of this made Page One; and the rest of the leader page was devoted to a studio picture of the woman of the hour, with a biography of her noble escort, Lord Brownlow.

When the first editions of our rivals came into the office no one had been as bold as the *Express*. 'Never mind,' I said, 'they'll copy us by the time they reach their finals.' Our rivals usually did.

Having got our own slant on Mrs Simpson's letter, the only question that bothered us now was how to make the story even more our own. So I rushed fifty copies of the first edition to the Café de Paris, where white-tied London cavorted in those days, and in our final edition appeared a three-column picture of the gay young Socialites surrounded by champagne and caviare, all of them reading the *Daily Express* first edition.

At 2.30 a.m., when the last edition had gone to press, Tom Driberg (William Hickey), Frank Owen, Bill Knott, the splash sub-editor, one or two others and myself went on the town at Frisco's in Soho. Frisco was an out-size coloured entertainer whose club was patronised almost exclusively by people like us. Driberg wrote words to the tune of the St Louis Blues:

> Say, boys, the crisis is over,
> Mrs Simpson's got it on the raw,
> Her situation is unhappy and untenable,
> Da-da-di-da-dida-da . . .

We formed a crocodile, with Frisco in his top hat, white tie and tails leading us round, and we sang and sang. Our tension was ended and all that remained was to tidy up.

But next day the song turned sour. The crisis was not over, although many others had taken our view: the stock market had recovered its nerve, one thousand divorced women in Austria sent the King a congratulatory telegram, and even M.P.s laughed at each other's jokes in a more relaxed atmosphere.

But Mr Baldwin was not in the House that day; he was with the King at Fort Belvedere. And soon Frank Owen was writing another leader column: 'Twenty-four hours have brought changes that may alter the way that King and people might have walked together. Pray for the King, to give him guidance and strength in the dark hour. . . .'

'How often have I said that you should not prophesy for tomorrow, only for six months hence!' was the Beaver's only comment when he finally came through on the telephone.

Frank Owen and Reggie Thompson, with the inexhaustible energy of those days, sat down together the very week-end the King was exiled and wrote a book telling the story of the Abdication as Fleet Street saw it. It was called *His Was the Kingdom*.[1] It is long since out of print, but some of its preface is worth re-recording today:

It is the press which will destroy future dynasties,' said Napoleon. He estimated that the power of a newspaper was equal to as many bayonets as it had readers.

What was the weapon which brought down King Edward VIII? And how was the thing done? Here we tell the story as it took shape under the eyes of newspapermen. For it was a newspaper story from the word go.

Only when it was all over, bar the shouting, did the principal actor, the ex-King, turn to the radio. Later still, the Archbishop of Canterbury. As for Parliament, our ancient forum was dumb until the day that the Bill of Abdication was read over to it for approval. Mr Winston Churchill, who tried to speak, was howled down.

1. OWEN AND THOMPSON: *His Was the Kingdom*. Published by Arthur Barker Ltd.

The newspapers of the country played a remarkable double rôle. Their part began with an open conspiracy among editors to protect the King from scandal, by saying nothing about his friendship with Mrs Simpson. It ended with a secret plot to force the King to give up Mrs Simpson or his throne.

Not all the newspapers acted together in this second phase. But the 'restraint' with which the entire British press handled the opening chapters of the Simpson story made only the more effective the vehemence with which the anti-Simpson section drove home their final demand. So effectively had the facts been withheld from circulation that the vast majority of the British public were dumbfounded when they were informed that there was a crisis over the King's intended marriage with an American woman.

From the morning when the British public read the first intimation that trouble was upon them, only ten days passed until they learned that King Edward had abdicated the throne.

But for newspapermen the story had begun ten months before, though none of them foresaw the end. . . .

Times have changed. Nowadays Prime Ministers go on to Press Conference on B.B.C. Television and allow themselves to be harangued for ITV on Sunday afternoon. It may no longer be possible for the Press to make or break dynasties. But no matter how many new media for the dissemination of news are created, there is one rule that should never be broken: TELL THE PEOPLE!

19 . . . There Will Be No War

Lord Beaverbrook gave a dinner party in my honour at Claridge's Hotel in December 1959 for one hundred and ten newspapermen. All of them had worked with or for me. Jack Frost, the chubby-cheeked and at sixty-two the perpetually young-looking shipping correspondent of the *Daily Telegraph*, counted twenty-one among the company whom I had sacked, including himself. But we were all good friends, and when I whispered to my host that he should drive away from the top table people still in his organisation and invite the twenty-one to the places of honour around me, the banquet was transformed into a bear-garden. The comings and goings gave Lord Beaverbrook the utmost delight; there is nothing he enjoys more than organising complete chaos in any sphere.

Eventually we were sorted out. But the re-seating joke had revealed many omissions in the invitation list. Where was my predecessor in office, Beverley Baxter? Where was Sir Leslie Plummer who was with me in the days of the Manchester *Daily Express* triumph? Where were George (Golden) Miller, George Scott and James Leasor, now well-known authors? Above all, where was Michael Foot?

I had forgotten that Michael Foot, the acidulated Left Wing orator, pamphleteer and telecaster, had worked on the *Daily Express* for a short spell. But Beaverbrook had not, and he had hoped Foot

would be present so that the story could be told of 'the only occasion
I had quarrelled with the Boss himself'.

'D'ya remember?' he asked.

'Yes,' I said. 'Over the release of Oswald Mosley from prison in
1944.'

'Quite right,' he replied, somewhat surprised. 'I'll tell the story
anyway,' and then proceeded to get up and do so.

His enemies – and some of his friends – will tell you that Beaverbrook does nothing without a hidden purpose, that with Beaverbrook nothing is as it appears on the surface, that every action,
every phrase, let alone every sentence, arises from the calculations
of a shrewd and purposeful mind. This may well be so; certainly
an idle, ill-thought-out comment by one of his circle can alter his
mood in a flash, so sensitive is he to the possibilities of hidden meanings even in the lightest and brightest of good intentions.

Beaverbrook's motive in telling the Mosley story? Perhaps as a
good example of the relationship between him and me; perhaps to
assert once and for all his political domination over me, which I
have always acknowledged.

'Christiansen and I quarrelled only once in all the years,' he said
to his hundred and ten guests that evening. 'It was over Herbert
Morrison's decision as Home Secretary to release Sir Oswald
Mosley from prison in 1944, even though the war was not then
over. Morrison was a great Home Secretary, a profound believer
in liberty and you fellows have good cause to honour him. He took
the view that Mosley was no longer a danger to the security of the
country and that Regulation 18B should no longer be invoked to
keep him under lock and key. I wanted the *Daily Express* to support
Morrison, because I subscribed to his view, too. But Christiansen
wanted to keep Mosley in jail. I had never had any difficulty in
carrying Christiansen along with me up to this time. And then I
realised why! Michael Foot was his leader writer at this time!

'So I removed Foot and I won the day, and while the other newspapers hurled abuse at Herbert Morrison, the *Express* stood by
him in staunch support of his policy of freedom.'

The Mosley fracas began with the usual telephone call from the
proprietor to tell me that 'I was entitled' to publish a leading article
recommending the release of Mosley. This form of words preserved

the editorial prerogative; if I felt that I was 'not entitled', then I had the right to refuse publication. Not a theoretical right, either, for since I was the person who might in some circumstances be committed to prison or to the Watch Tower under Big Ben, I was 'entitled' to approve every word that was printed, even in the advertisement columns.

I had no strong views about Mosley's continued imprisonment, but I had a long memory of the disastrous effect which support of Mosley had had on the sales of the *Daily Mail* in the thirties. At that time, the *Express* reached record sales as Beaverbrook stumped the country propagating his twin policies of Empire Free Trade and No European Entanglements; while the circulation of the *Daily Mail* dropped and dropped when, at the same time, the first Lord Rothermere campaigned for the resumption of the monarchy in countries like Hungary, and for support of Mosley's Blackshirts ('they are neither Nazis nor Fascists').

I told Lord Beaverbrook that just as public opinion would not tolerate Mosley in the thirties, it would not support a move to release him while Britain was still at war. I was summoned to his penthouse in Arlington House (he had been bombed out of Stornoway House). Here we quarrelled so violently that I can well believe the story which reached me many years later that only the most persuasive pleadings by the managers saved me from dismissal.

When I got back to Fleet Street, I was in a highly emotional state. Michael Foot came into my room and I told him what had happened. Thereupon he began to argue the case for Mosley's release, but gently, a method that contrasted sharply with the Beaverbrookian bludgeoning. Michael was *not* at that time in favour of Mosley's release, but he argued the case in an attempt to solve the *impasse* that had arisen between proprietor and editor (at least that is the view that we both now hold). Under the combined weight of the Right Wing proprietor and the Left Wing leader writer, I caved in. Michael wrote a grudging leading article of endorsement; I sent it to Lord Beaverbrook; it was approved; into the paper it went.

The next day when the issue was debated in the House the leader column became more enthusiastic in tone. The Christiansen Mutiny was over.

Was it the first in the eleven years for which I had then edited the *Daily Express*? I expect so. I remember feeling sick when Neville Chamberlain over the radio described Czecho-Slovakia as 'a far-away country' and I remember expressing my revulsion to Lord Beaverbrook over the telephone. But when he said in a harsh voice, 'Well, isn't Czecho-Slovakia a far-away country?' I agreed that it was and got on with my job of producing an exciting newspaper. I regarded that as my purpose, and Beaverbrook's to adumbrate, formulate and pursue the political policies.

Tom Driberg in the preface to his book *Colonnade*[1], a collection of his 'William Hickey' contributions to the *Daily Express*, expresses his sympathy for me in my job.

'Within limits,' he writes, 'I was given freedom to express, or at least to imply, political views different from those of the newspaper I was working for. The limitations were more rigid, and more galling, during the Munich period. I often felt that I ought to leave; but many friends (including John Strachey) urged me to stay, partly because I was part of the open underground resistance within the *Express* office. . . .' To which Driberg adds the footnote: 'There was no deception; we had our fierce arguments daily, often triangularly – proprietor, editor, columnist. In retrospect, I pity the editor most.'

Driberg and I had an arrangement whereby he was honour-bound to show me political or controversial matter before it went to the printer. He was scrupulous in observing the agreement and I helped him to rewrite in suitable 'implied' form more Left Wing stuff than I ever put on my spike. I enjoyed these almost nightly exercises, but my purpose was anything but political. I wanted to produce a 'William Hickey' column that I liked myself, in the belief that it would attract readers. I was more eager to perform my tricks with type and to back my prescience about where the news was going to happen and how it should be projected than with political views.

The *Express* had developed a new journalism. The yards of 'No More War' articles, the columns and columns devoted to the row between the *Express* and the League of Nations Union – even these were served piping hot. An article by Lord Castlerosse calling

1. TOM DRIBERG: *Colonnade*. Published by The Pilot Press Ltd, 1949.

on his First World War comrades to resist European entanglements was dressed up with little rows of white crosses to memorialise the 1914–18 dead, with the words 'All in Vain' repeating themselves remorselessly through the text. The League of Nations Union published a 'Peace Ballot'; the *Express* re-christened it the 'Ballot of Blood'. An Armenian financier named Garabed Bishirgian, who was trying to corner the world's pepper supplies, was found to be also a pig-breeder in Surrey, with a flat in Park Lane. By the time he went to prison for a £1,000,000 fraud the *Express* had made him known everywhere as 'the Park Lane pig-breeder', and as such his discovery and sentence were read about further and wider than if he had remained simply a financier with an unpronounceable name indulging in complicated financial transactions.

That was the technique. Make the news exciting, even when it was dull. Make the news palatable by lavish presentation. Make the unreadable readable. Find the news behind the news. Find the news even before it has happened. For instance, on the notorious 'Night of the Long Knives', when Hitler bumped off scores of homosexuals and 'traitors' in the Nazi Party, I had sensed 'something', and on a hunch had sent Sefton Delmer, then the newspaper's Paris correspondent, back to Germany to be on the spot before the story broke.

That was what editing the *Daily Express* meant to me: a tough, exciting technical job of news presentation, preferably of exclusive news presentation. Be first! Be there!

Should I have taken a more political line in my conduct of the paper? Certainly I had every opportunity to do so. Political discussion went on between Beaverbrook, Robertson and myself incessantly and we agreed policies before they were launched. But I was a journalist, not a political animal; my proprietor was a journalist *and* a political animal. The policies were Lord Beaverbrook's job, the presentation mine; and when, for example, a decision was taken to use the slogan 'There will be no war', I projected it so violently that there was no escaping it.

Publication of that slogan in 1938 and 1939 is still used to attack the *Daily Express*, Beaverbrook and myself – although hindsight now informs the attackers. Many public men and newspapers from 1936 onwards declared that there would be no war. Many said so even in 1939 (Tom Driberg in his 'William Hickey' column 'fell' for the belief that war could be averted as late as August of that year) but it was the *Daily Express* that was castigated for such a whopping error of judgement. Why? Because the *Express* banged the drum loudest.

It is said that in 1939 I suggested the addition of the words 'or next year either' to the 'No war this year' slogan. It may be so; I do not remember. I certainly did not seek to suppress the publication of the slogan. It seemed to me to suit the spirit of the time and the spirit of the people. It gave hope and reassurance that the worst need not befall. Was that so very wrong? The slogan gave Beaverbrook's critics a pretext for abuse when war broke out – and since – but it in no way impaired the will to battle when the tragic day came.

The *Express* itself revives the 'No war' issue from time to time. When Kruschev and Bulganin came to England in April 1956, my name made one of its rare appearances in an article headed WHAT ARE THEY UP TO? WHAT SHOULD WE DO? which put the view that Russia had passed from threatening war to seeking peace, and that it would be preposterous not to respond to the peaceful advances of Moscow.

The article called the war of 1939 the 'Unnecessary War'. It argued, 'No country gained freedom. Many lost it. . . . If only Chamberlain's will to peace had held strong and firm those dictators (Hitler and Stalin) would have destroyed each other without any sacrifices by Britain.'

People from every part of the country wrote to me enthusiastically. The article was republished as a pamphlet and had a widespread distribution.

Wrote A. P. Wadsworth, Editor of the (*Manchester*) *Guardian*: 'We can only applaud and agree when Mr Arthur Christiansen, the distinguished editor (and a great journalist) says across a whole page that we ought to "respond to the peaceful advances of Moscow" . . . alas, Mr Christiansen, for once forgetting the maxim about the deadness of yesterday's news, spoils the effect by a retrospective defence of his paper's attitude in 1939.'

Wrote Sir Linton Andrews, the Editor of the *Yorkshire Post* (and then chairman of the Press Council): 'I rejoiced to see that Mr Arthur Christiansen, the Editor of the *Daily Express*, had declared with the utmost emphasis in a leading article, across almost the whole breadth of his editorial page, that Russia had passed from threatening war to seeking peace . . . it is a most welcome encouragement to common sense that so vivid and vital a paper should proclaim this thought throughout the country . . . Mr Christiansen is on more uncertain ground when he goes on to defend his attitude towards Hitler's intentions before September 1939. . . . Fancy an editor of Mr Christiansen's seniority – he is, I think, senior to any other editor of a London daily – being content with the word of Sir Thomas Inskip. . . .'

But let me now confess. Just as, when a young man, I 'ghosted' articles for people like Nazimova and Harry Lauder, so that article was 'ghosted' for me. The article which inspired so much praise from such distinguished journalists as Wadsworth and Andrews, was written in Lord Beaverbrook's villa in the South of France, and reached me in Fleet Street by courier. I was asked if I would allow my name to be attached. I said 'Yes'.

Why not? I did not disagree – I agreed with the *Express* policy in 1939 and in 1956. Beaverbrook never forced me to publish one word I did not want to publish. As you will certainly have learned from these pages, Lord Beaverbrook is not a man to be thwarted in his beliefs. By devious ways, by pressures of all kinds, by kindness or by ferocity he tries to achieve his goal. No doubt if an editor opposed him with equal fanaticism, that editor would not long be bringing out the *Daily Express*, but would join some rival newspaper with which his convictions were more in sympathy. Would not a proprietor be a fool to employ as his editor a man with whom he had to do daily battle on matters of conscience and principle?

My retirement from the Beaverbrook payroll in October 1959 got lavish coverage. The *Daily Worker* chortled with delight in attempting to make me the victim of some filthy capitalist intrigue. In the *News Chronicle*, James Cameron wrote about 'this astonishing newspaper genius who changed the face of British newspapers.' The *Daily Telegraph* sneered in its Peterborough column that at least I had not influenced the appearance of the *Telegraph*. The *Daily Herald* wittily forecast that my reminiscences would not be published 'this year or next year either'.

But it was when I found myself the central figure of the famous Friday evening television programme, 'Press Conference', in January 1960 that my retirement and the hostility to *Express* policies really got the full treatment.

My inquisitors were Francis Williams, roly-poly Liverpool friend of years ago; Sydney Jacobson, the ascetic political editor of the *Daily Mirror*; and Brian Inglis, the Left-Wingish editor of *The Spectator*. They gave me a rough time, but from their grilling emerged a picture of my workaday philosophy, some of which may perhaps go on record here as a summing-up.

Williams: 'You were editor for around twenty-five years of the *Daily Express* and during this period its circulation rose from under 2,000,000 to over 4,000,000. You are, in fact, one of the architects of this fascinating social phenomenon of the rise of the modern large circulation press with all that it involves. What do you yourself put down the success of the *Express* to?'

Christiansen: 'In relation to myself, you mean, I suppose, not in relation to my colleagues? I think possibly that I was the Common Man, the typical *Express* reader. It was said by Alexander Woollcott of Harold Ross, the Editor of the *New Yorker*, that he had the utmost contempt for anything he did not understand. I did not have the utmost contempt, but there were so many things I didn't understand that I thought the public should know about, that I tried to simplify news in such a way that it would be interesting to the permanent Secretary of the Foreign Office and to the charwoman who brushed his office floor in the morning. I tried to make news exciting, and on that account I had to change the typography of the British popular newspaper. My approach to newspapers was based on the idea that when you looked at the front page you said: "Good heavens", when you looked at the middle page you said: "Holy smoke," and by the time you got to the back page – well, I'd have to utter a profanity to show how exciting it was.'

Jacobson: 'Was this largely technical or had it some relation to the social changes and the people you were producing for?'

Christiansen: 'A newspaper is a record of the times. Any newspaper is a record of the social changes going on. I had a tremendous urge to educate people and help them to better themselves. In fact, I aimed the paper at ambitious young men – at a young man with two children who wanted to get on in life. And I wanted him to know what was going on and to know the difference between Budapest and Bucharest.'

Inglis: 'You are talking to some extent about creating policy; how far did you have control?'

Christiansen: 'I did not have control of policy except that I controlled every word that went into the newspaper.'

Williams: 'You were concerned mainly with the presentation, not with the policy?'

Christiansen: 'The policy was laid down by the proprietor, Lord Beaverbrook, and I was the man who made the policy attractive to the people by presentation.'

Inglis: 'Do you think this was a good idea for an editor?'

Christiansen: 'This always raises the question whether an editor should have divine rights. I believe if Lord Beaverbrook had not been a proprietor, he would have been an editor, and then God help all the editors in Fleet Street. I was perfectly prepared to follow his political policy and at the same time project it.'

Williams: 'What about "There will be no war this year or next year either", which you ran up to three weeks before the outbreak of war?'

Christiansen: 'I have no apologies to make for that well-known slogan which is hurled at the *Express,* and I can only say if only the policy had proved to be accurate there would have been many happier people in the world to-day. The policy never, in fact, was tried out. The policy underlying that slogan was based on the policies of Mr Neville Chamberlain who wavered in his determination until eventually the country was driven into war. For what purpose I really wouldn't know, because Poland is not free, which was the pretext. The war created another dictator in Stalin who was just as ruthless if not quite so wicked as Hitler.'

Williams: 'Your real complaint is that appeasement had not gone on long enough?'

Christiansen: 'Chamberlain failed in carrying through his policy
to the point where Hitler would probably not have dared to
make war.'

Williams: 'Most of the Government people who had, in fact,
put over the policy either retired from public life or were
moved out. Did you ever feel those associated with it in the
Express, having misled the public up to three weeks of war,
should have moved away?'

Christiansen: 'The public always had the sanction. They could
have stopped buying the *Express* if they felt we were failing to
serve the country.'

Inglis: 'Do you suggest you as editor were a kind of prosecuting
attorney for your paper, even if you did not agree with it, and
pushed it to the best of your ability?'

Christiansen: 'I would have said that the editor of any paper has
the right to sack his proprietor just as the proprietor has the
right to sack his editor. If the editor feels deeply enough he
can at any time of the day or night say, "I will quit".'

Williams: 'In a sense, your whole career as far as policy is concerned was one of capitulation where you always felt you must
agree in the end with what Lord Beaverbrook thought.'

Christiansen: 'Capitulation? No. Understanding? Yes. I was a
Beaverbrook man. I joined the Beaverbrook Press when I was
twenty-one, and I do not suppose if I had not thought in the
way of the proprietor that I would have been appointed
Editor. I thought as he did. I followed him. It may have been
wrong for the Beaver to have supported Neville Chamberlain,
but certainly it was not wrong for me to have supported the
Beaver.'

Williams: 'Now you have severed your connection with the
Beaverbrook Press, do you feel a little lonely in the world on
your own without Lord Beaverbrook to talk to?'

Christiansen: 'Not at all.'

Williams: 'You don't feel the need to have a chat with Beaverbrook to decide what you should think?'

Christiansen: 'That is a pretty offensive thing to say, if I may
say so.'

Williams: 'I am trying to get at this because you have said, if Beaverbrook insisted, it was your job to carry out and express his policies.'

Christiansen: 'Certainly, and I have said I always had the right to resign my job.'

Williams: 'But you never exercised it, so you found this relationship of being the spokesman a satisfactory one?'

Christiansen: 'Certainly. It was a warm and fine relationship. And as I say the policies were discussed and laid down and projected by me and I have no regrets about my career in any form whatsoever. It was great fun and more than four million people – probably, according to some surveys, fifteen million people a day – were interested, and may be learned a little more about the world than if the *Express* had been a fuddy-duddy paper edited by a committee.'

Inglis: 'Can we get on to this business of news presentation? Always through a personality. Now there are certain cases where the story would get lost as a result. Do you think this was a good way of setting about what you were trying to do?'

Christiansen: 'Every technique of presentation of news is liable to falsification in some way or other. What I tried to do was to publish serious news alongside news which would attract, say, the woman reader, so that I could lead her eyes to the heavy news of the day.'

Williams: 'I notice, looking through some of the famous daily bulletins which you used to issue, something like this: "You cannot just put news in the *Daily Express*. It must be projected." Doesn't that philosophy mean that the news must be made to fit the paper? Does it not follow from this that there is an angling of news?'

Christiansen: 'No. It means that the news must be made exciting on the dullest day. I picture my own home town, Wallasey, which is not so dull as Derby, or perhaps the East End of London, and I like to think of the newspaper dropping through the letterbox and bringing some excitement into the lives of people living in these places. I believe there is an immense reader-resistance to newspapers and to magazines and that my job was to get people to read every line if I possibly could.'

Jacobson: 'How do you reconcile that with the earlier statement that you produced a newspaper aimed at the Common Man going places? Is there not a clash?'

Christiansen: 'None whatsoever. Obviously one hundred per cent of any newspaper cannot be devoted to one particular image. When you create one image, you have also to create other images in the realm of, say, finance and sport. Perhaps half your readers don't read the financial or the sports pages – but if you create and keep to the idea of a paper read by ambitious people, by and large you will succeed.'

Williams: 'You also said we must try to make the paper suit the optimism of the masses. You said that the *Express* should "make everyone feel it was a sunny day". An admirable ambition, but events do not always fit into that optimism. Were you under any temptation to shade the blackness?'

Christiansen: 'You know perfectly well that the general optimism of a newspaper is always overshadowed by some tremendous disaster. You cannot have a submarine sinking and get sunshine all over the paper. But you can in recording the news see that the seamier and more tragic side of the world is not unduly emphasised, although it is recorded.'

Williams: 'Another charge against the *Express* is one of triviality, that the paper tended through its technique, such as the brilliant development of the gossip column, to promote the trivial things of life.'

Christiansen: 'What I tried to do was to present a fair amount of entertaining news, and I did it quite prominently to get the whole of my newspaper read. The Royal Commission on the Press said the *Express* presented the longest reports of Parliament. Certainly by comparison with the Socialist *Daily Herald* we had much fuller coverage. There may have been trivia in the *Express* but there are trivia in every paper. It was for the purpose of making the whole readable.'

Well, there it is. Not the least tribute to the way the *Daily Express* has always been conducted is the way in which it is always being discussed.

20 . . . Flick through the Files

Great events make less impact on editors than on individual members of their staff. The reporters who cover the news will remind their editors years later of some incident or some comment the editor made at the time, which have long since vanished from the editor's memory. Editors are too close to the day's news. Even on important days there are a dozen trivial events that must be given personal attention. It is no good relying on the paper to fill itself with good stuff. To the diligent editor the last news page must be as vital as the first.

I consoled myself for the fact that I had no time to keep a diary by the thought that the *Daily Express* was itself my diary. I imagined that if ever my reminiscences were to be thought worth writing, all I had to do was to take the bound volumes of the paper from the office library and hey presto! the 'inside dirt' that I knew at the time would be recalled as fresh as a first edition off the presses.

But it does not work: I tried it with the year 1935. It opened with the Saar plebiscite which returned that territory to Germany, and the trial of Hauptmann, the Lindbergh baby kidnapper. My memory stirs little at either event.

It was Silver Jubilee Year for King George V and Queen Mary. The files tell me that the *Express* published a Souvenir supplement printed in colour, no doubt a bold idea at the time; that we

organised a competition to find Miss Jubilee; that we sponsored a
vast Thanksgiving Service in Hyde Park. But I have no memory of
these events, only of receiving an invitation to be present with my
wife at the official Thanksgiving Service in St Paul's. We went –
and I recall we were in such a remote corner of St Paul's that we
were completely out of sight of the Royal Family, and would have
enjoyed ourselves and seen more from my office window or with
the crowds in the sunshine on Ludgate Hill.

Here is an item by a pretty (I remember that!) girl reporter named
Molly Castle, naming a Mrs Ernest Simpson, wife of a London
stockbroker, as 'the world's best-dressed woman'. Here is Jack
Hobbs announcing his retirement from first-class cricket; James
Douglas protesting over Epstein's 'Christ'; an artist named Robb
drawing his first fashion sketches; an article by Lord Castlerosse –
part of the Splendid Isolation campaign – entitled 'Bombs will
never win a War'; Sir John Simon and Anthony Eden meeting
Adolf Hitler; Lord Beaverbrook writing on the leader page, 'The
Socialists Mean War'.

But here is something; 20 May, Page One:

TO-DAY'S 'DAILY EXPRESS' IS DIFFERENT

I remember that all right. It was the day that the *Express* re-
shaped its style and *omitted full stops* from headlines. Now that was
a BIG day! An editor does not lightly take such a step. Seriously,
he does not lightly make such a revolutionary change. The chances
are that it was discussed for weeks, was referred finally to Lord
Beaverbrook for O.K., and that Percy Pratt, the Head Printer,
thought the whole idea outrageous.

Here is an item that recalls a tense moment:

'AQUITANIA' TRAPPED ON MUDBANK

I had thought, 'What a good job Cedric Belfrage (our film critic)
was sent to Southampton to meet the *Aquitania* because of her
cargo of film stars! He will obviously hire a speedboat to cover the
story.'

But did he? He did not. At seven o'clock that night the apocryphal story of the reporter who returned to his office with the news that he had not stayed to cover a wedding because the church had caught fire, came true. Belfrage got back to Fleet Street with the news that he had been unable to interview his film stars because the ship was aground ten miles from Southampton. He had, therefore, come home.

A rum case, Belfrage. I was giving a cocktail party that night and pulled his leg by telling everyone of his classic boob. I sneered that he had rushed back to London in order not to be late for my party, instead of getting stuck into the job and making a new name for himself. To this he was impervious. He sneered back that it wasn't his job to report a ship aground; that could be left to the general reporting staff. But I wanted film critics who could cover shipping disasters, and general reporters who could interview film stars.

As I flicked through the 1935 newspaper files, I wondered what would have happened if I had sent Cedric Belfrage to cover the Abyssinian war which came at this time. As a sensitive Left Wing political animal, he should have been a first-rate choice; but like Evelyn Waugh, the novelist chosen by the *Daily Mail* for this assignment, I suspect he would have been weak on news coverage. Waugh wrote a brilliant novel with an Abyssinian background called *Scoop*, a rich and witty satire on newspaper reporting, but when it came to the business of gathering real facts and grinding them out against real edition times, he was beaten by the old contemptibles of our craft, the general reporters.

Vivien Leigh made her stage debut; Ramsay MacDonald resigned in favour of Mr Baldwin; a curious little French freak airplane called The Flying Flea was toured by the *Express* around the seaside resorts; unemployment fell to just over two millions (2,000,110 was the figure for June) during the summer of 1935.

It was at this time that I met Baldwin for the first and only time. I was too busy producing the newspaper to pay much attention to politics – if a politician seeks out an editor he is usually after something. The more important the politician, the more certain it is that he seeks support for himself and his Department's policies. But Baldwin was the exception. *He* was all charm.

Guy Eden, the newspaper's political correspondent, was my host at lunch and Baldwin was the guest of honour.

'This is my Editor,' said Eden, his nervous grin very much in evidence. Baldwin and I shook hands and eyed each other.

'An interesting paper, yours, and an interesting job,' said the Prime Minister (that day the leader column had attacked him furiously). 'Tell me, do you deal with Strube personally?'

I told him about the great cartoonist's habit of sitting at the side of my desk on the waste-paper basket, never on a chair, while we discussed the day's ideas.

'Strube is a gentle genius,' said Baldwin. 'I don't mind his attacks because he never hits below the belt. Now Low [David Low, then the cartoonist of Beaverbrook's *Evening Standard*] is a genius, but he is evil and malicious. I cannot bear Low!'

With that, others joined us and the talk returned to, maybe, the weather. But the mellow voice, which I was to hear again on the radio at the time of the Abdication, still rings clearly in my ears. I do not think I have ever heard such a beautiful speaking voice before or since. Gielgud and Olivier have nothing on Stanley Baldwin.

Flick the files again. Here is an interview with Mussolini which confirms my point that politicians (or Dictators) do not seek the favour of newspapermen unless for propaganda purposes. Harold Pemberton, one of the much-venerated older members of the staff (I suppose he was fifty!) suggested this interview to me. I was never much in favour of the big interview technique. I considered that the interviews Hitler had given to the veteran G. Ward Price of the *Daily Mail* had done that newspaper positive harm; and that Ward Price's audience with the Emperor of Japan which contained one direct quote something like, 'I wish the people of Britain much happiness', in three columns of descriptive matter was the big flop interview to end all big flop interviews. Just the same, I let Pemberton have his head. The result was propaganda for Italy, except for Pemberton's nice description of how long it took him to walk the twenty-five-yards-that-seemed-five-hundred to the Dictator's desk.

Here is Frank Owen's leading article on the night Mussolini marched into Abyssinia. It makes fine reading still, a model of narrative writing that has lamentably disappeared from leading articles. Thus: . . . 'the barbers stop their gossip, the half-shaven customers rush home for their black shirts and their rifles . . . and down comes the rain.' It was a piece scornful of Italian pretensions, yet fearful for the Abyssinian underdog. Lord Beaverbrook, who supported the Hoare-Laval Pact to carve up Abyssinia (which carved up also the Beaver's friend, Sir Samuel Hoare) had yet this curious political liberalism in his make-up. He allowed Owen to run a leader column that was to all intents and purposes interventionist in Abyssinia (and later in Spain), while at the same time he himself was writing isolationist articles.

A new name was blazoning forth from Addis Ababa: O'Dowd Gallagher.

'Who's this O'Dowd Gallagher you've sent to Abyssinia?' growled the Beaver. 'Is he Irish?'

'A discovery of mine,' I replied. 'Only twenty-four. Knows his Africa. Born in Johannesburg. He will be a credit to us.'

'Then if he's not Irish, or even if he is, you are entitled to change his name. You are entitled to give him his initials instead of his Christian name.'

Whether Beaverbrook thought that a war correspondent with an Irish name suggested recklessness, I do not know; but I changed Gallagher's by-line. 'O. Gallagher' seemed inadequate, despite the precedent of the immortal 'O. Henry', so O. D. Gallagher he became. (A year later I changed the name of another *Express* correspondent, this time in the Spanish Civil War, from Solomon Charing to Stephen Charing, only to receive this cable from Charing: AM PROUD TO BE A JEW STOP PLEASE BY-LINE ME SOLOMON OR LEAVE ME ANONYMOUS. But Stephen is still the name by which he is known.)

O. D. Gallagher was *Daily Express* Chief War Correspondent in the Abyssinian campaign at the age of twenty-four. He had come to my notice when he got us a world exclusive interview with the white man who had been flogged by Chief Tshekedi in Bechuanaland. With the bonus he was paid for this he came to England in a sugar-boat, and we gave him a job on space rates (you get paid only if your stories are used). I was not very far from speaking the exact truth when I told Lord Beaverbrook that Gallagher had been sent to Abyssinia because he 'knew his Africa'! There have been stranger reasons for appointments to high responsibility in Fleet Street.

I lost my nerve slightly when the big guns of the Hearst Press arrived in London on their way to the Abyssinian war: Carl Von Wiegand, with an anti-British reputation dating back to World War One, and H. R. (Red) Knickerbocker, who made up for Von Wiegand in every way. Von W. was the first to arrive and I lunched him and Gallagher at the Savoy Grill. The German-American looked as old as sin and could scarcely conceal his disdain for my boy. But it was my boy who saw the war out and stood up to the fiery challenge of the world's best reporters. He finished the campaign by interviewing Haile Selassie in exile in Palestine – a 'big' interview that was worth getting – and established himself as one of the best foreign correspondents of his generation (even to his prodigious expense accounts – the *Daily Express* still owns with *Politiken* of Copenhagen a camel and a caravan jointly purchased during the Abyssinian war).

I have been wondering what 1935 meant to me, apart from the anxieties created by the news that was climaxed in its final month by such headlines as: SIR SAMUEL HOARE RESIGNS OVER HOARE-LAVAL ABYSSINIA PEACE PLAN. GENEVA BURIES OIL SANCTIONS. ANTHONY EDEN APPOINTED FOREIGN SECRETARY.

I believe now that this was the year when the new journalism began to be evolved. I had been editor for two years, which is just about the minimum time in which a man can mould people to his will. Now the time had come to move on. Backed by Beaverbrook, supported by a zestful and brilliant staff, the *Express* set the pace for what was then a fresh and startling approach to the news.

Let me quote with all immodesty from a pamphlet[1] on Fleet Street which seems to sum things up. The *Daily Express* was described herein as 'the country's most volatile, irritating and widely copied newspaper. The daemon which possesses it is Beaverbrook's, but its success is due to sheer professionalism. In Arthur Christiansen . . . it found a journalist of mettle rare enough to withstand his proprietor's all-consuming energy. In him, too, it found the incarnation of its own semi-mythical Average Reader; in its editor

1. DENIS THOMAS: *Challenge in Fleet Street*. Published by the Truth Publishing Co.

was embodied the twentieth century genus *Express* Man. . . . Here is a journal which has built up an enormous circulation without reaching for the lowest common denominator. Instead, the *Express* has created a new journalism, of which the dominating characteristic may be described as dynamic curiosity. The *Express* reader is never allowed to feel that he is anywhere but out in front – not so much abreast of events as part of them.'

That is what the *Daily Express* started to try to do in 1935.

21 . . . The Daily Bulletins

Of Henry Luce, the originator, proprietor, and editor-in-chief of the American news-magazine *Time*, it is said that when he left college he was curious about everything. In the early days, I was told Luce would listen even to the views of an office boy, and ask for his comments on the latest issue of *Time*. Nowadays the cynics say he still asks, but only pretends to listen, because he knows it all.

Many men develop in this way; success and age beget dogmatism. But I was always pretty dogmatic, even in my early thirties; probably that was why I was a good editor. Henry Luce's magazine described me in its Press Section as 'plump, pink and self-confident. ... When he took the job he saw his goal was to increase the *Express* circulation by one million in ten years. He almost did it in five'.

This article caused me much pain and grief. I had made no such boast, staked no such claims, but Lord Beaverbrook was furious, and I was in the dog-house for a week or two. To Robertson, the General Manager, he said, 'You and I have had something to do with the success of the *Daily Express*'; and I was told that he beat his breast fiercely and repeatedly as he spoke. This is a gesture which Lord Beaverbrook makes at times of acute emotion. As the fists flail at his frail body, he shakes his massive head and growls like a bear, grunting the word 'No, no, no, no, no, no'.

In this case there was nothing I could do except wait patiently for the storm to subside. Eventually we resumed our father-and-son relationship, he driving me crackers with his explosive maelstrom of ideas and criticisms affecting every department of the newspaper (except the sports pages), and I in turn driving my staff round the bend with the proprietor's views (when I agreed with them) and my own (whether he agreed with them or not).

In my early days on the *Sunday Express*, the staff was huddled together in so little space that I gave orders, criticism and praise in a voice loud enough for all to hear. But on the *Daily Express* this was not possible; and in any case, we had printing centres with complete editorial staffs in Manchester and Glasgow, as well as bureaux all over the world. It was for this reason that I started what became known as 'The Daily Bulletin'.

There is nothing particularly novel about the use of an office notice-board, in journalism or any other trade or profession. Lord Northcliffe used the device. But Northcliffe's notices were spasmodic, depending on his mood. My Bulletins came out nearly every day from the early thirties until 1956, when I actually sent one from the Bahamas. They analysed the newspaper almost line by line. They praised and they blamed. They stated general principles. They raised the temperature when we were up against it (for every newspaper has its runs of bad luck). They reduced the temperature when we were riding high (which is the time when arrogance can induce bad judgement), and they taught my brand of journalism to the staff.

William Barkley, the Parliamentary reporter, wrote to me recently, 'Do you know, my new assistant, George Lockhead, tells me that in five years on his old paper he never had any comment from his office, either adverse or favourable, and never any suggestions. I gather that most of the Gallery men have spent their lives that way. So never forget the firework displays and the immense sense of adventure you gave us all during these long years....'

The Bulletins were the beasts of burden throughout the years that Barkley describes. They were dictated as my last task each day before lunch and they were pinned up in a locked, glass box outside the News Editor's room when I got back from lunch. Copies were sent to Barkley in Parliament, to the provincial offices, to heads of departments, to the ends of the earth, wherever the *Express* had a correspondent.

I quote from a few post-war Bulletins in the belief that not only newspapermen, but newspaper readers, will be interested and may learn at least two things. First, that a tremendous and sincere effort goes into the production of a morning newspaper, to get the facts right, to keep the right balance, to instruct as well as to entertain. Secondly, that a capacity to spell, to punctuate and to write decently is only the foundation of one of the world's most exacting professions.

*   *   *   *   *

I detect in my travels a great thirst after knowledge on the part of the humble people.

Watch them on the railway bookstalls, picking up serious books – books on philosophy, politics, culture. Watch them in the trains, and see how much reader-resistance there is to the newspaper. The reader can 'gut' a newspaper in about ten minutes, after which some of them settle down to the crossword, while others read a book or play cards.

So much for our efforts! So many more reasons why we should redouble them to make newspapers read.

Big type is not the answer. Ideas are. After the ideas comes the projection, a balance of excitement and thoughtfulness. Watch out for the unexpected and the unusual – the story which will occasionally take people's minds far, far away into distant lands or on to distant problems.

Always, always, the news should be presented fairly in our columns. We will, of course, give prominence to those who support Empire policies and that sort of thing, but we will not be unfair to those who oppose us. So far as the news columns of the paper are concerned, we seek only one thing – absolute objectivity. And I call upon the staff to help me in this task.

Dear John Macadam,

You have written one of your greatest sports columns. You owe a lot to George Allison, but George 'Arsenal' owes a great deal to you for the brilliant projection of his reminiscences.

Now, my dear John, can you tell me which football team Graves and Beaune play for? If a lot of your readers write letters to George Arsenal without full stops or any sense of grammatical construction, you must also expect them to think that Graves and Beaune will be playing football for England when they have had more experience!

A batch of 1948 clichés:

> *Couldn't care less*
> *Couldn't agree more*
> *Priority number one*
> *More than somewhat*
> *Okay by me*
> *Jumping to it*
> *Action stations – as applying to anything but action stations*
> *Giving the air to*
> *Niterie*
> *Giving the works*
> *Stole the show*
> *Made the grade*
> *New look – as applied to anything but women's clothing*
> *Giving the once over*
> *Good-time girl*
> *Teen-ager*
> *In the red.*

One of the things which we must overcome is the general Fleet Street idea that news told in a warm, human and friendly way is a cynical trick invented by a hard-boiled lot of clever fellows for the purpose of fooling the simple reader.

A paper that creates an understanding between itself and its readers has to make every line of type work for it. This human link is not just an angle for a sob story. It is an editorial attitude of mind, to which readers respond. We want readers to turn to us automatically with their confidences, their grievances, their triumphs, or the wrongs that are done to them which they want to get put right.

When a story goes over the top in slush, then it arouses nothing but contempt and distrust. When a story – shall we say about animals – is omitted altogether or given impoverished treatment, then the friendly link remains unforged.

I want to spread the idea among the staff that this paper must comport itself with great sincerity in everything it does. We must never be defeatist in approaching the problems of sincere news presentation.

It would be a good thing for all those who work on the 'inside' of newspapers to go regularly to one of the provincial centres so that they could observe conditions at first hand. No wonder the *News of the World*, the *Daily Mirror*, the *Sunday Pictorial* and *The People* sell in such vast quantities, for they constitute escape from reality in towns like Derby!

We on the *Daily Express* have not the same weapons as the above papers with which to fight. But we have, over the years, sought to produce a newspaper which livened up the day, within the limits of responsibility and complete news coverage.

The *Express* must aim at lively make-up, at good, controversial ideas, at the vigorous talking-point, the picture with sunshine in it, the viewpoint that is optimistic and provocative – for the sake of the millions who live in Britain's dreary cities.

Any page that looks as drab as Derby can be counted a dead loss – and even we produce them from time to time.

In the handling of every single story, whether it be high politics or broad humanity, we should never fail to have the COMMON TOUCH.

The question arises as to what women read and whether much of the stuff published as woman's interest is not, in fact, basically masculine interest? Are women more interested in pictures of beautiful women than men? I doubt it.

On the other hand, women are far more interested than men in pictures of good-looking men. I know women whose morning paper is not complete without a picture of Denis Compton either on the sports page or in the Brylcreem ad.

Never underestimate the interest of women in news which is supposed to be outside their purview.

The gigantic sale of the *Daily Express* should never be used for belittling or mocking or cheapening little people. We must go for the big shots when we want to criticise.

A story starts with the statement that when Parliament sits every word spoken is recorded by a staff of shorthand writers. Where is the news in that? The news is about a complaint that a woman shorthand writer on Hansard staff is not getting as much money as the men shorthand writers.

I saw the manuscript of a reporter's story about Mr Churchill's meeting at Woodford last night. It opened with an amusing incident about the electric lights failing. But, of course, it was a most important speech and the introductory angle was wrong. In fact it sacrificed the substance for the shadow. It was rather like saying 'Nibbling an olive and holding a glass of vodka in his hand, Stalin declared war on Britain last night'.

I wish there were some way for newspapermen to diagnose how much of any single issue of a newspaper is read. Are there people who read every line of it, as we must? Do most people 'dip', reading only that which appeals to them? I take the view that these are the majority.

I have just come across a saying by Charlie Chaplin on films which seems to be the basis of good journalism, good writing, good lay-out, in fact everything good in our craft. It is this:
'I cut, I rewrite, I cut again . . . simplicity is no simple thing.'

It would do everyone connected with Fleet Street – especially editors – a power of good if they spent an occasional day off in unfamiliar territory, seeing the newspaper reader as he is at work and play. In familiar territory, in the neighbourhood of your own home, you don't get the same perspective.

I journeyed from Rhyl to Prestatyn on Sunday, past lines of

boarding-houses, caravans, wooden huts, shacks, tents and heaven
knows what else. In every one of them there were newspaper
readers. Happy citizens, worthy, fine people, but not in the least
like the reader Fleet Street seems to be writing for.

These people are not interested in Glyndebourne or vintage
claret or opera or the Sitwells, or dry-as-dust economics, or tough
politics.

It is our job to interest them in everything. It requires the highest
degree of skill and ingenuity.

The Man on Rhyl Promenade says:
'What's this Chateau Yquem and garlic stuff in the *Express* to-
day? My champagne touch is a bottle of Guinness and a plate of
winkles.'

The Man from Rhyl asks:
'What is the Civil List?' and 'What is the Privy Purse?'

The Man on Rhyl Promenade says:
'What a lot of French there is in the paper to-day! *Mot juste*,
bon mot, and all that sort of stuff – on the sports page, too. Why
can't the *Daily Express* joke in English, especially with this
American Election running, which I don't understand a word of.'

The other night I met a public man of considerable influence.
He told me that he takes three papers at home – the *Daily Express*,
The Times and the *News Chronicle*. He says that he reads the
Express first because it gives him an overall picture of the news
more graphically than any other newspaper.

We must never forget our responsibility to these people, who are
legion. Our Page One purpose is to give the hard, cold, complicated picture of real events in bright focus, as well as to project the
human twiddly-bits that make for conversation in the pubs.

At whom should the *Express* be aimed? The *Express* should be
aimed at the young and ambitious in every walk of life. The young
people with their own car and their own home, with a desire to
improve their social circumstances. The young couple who do not

M

possess their own home or their own car, but have the ambition to do so at the earliest date. The adventurous people who seek their fortunes by daring and boldness.

On that account the *Express* should encourage the kind of adventure story told of the corporal in Hong Kong who went exploring and found a rare mineral called beryl. Our reporters everywhere should be on the look-out for such stories and our executives should 'play' them with imagination and distinction.

The *Express* wants people to get away from the back streets of Derby. It respects these people deeply and seeks to write in language that they can understand.

The *Express* respects the Welfare State, but has no time for people who expect to lean on it from the cradle to the grave.

The *Express* should make people reach for the stars.

Good stories flow like honey. Bad stories stick in the craw. What is a bad story? It is a story that cannot be absorbed on the first time of reading. It is a story that leaves questions unanswered. A good story can be turned into a bad story by just one obscure sentence.

Keep typographical lay-out tricks under control. There is much virtue in simplicity. Always the reader *outside* Fleet Street should be considered.

You cannot just put things into the *Daily Express*. By and large, they must be projected. We have always got to tackle the news emphatically, with boldness and confidence. On each page there should be a feature that attracts the eye. This does not necessarily mean the use of ever-increasing type size. It means the correct use of white space, the display of pictures, the headline that intrigues the reader.

When a man under fifty dies, give the cause of his death.

Are we not in danger of becoming a nagging paper, simply because it is much easier to criticise than to praise?

There are too many stories about things and not enough about people. 'Significant' news predominates – and while that is fine, you will never get people to digest 'significant' news if there is nothing else on the diet sheet.

Take an interest in diet. More people weigh themselves now than ever before. I know the man who owns the weighing machines in Woolworths and other big stores. It is quite a normal day's business to have 3,000 pennies placed in one machine.

Here is an old three-fold rule of conduct for our paper:
1. Never set the police on anybody.
2. Never cry down the pleasures of the people.
3. Remember our own habits and frailties when disposed to be critical of others.

News, news, news – that is what we want. You can describe things with the pen of Shakespeare himself, but you cannot beat news in a newspaper.

It is journalistic fashion to concentrate on the first paragraphs of stories. I believe in that. But I believe just as emphatically in the perfection of the last paragraph.

In one of the papers to-day, there is a headline CRYSTAL SET BAND-LEADER MADE HISTORY, which reminds me of the head-line written by the *Liverpool Echo* when Lord Leverhulme died – DEATH OF A WELL-KNOWN CHESHIRE PEER. It is good to work on a newspaper whose headline reads simply DEBROY SOMERS DIES AT SIXTY-TWO.

Most of the papers had good headlines on the enticement case, but top of the class goes the man who wrote: THE MAN WHO CAME TO DINNER STOLE THE COOK.

Good headlines are written in vigorous conversational idiomatic language. Good headlines should be capable of being read aloud – which the mind does subconsciously.

I wonder what luxury vegetable Fortnums are selling to-day and what price they are? There is often a lot of news to be got out of shop windows.

The *Daily Express* likes and practises the cult of the short sentence. But don't let this lead you into the adoption of a style so breathless, so staccato, that the reader feels he is being treated as a child in the 'Cat Bites Rat' stage. A story can be brisk, have pace, indulge in short sentences, and still flow.

*　　*　　*　　*　　*

Thus in the Bulletins, day by day, I sought to establish a way of newspaper production which would be foolproof. Of course, I never succeeded. The newspaper is an intensely personal thing. What interests one reader bores another, and so it is with managing editors, night editors, chief sub-editors, news editors, foreign editors and all the other editors to whom The Editor must delegate his authority. But on the *Express* we had a good stab at perfection *every* day, and we never let up.

Here is a Bulletin that I did *not* dictate. It was posted in the glass case outside the News Room one morning in 1939:

A magnificent paper this morning, edited with great skill, vigour, dash and aplomb.

It is a credit to all, particularly to the Editor. He has a sure touch, firm and resolute, never faltering in moments of stress. I cannot criticise anything he does.

I particularly liked the way he handled the splash stories on pages 1, 2, 5, 7, 9, and his choice of leaders, the leader page article, the Daily Sportlight, Course Jottings, and his seven-column heading to the Classified Advertisements. Pages 3, 4, 6 and 8 and the back half of the paper missed his warmth which unhappily is not instilled into stories by anyone but the Editor. . . .

Just the same, I would be obliged if the Editor could be relieved of some of his work. He must be given time to train up young men, although Lord knows where we are going to find young men who are one-fiftieth as good as the Editor was when he was a young man.

The financial page is very good to-day, largely as the result of advice from the Editor, who surprises one and all by knowing all

there is to know about finance. In future he advises that all Stock
Market prices be printed incorrectly. We have printed Stock
Market prices correctly for thirty years. To hell with it – don't
let us be slaves. The *Express* depends on these touches to bring
the paper to life. . . .

I want you all to remember that the *Daily Express* is printed
for the people, as the Editor says in his usual witty fashion.

My secretary discovered this exquisite parody being read by a
crowd of grinning reporters, all of whom had been on the penitent
bench from time to time.

'Shall I take it down?' she asked.

'No,' I said, 'leave it up. I won't do a bulletin to-day! Get Gunn
on the telephone.'

Herbert Gunn, the Managing Editor (later Editor of the London
Evening Standard, the *Daily Sketch* and now Editor of the *Sunday
Dispatch*) was the author. 'Congratulations, Bert,' I said. 'I wish
I could write like that!'

22 . . . Merrily We Go to War

A home movie shows a Christiansen birthday party the week-end after the 1938 Munich Conference, from which Neville Chamberlain brought back the message that was supposed to mean peace in our time. The movie is in Kodachrome, which picks out the colours of the jam tarts, the cakes, the sandwiches, and the salads on the tea table.

Around the table are my wife, our four children, my mother, my wife's mother, my younger sister, 'Nanny' Harvey – with me bobbing in and out of the picture as I alternate with eleven-year-old Michael, our eldest son, as cameraman. The children wear fancy hats; I teach them bad manners by doing a circus trick from a bowl of tomatoes. One, two, three tomatoes fly high to the ceiling and are caught in my mouth to the applause of the rest of the party.

Only a few hours previously it had looked like war. Now the nation's mood had swung dramatically into complete reverse and it was certainly, surely, positively, PEACE! Do you remember (even the minority who still feared war) the wave of relief that swept through every home in the land? It had been expressed in the *Daily Express* in a size of type that we did not even possess.

How was that possible? The word PEACE! was set in the biggest available type, one inch deep. Then a block was made by the photographic process department. 'Make it five columns wide, and we'll see how deep it comes,' I said; and to my delight it was more than two inches deep, including the exclamation mark called a 'striker' by printers, and it really did look striking! Above this gigantic word, the biggest type ever used in an English newspaper up to that time, appeared the words: 'The *Daily Express* declares that Britain will not be involved in a European War this year, or next year either.' It caused no commotion, or even comment, because everybody wanted to believe it.

Our new home was safe again, our children could grow up in peace – and prosperity. For prosperity had come to us – and the nation was booming, too. We had now bought a house standing in four acres of land on the Essex coast, with a lake, a tennis court, peach trees on the south wall, a rose garden, a paddock, fruit trees, daffodils in the spring, separate bedrooms for the four children and to spare. The staff consisted of a gardener and an under-gardener, a chauffeur, a cook-housekeeper and a nanny. All this, and a flat in London just off Fleet Street itself so that I need never be far away when the big news was breaking.

If hindsight had been granted to us, would we have acted differently in 1938? If I had foreseen that in a few brief years one of my sons would be fighting in the Navy, and that his young brother would later on be a peace-time conscript, would I have acted differently? I don't know. On the paper, we worked for peace and prepared for war. We told the nation that we did not believe there would be a war and we strove to get re-armament going. Some people will tell you to-day that the *Express* policies weakened the nation's will to fight; but of course that would mean the *Express* had power which even *it* has never claimed for itself. The facts are more simple: as in my home on the day my colour movie was made, in humble and in grander homes people wanted peace, wanted to believe in peace, and rejoiced in the achievements of Neville Chamberlain, the man they believed *was* achieving peace.

On the day the Germans marched into Austria, 12 March 1938, the front page of the final edition bore a heavily-scored label:

BIG FIGHT EDITION

Nothing to do with the gathering war clouds; the catch-line referred to a boxing match in which Max Baer, the American heavyweight, defeated Tommy Farr, the British champion, at Madison Square Garden, New York.

That was the way of it. Mix it up. Cater for all tastes, even though the emphasis was then violently political. That morning's leading article quoted *Mein Kampf* and asked where Hitler would strike next for the purpose of bringing the German minorities in other lands back to Germany. Perhaps it would be Czecho-Slovakia, Poland, Danzig, Denmark, Lithuania, or even Switzerland.

'What does it warn us? That we must require now a renewal of the pledge to make this country's air strength equal to the strongest in Europe WITHOUT DELAY.'

That was the way of it. Mix it up. Cater for all tastes . . . I started the first-ever Entertainment Page at the back of the newspaper (look after the back pages and the front page will look after itself).

I put the page under the direction of Paul Holt, a £2,000 a year hornet-of-a-journalist, whose sting was lethal, even in that era which was pretty tough and hard-hitting. In the chameleon-like way of good newspapermen, Holt later became a fine war correspondent in Russia, where he reported the battle all the way to Stalingrad and some of the way back. But he sharpened his lance first in the battle of Wardour Street and the West End.

Mix it up. Cater for all tastes. Here is a headline on a man-hunt story to cap the lot:

MAN WITH STARING EYES HAS EGG-SHAPED HEAD

Christiansen: 'Who wrote this headline?'
Gunn (the Managing Editor): 'I did.'
Christiansen: 'You would, you yellow bastard. Take it out of the next edition, Bert.'
Gunn: 'Why? It tells all the news in one sentence. Isn't that what you want?'
Christiansen: 'Oh, all right. Let it go.'

The scene is morning conference and I am calling for a series of articles for the autumn which will provide a home university course in the arts, literature and philosophy, that will be comprehensible even to myself. It is to be called 'Smith into Superman'.

What else can we get up to? Why not get Kitty, Fleet Street's flower girl, to be a Lady-for-a-day? Dress her up from Moss Bros. and put her up at the Savoy. Fine idea.

Any member of the staff having a baby? Yes, Martha Blount. Ask her to write about it week by week, and we'll 'adopt' the off-spring when it's born. Fine idea.

There must be a man somewhere in the British Isles who re-sembles Strube's Little Man. Let's have a competition to find him. Fine idea. (He is duly found – a plumber, complete with umbrella, and the climax of this stunt is that he is introduced to the audience from the stage of the Palladium.)

Next Christmas let us elect Britain's Ideal Mother. Fine idea. (Put it in the 'futures' book to be discussed about the middle of November.)

Send for Emrys Jones and tell him to take the readers behind the scenes in the *Daily Express* office. We'll call the article

. . . SO THAT YOU COULD HAVE THE NEWS

Jones writes his article which reports that as the Editor was rush-ing home from a holiday in Copenhagen a vast number of his staff were being rushed abroad. . . . 'C. V. R. Thompson walks in from New York and immediately walks out again, hopping a plane to Munich' to cover the meeting between Hitler, Chamberlain, Daladier and Mussolini.

'Here is Sefton Delmer on the telephone from Madrid', the article continues, 'to ask why he was bothering with the Spanish War when the greatest war in history is blowing up in Central Europe. . . . What a life. He is leaving Madrid where he has been bombed for months to go to Czecho-Slovakia where he will find Sudeten Germans pointing rifles at his chest'.

'Fifteen calls to Paris', says the article. 'Sixteen calls to Berlin; four to Geneva; three to Warsaw; three to Metz; two to Bayreuth; one to Teschen; one to Belgrade; one to Vienna; four to Brussels.'

My secretary buzzes me; Lord Beaverbrook is on the telephone again. What now? It's the fifth time this morning. Clear the conference room so that I can talk in privacy. 'Sorry, chaps, don't any of you go out for one – I want you all back as soon as the Old Man's through.'

'I congratulate you on the net sales figure for February,' says the Old Man. As I have not seen the figure, and as February with its snow, frost, fogs and dark mornings, is a bad circulation month, I am puzzled. But soon all becomes clear: the Old Man has a Page One manifesto to unload and the net sales certificate is the topical peg on which to hang it.

Next morning a two-column headline on Page One reads:

UNPOPULAR
POLICIES

2,467,037 *people trust the*
DAILY EXPRESS

Writes Lord Beaverbrook:

'The popularity of the *Daily Express* is demonstrated again to-day by the publication of the net sales figures.

'What is the reason for the supreme position in journalism held by this newspaper? Why is it the very largest newspaper in the world? . . .

'Is it because the *Daily Express* advocates popular policies and panders to public opinion? Not at all.'

Then follow a list of unpopular policies – a very impressive list. FOR the return of the German Colonies. FOR tariffs with taxes on foreign food for the protection of agriculture. AGAINST a National Home for the Jews (Zionism). AGAINST the League of Nations. AGAINST chain stores and the Co-op. in favour of the small shop-keeper.

None of the more senior members of the staff care much for the idea of returning the pre-First World War African Colonies to Germany.

'Would you fight for them?' growls Beaverbrook, who is preparing public opinion for another peace concession by Neville Chamberlain.

'No, we wouldn't.'
'Well, then, what's the argument?'

Mix it up. Cater for all tastes. Let us now find 'the *Daily Express* Man'. I assign James Bartlett, a lively young feature writer, to this task and with some ingenuity he produces a series of statistics giving not only the height, weight, colour of hair and eyes of this typical reader, but also the round-the-seat-of-his-trousers measurement. (To-day the word 'backside' is used in newspapers, but not then!)

The winner is a man called Robert Barlow Neve, an Air Ministry radio operator living in Watford. He and his wife are brought to London and housed at the Savoy. They dine in the Grill, go to night-clubs, the theatre, Broadcasting House, the Old Bailey. And with that luck which attends well-run newspapers, a high drama develops. It transpires that Neve had quarrelled with his parents because he had kept his marriage secret from them; neither side had spoken to the other since the wedding-day. But Neve's father now gets in touch with me and a family reunion is organised. It is a great success, and no one enjoys the pleasures of the West End more than Neve's father – a tough little stevedore from London's Albert Docks, earning about £6 a week and running his own motor-car.

Lord Castlerosse philosophises over the Neve romance in his *Sunday Express* column. The *New Statesman* pulls our legs. And the whole thing ends with Neve dictating an article which concludes: 'Give me my own little home and our way of living. I am content as I am.' With that he returns to obscurity. (When I last heard of the Neves, the family had moved to Yorkshire and were earning far more money but wishing they were back in the old days. 'Every man is an average man nowadays,' Neve ruminated.)

'Newfoundland is broke,' says Lord Beaverbrook. 'Britain has deserted her oldest Colony. Send a man there and stir things up.'

A young reporter who has joined the *Express* from the Press Association gets his big chance. His name is Morley Richards and in the post-war period he is to become News Editor of the paper for 14 years. For day after day in the freezing depths of winter his despatches come in from the townships of Newfoundland, until finally the British Government announces a grant-in-aid of £400,000. We had asked for a couple of millions, but even the smaller sum is a triumph.

Home again comes our hero, and returns to the reporting staff. At morning conference we decide to campaign for an increase in the Old Age Pension. Who shall lead the campaign? Our Newfoundland campaigner, of course. Richards is sent for. He is a plump, Pickwickian type, even in his thirties.

'Another campaign for you,' I say. 'Only this time much worse than freezing on the fat of the land in St John. I want you to live on an Old Age Pension for a fortnight and report your emotions daily.'

Richards starts next morning. He is a six-pints-of-beer-a-day-man on Monday – and a teetotaller on Tuesday. In ten days he loses ten pounds in weight and suffers the agony of real hunger. We have him photographed looking longingly, like a Bisto Kid, into the window of a baker's shop. He says to-day that this was his worst assignment. But . . .

Two months later the Old Age Pension is increased.

Frank Owen is late in the office and the leader column staggers to press even later than usual. 'Where have you been, Frank?'

'You can't blame me this time, Mister,' says Frank. 'I've been to tea at Churt with Lloyd George and the Beaver.'

He tells me of the conversation between the two wily men.

'How many chickens have you got here, L.G.?' asks Lord Beaverbrook.

'Twenty thousand, Max.'

'How many pigs?'

'Seven hundred and fifty, Max.'

A pause while these impressive statistics of Lloyd George's farm are digested. Then it is L.G.'s turn to quiz;

'And how many chickens have you got at Cherkley, Max?'

'Thirty thousand.'

'Really! And pigs?'

'Twelve hundred.'

Another pause. . . . On the way back to Lord Beaverbrook's home, Frank says, 'You haven't got all those chickens and pigs, have you?'

The Beaver grins. 'No, I haven't,' he says, 'neither has L.G.'

I have been editor for five years all but one month when a big day arrives. On 7 October 1938 it was announced that the sales of the *Daily Express* have for the first time topped 2,500,000. To celebrate the achievement, a double-column unsigned announcement declares that our popularity was due to two factors – to 'the policy of restrained optimism' and because we 'kept more correspondents in foreign countries covering the world crisis than any other newspaper.'

(That was true enough. In fact, we had more of everything, except for bosom pictures and smutty reports.)

I go to dinner parties with Lord Beaverbrook at Stornoway House. There are always more Left Wing than Right Wing politicians at table. Aneurin Bevan is a regular guest, and the two men obviously fascinate each other and have many, many things in common. As for politics, they use this subject to sharpen each other's wits!

One night Beaverbrook serves a Veuve Cliquot champagne of 1904. He announces that to get four drinkable bottles, nine had to be uncorked because of the wine's great age.

'How do you like it, Nye?'

Nye appraises the still old wine with the eye of a connoisseur. 'Well, since you ask me,' said Nye solemnly, 'I don't like it at all. I like champagne young, fizzy – and cold.'

The Beaver is not to be outmanœuvred. He bawls for his butler. 'Bring the Bollinger Bolshevik a bottle of young, fizzy, cold champagne, all to himself,' he orders.

I find myself next to the Lion of the House at lunch in the House of Commons. My host is Guy Eden, our Political Correspondent, and Neville Chamberlain, almost fresh from Munich, sits between us.

Chamberlain is remote, cold; not unfriendly, but far, far away. My attempts to talk politics to him are disastrous, so I draw him out for a sentence or two on fishing. But neither fishing nor politics are my strongest interests.

I do not shine in the company of politicians: Herbert Morrison invites me to lunch with him in his top-floor suite in the Norfolk Hotel, off The Strand; Maisky, the Soviet Ambassador, has me to the Soviet Embassy regularly; Geoffrey Lloyd, one of Stanley Baldwin's bright boys, invites me to the Savoy Grill; Sir Albert Clavering, the cinema tycoon and Tory Central office propagandist, says, 'You must meet R. A. Butler', and I do, in the Savoy Restaurant; but always I come away from these occasions conscious that I am a Back Room Boy with little desire for the political limelight.

A call from Stornoway House to drop in on the way home and bring a few copies of the first edition with me.

In the corner Lord Beaverbrook and Brendan Bracken, a young carroty-haired M.P., are playing backgammon. Standing with his back to the log fire is Winston Churchill, who is clearly bored at being neglected by the backgammon players. It is our first meeting and I notice that he is smaller than I expected, but just as pink and baby-looking. He shakes me limply by the hand, but in spite of this he is enthusiastic to have me for his audience, an audience of one only but that is better than none. It is Thursday, 6 April 1939, the day before Good Friday in that year.

'Where is the – ah – the British Fleet to-night?' he asked me, rolling the words around his palate and licking them before they are uttered. 'It ish lolling [what a beautiful Churchillian word!] in the Bay of Naples. No doubt, the – ah – the Commander of the British ships at Naples is – ah – being entertained ashore, entertained no doubt on the orders of – ah – Mussholini himself at the Naples Yacht Club.'

Churchill glowered at me and chewed his cigar before continuing: 'And where should the British Fleet be to-night? On the other side of that long heel of a country called Italy. In the Adriatic Sea, not the Mediterranean Sea, to make the rape of Albania imposhible.

'That is why, my boy, Mussholini is entertaining the British Fleet ashore at Naples to-night.'

On the following day, Italian troops were disembarked all along the Albanian coast and began to march on Tirana, the capital. King

Zog fled with his Queen, who had just given birth to a son, and he never got home again. The Italian losses totalled twelve killed and fifty-three wounded.

A good story reaches me but from a source which I cannot recall:
King George VI gets pleasure out of telephoning Mr King, his bank manager, personally, without interception through switchboard operators, so that he can say:
'Is that George King? This is King George speaking.'
Almost every morning when the King is in London the joke is solemnly, and hilariously, repeated.

Mix it up. Cater for all tastes. Get the news, all the news.
'Hoskins,' drawls J. B. Wilson, the News Editor. 'Why can't you find out where these I.R.A. bombs are being made? Chris is tearing his hair out. This is the fifth day he's asked, and he wants an answer to-day.'
'Well, J.B.,' replies Hoskins, the crime reporter, 'I've got some bad news for you. They're being made in your own cellar. The Special Branch are there now, taking away the explosives – and your butler.'
Newspapers have got to be both efficient and lucky. J. B. Wilson, the best News Editor in the country, never had such a lucky break as when the Special Branch, inquiring into the source of the I.R.A. balloon bombs which were being deposited in railway cloak-rooms all over London, traced them to the house in Brunswick Square occupied and owned by J.B. himself.
J.B. had never been known to go out on a story before, but he seized a movie camera and not only reported the raid on his own house but took a film of it as well. What is more, after the raid was over and his Irish manservant locked away, he was responsible for the arrest of another member of the gang. Just as he was about to leave his home and return to Fleet Street, J.B. saw a man slip down the area steps carrying an attaché case. He telephoned the Yard. The man was arrested, and in the attaché case were sulphuric acid, potassium chlorate, detonators and balloons. (They had to be described in the newspaper as balloons; in fact they were what are

called *capots anglais* in France, and are still unmentionable in to-day's newspapers.)

August 1939. . . . The nation breathes an uneasy sigh of relief as the Bank Holiday period passes, and Hitler has not emulated the Kaiser's action in 1914. But in every newspaper office in the world there is the smell of gunpowder and every man has his orders, especially the men on duty in Berlin, Vienna, Prague, Danzig and Warsaw. In the *Daily Express* office, Robertson and I are summoned repeatedly to Stornoway House, and despite Robertson's objections, we decide to run the 'No War' slogan yet again.

'We've *got* to reduce the temperature,' argues the Beaver fiercely. 'If it keeps on going up there will be no hope at all. We've *got* to curb the war fever.' He expresses no view on the accuracy of the slogan, but he may well believe in it, for soon afterwards he leaves for Canada. Newspapermen often fall for their own propaganda.

I fall for it myself and refuse to cancel a 28 August booking on the *Queen Mary* until a couple of days beforehand. But by then the inevitable dawns on us. This time there seems to be no reprieve. Lord Beaverbrook comes back from Canada on the advice of Robertson, and wisecracks: 'Robertson is carrying his umbrella as though it is a rifle'. Leslie Hore-Belisha, the War Minister, rushes his few 3.7 anti-aircraft guns hither and thither around London in a blaze of photographic publicity, hoping that the deception will convince Von Ribbentrop, the German Ambassador, that London is well defended from air attack. Sam Hoare, the prune-mouthed Home Secretary, invites the editors to Whitehall every day, to give us the news of the Government's hopes and fears, its evacuation plans, its mobilisation plans. Sandbags, black-out: you will recall it all as well as I.

Some friends are on holiday at Hartland Point in Devon, and it seems wise to accept their invitation for my wife and children to join them. Off they go with the rest of the evacuees, and I am relieved that I can carry on without worrying about their safety in the tin-pot air-raid shelter we had dug 'for fun' in the grounds of our lovely Essex home.

Parliament was sitting on that fateful Saturday, 2 September.

And Arsenal were playing Sunderland at Highbury. There was nothing for me to do, as it was publishing day for the *Sunday Express*, so I went to the football match. Afterwards I telephoned the office for news. The first edition of the *Sunday Express* had not yet gone to press, and I gathered that the intention was to prophesy even at that time that war would be averted. I telephoned William Barkley at the House of Commons Press Gallery. 'It's madness,' said Willie, whose judgement of the mood of Parliament was immaculate.

That night I dined at Scott's in Piccadilly, and it was after eleven when we left the restaurant. Lightning was bringing daylight to the blacked-out streets, and thunder made the noise of a million guns, as though God Himself were rumbling in rage at human folly. Hitler's bombers never put on a show like this.

Next morning the sirens sounded their first alarm. William Barkley came on the telephone when I got to the office at noon, with a great joke to tell me.

'Chris,' he said, 'you should have seen all the M.P.s squashed together in the terrace corridor. If anything had happened, my dear, we'd all have been crushed to death or drowned in the Thames.'

'Go on, Willie,' I said, 'where's the joke in that?'

'Well,' said Willie, 'it suddenly occurred to me that the whole thing must be a false alarm organised by Neville Chamberlain.'

'Why, Willie?'

'Because, my dear, he's afraid to face the House!'

23 . . . The Bombs Scream

By all accounts, there will be no time to produce a newspaper, let alone an inclination to read one, if ever war should curse this planet again. By all accounts, one bomb will finish things. By all accounts, the mess might take anything from three days to three weeks to tidy up – if there is anyone left to clear up the mess.

But be not deceived by the prophets. In September 1939 the British Government was so convinced that there would be 50,000 casualties from air raids in London alone on the first day, that every hospital was emptied so that these casualties could be dealt with. I was a victim of this gross misjudgement, for I broke my leg in the black-out during the phoney war period and could not be treated at St Mary's Hospital. That was seven months after the outbreak of war on 3 September, and up to that time all we had had was an air-raid warning on the first morning, a declaration by Field-Marshal Ironside to an American News Agency that Britain would welcome an attack by Hitler – the *Express* printed the declaration exclusively and it caused the usual commotion – an incredibly efficient evacuation of children from the big cities, a mess in other directions as food rationing, newspaper rationing, the black-out and other 'don't-do-this' regulations became the British way of life.

The one tragedy that fitted into the true pattern of war as we had

known it in 1914–18 was the sinking of the liner *Athenia*, but we
were not to know in those days that this was in fact a mistake.

It may be that the prophets will be equally wrong if there is a
third war. It may be, for example, that by outlawing the H-bomb
and the A-bomb and the space rockets, man will be able to indulge
in his favourite pastime of self-destruction with what are known
as conventional weapons such as flame-throwers and block-busters,
that do only a teeny-weeny bit of damage like killing or frying a
couple of hundred at a time. It may be that even those weapons
will be held in check until one side or the other thinks it has overwhelming superiority.

If so, I warn future editors not to be Maginot-minded. What
does that mean? I was shocked the other day when my six-year-old
grand-daughter asked 'What is an air-raid?' so I had better recall
that the Maginot Line was an impregnable strip running the
length of the French frontier in 1939, which the Germans in due
course simply went round and conquered from the rear, so that the
term in 1940 for an old-fashioned, hide-bound, dug-out mentality
became 'Maginot-minded'.

I was definitely Maginot-minded; I saw this new war in terms of
the last one. What was the most popular newspaper idea in 1914?
Bruce Bairnsfather's Old Bill, that walrus-moustached Old Con-
temptible who had joked from shell-hole, trench and dug-out. All
right, get St John Cooper, who draws the Home Page Cat, to invent
a character. Call him Young Bert. The size of the paper is cut down
from twenty-four to twelve pages (and will get even smaller), but
we must keep the *Express* spirit strong. Everybody is singing a song
called 'We'll hang out our washing on the Siegfried Line'. Feature
it, make it the 'Tipperary' of the 1939 war. Bud Flanagan is singing
a catchy tune called 'Run, rabbit, run'. Feature that one, too; we'll
make it as popular as 'Pack up your troubles in your old kit-bag'.

One old boy on the sporting staff took off to Cornwall the day
after war broke out and was never seen again, but he was the only
deserter: the others who disappeared were the young men – sixty
in all – who volunteered for the Armed Forces. The windows of our
Fleet Street glass-house were blocked up – my secretary worked for
several days between two ladders bridged by a plank, from which
an aged builder showered her with plaster and reminiscences of his

days in San Francisco after the earthquake; and for a week or two, after the issue of tin hats to the chief executives, several of us slept on the premises in specially constructed dormitories, just in case the real war started up.

But soon things became 'normal' again, and we were campaigning against food rationing and the black-out and all the other irksome restrictions. Lord Beaverbrook was morose and mischievous, harsh and quarrelsome with us all. He could not get on with this war; he kept calling it the 'Unnecessary War'. There was at this stage very little war to get on with, and he was difficult to handle.

At London University in Bloomsbury, a Ministry of Information was set up with a Censorship Division, headed by a retired admiral named Usborne, who recruited his censors largely from retired naval commanders and army majors. In turn the newspapers set up their own censorship departments to keep liaison.

Soon things were in chaos. In the second week of September the War Office released the news that units of the British Expeditionary Force had landed in France. Usborne's Chairborne Warriors went into battle over the *Daily Express* story telephoned by Geoffrey Cox, our man in Paris. With World War I punctilio, the censors blue-pencilled phrases that might reveal to the enemy the size of our army, even to the fact that they were transported in trucks marked '40 men, 8 horses'. Out came details of equipment. A sentence which stated that the sight of 'the heavy-tyred camouflaged guns and pontoons set the French people cheering madly' was mutilated completely, as though our troops were armed only with the pikestaffs which were later dished out to the Home Guard.

But from the ten lines that were spared the blue pencil, we made these enormous headlines:

Men in khaki lean from a train as it rumbles through a
village, revealing to the world –

BRITISH TROOPS IN FRANCE

French folk run to cheer the Tommies

'TOGETHER IN MAGINOT'

This was IT! Too true, it was; for at midnight Field-Marshal

Ironside changed his mind and cancelled the authority to publish the news!

For the purpose of creating confusion, Whitehall can act much more quickly than any other known human agency. Within half an hour I had a visit from a florid Police Inspector wearing a First War D.C.M. ribbon, carrying a tin hat and a gas-mask in his hand. No papers, he said, must leave the premises.

'But the first edition is already in the trains to places like Cornwall, Wales, East Anglia,' I argued.

'In that case,' said the Inspector, 'they will be seized on arrival.'

In a 2 a.m. frenzy, we prepared a new front page. But this was no sooner on the machines than the Field-Marshal changed his mind again and we were allowed to restore our original headlines! I seized my pen at three o'clock and wrote an exposure of the muddle of Defence Regulations for a special final edition that would circulate only as far as the sand-bagged War Office. 'You'll be liable to go to jail for this,' warned Mark Goodman, the late-duty lawyer, whose business it was to keep me on the rails. 'The public isn't supposed to know that such things as Defence Regulations exist,' to which I snarled, 'Jail would be peace, if this is war.'

Next day the editors were invited to meet Sir Samuel Hoare at the Home Office to be assured that such a situation would not occur again. It never was quite so bad thereafter until, one day during the Battle of Britain when the bombs were falling on an almost undefended London, I ran a Page One streamer in our biggest type:

THE FLEET'S HERE!

A destroyer – ONE destroyer! – had arrived in the Thames. Her guns pooped off through the night. It was a new sound to battered London. It gave us all the feeling that even though the shells weren't hitting anything at least the bloody bombers weren't quite having it all their own way.

That morning I was threatened with prosecution for revealing to the enemy that London was so defenceless that a destroyer had had to be brought to the rescue.

'Do you think,' I sighed, 'that the German airmen don't know London is defenceless? If you want to prosecute, go ahead. I shall plead extenuating circumstances. I shall say that the fact that the Fleet was brought to London's rescue was wonderful news for the Cockneys and that the *Daily Express* was letting a little sunshine into their lives by telling them that at least the Navy hadn't forgotten them.'

In time we got a new Chief Censor appointed. He was another Admiral, but of a very different kind. George Thomson, a retired submarine wallah with a grey face caused by a stomach ulcer, was prepared to learn, and learned to such good purpose that he became Fleet Street's champion with the Service Departments instead of our enemy. He fought for the publication of news so strenuously that even when he was obliged to say 'No' there always seemed a hope. Giving me a prodigious wink, Willie Crumley, the *Daily Express* Censorship Desk chief, disappeared one night in the direction of London University for a personal visit, uttering a Scottish incantation that 'Once Admiral Thomson has made up his mind, no power on earth can make him stick to it!'

Just the same, Fleet Street was seething over the whole Ministry of Information set-up. Lord Camrose, the owner of the *Daily Telegraph*, a genial but tough character, set up office as Director-General in the University for a week or two. I called on him with my grievances. 'Why don't you take the law into your own hands and print what you like?' he demanded. This was all very well for Lord Camrose, especially as he washed his hands of the job a couple of weeks later, but under war-time stringency his advice was not really practical.

Then Fleet Street set up an agitation to make me Minister of Information. A. J. Cummings, Political Editor of the *News Chronicle*, and Bob Cruikshank, Editor of *The Star*, jointly signed an article which said that whenever there was a shake-up of 'Minnie' (the Ministry of Information) a number of inoffensive minor functionaries were sacked and in their places 'some expert on Egyptian Hieroglyphics is appointed to take charge of British publicity in the Straits Settlement; the late Vice-Consul at Timbuctoo, for whom a job must be found, because he is Lady Bracknell's nephew, is appointed Director-General of Relations to the Collar and Tie Trade Papers.'

The article made an appeal to Mr Churchill: 'You who are so great a journalist . . . would understand better than anyone else, if only our words could reach you, that *journalism* demands above all things *journalists*, and *news* requires *newspapermen.* . . .'

The article described the kind of man the writer had in mind: 'He needs to be young, yet experienced, tough, yet imaginative. He needs to possess the intuitive flair for knowing the interests of our people, and the restless driving force that claws down stones from the reluctant air. He also needs a supreme disregard for the inhibitions of the Ancient and moth-eaten Old School Tie.'

At this point it was suggested that I should be conscripted in a 'Ministry of Newscraft Production which is as vital to us as the Ministry of Supply. . . . He is a professional. We respect him. And we are sick of amateurs.'

The campaign was so strenuously developed that the idea was even put forward that to save me the fuss of finding a seat in Parliament, I should be co-opted as a 'Member without constituency'.

Duff Cooper, the Minister of Information, took all this with unruffled indifference. When some of us dined with him, he gave the impression that he hated his job so much that he would have been glad to leave it for a Department which dealt in deeds, not words. As for my succeeding him, the idea was ridiculous. I was a journalist, and the politicians would have devoured me.

In April I stumbled in the black-out, fell and broke my leg in five places. Before I was back in Fleet Street, Hitler had invaded as many countries as my leg had cracks: Norway, Denmark, Holland, Belgium and France.

Thus I saw the phoney war end and the real war begin from a bed in Miss Ellis's Nursing Home in Manchester Square, W.1. I occupied the room in which J. M. Barrie died. That secretive, publicity-shy little man must have turned in his grave as hordes of friends and newspapermen called to see me day by day, laden with gifts, most of them liquid. At one time I had seven bottles of scarce Scotch in the wardrobe, as well as supplies of even scarcer champagne. 'You'll get this place struck off,' I protested. 'It's getting to be known already as Miss Ellis's Boogie-Woogie Club.'

But even here we worked hard. Every day 'conference' was held around my bed and ideas discussed. I was in telephone communication with the office, and tried to get through as much of my normal routine as one can with a leg in a cradle suspended from the ceiling.

Bert Gunn, the Managing Editor, brought me the news that the Maginot Line had been outflanked.

'Instruct our chaps not to get themselves captured,' I ordered. 'Prisoners of war are no use to a newspaper.' Already we had lost two men: Giles Romilly, a nephew of Winston Churchill, had been caught at Narvik, in Norway; and Selkirk Panton, our Berlin man who went to Copenhagen when war was declared, had failed to escape from Denmark. Later I learned that Panton had the agonising decision to take as to whether to leave his wife behind – she was in labour with a child when the Germans struck – or stay with her and spend the rest of the war in a prison camp.

By the time my leg was out of plaster, more than four months later, Miss Ellis's Nursing Home had been blown to bits by a German bomb. As I hobbled around the streets on my crutches, I was often mistaken for a Dunkirk veteran in mufti and shown so much sympathy and consideration from the Londoners who were soon to be in the front line of the blitz themselves that I felt ashamed. On my return to Fleet Street my staff presented me with an X-ray photograph of my broken leg, mounted on a white border which everybody autographed, and captioned: *One more score we have to settle with Hitler.*

Lord Beaverbrook had meanwhile joined the Government as Minister of Aircraft Production and was showing his genius not only as a producer of planes, but as a propagandist, too. His Spitfire Fund, for example, became one of the biggest morale boosters of the entire war.

The Spitfire Fund was not, in fact, Beaverbrook's invention, although his was the inspiration that made the fund such a smash-hit once the idea had been born. It started when a cable came to him from the Editor of the *Jamaica Gleaner* in the British West Indies enquiring the cost of a bomber. The reply was sent, and back came the money, £30,000 subscribed by the *Gleaner*'s readers.

Most of the newspapers found space for a small paragraph about this gift, but nothing more was done until another newspaper called *Express*, the *Wolverhampton Star & Express*, decided to ask its readers to subscribe the money for a fighter plane, about one-

quarter the cost of a bomber. This in turn was publicised briefly
and came to the notice of Harry Bradbury Pratt, an old West End
friend of mine who was then living in Brighton. Harry wrote to me:

> 'I know that I would be very interested in the exploits of an
> airplane given by Brighton for which I had helped to pay, and I
> feel that most of us here in Brighton would be the same.'

Not realising what a seam of gold I had struck, I published the
letter modestly with a footnote which said: 'Now then, Worcester
and Wallasey, Gloucester and Greenock, Wigan and Wimbledon!
Who is first in the field?'

Within a few days Worcester had raised enough money for two
Spitfires, and before long every town and hamlet in the country was
in on the campaign; indeed Lord Beaverbrook whipped up the
enthusiasm as far afield as the Argentine, from which three
'*Pamperos*' (the nearest Spanish word to Spitfire, I gather) were
subscribed!

Lord Beaverbrook had taken with him to the Ministry J. B.
Wilson, my faithful News Editor. He and Wilson were soon up to
more of the 'reader participation' ideas of the kind that sell newspapers and keep people interested and loyal. They launched the
aluminium drive and called on the population to hand over their
pots and pans to make airplanes. The fact that the shops were filled
with aluminium pots and pans was churlishly pointed out by some
sour-pusses, but it made no difference. Even hard-bitten journalists
joined in. Brian Chapman, one of my executives, drove his
aluminium-covered Railton sports car to a depot in Chelsea and
left it there to be dismantled. I stripped a kitchen shelf and a
Hoover vacuum cleaner of its vital parts. We were all in it, and
looked, if you remember, with the pride of possession on the planes
taking part in the first of those daylight air battles that preceded
the blitz proper.

Immediately war broke out the *Daily Express* had been reduced
from twenty-four pages to twelve; then to eight, then six, until,
when the blitz on London began, we were working on only four.
It was then that we really learned what compression meant: thirty

items to a page was the rule and if we fell below that number there
was an inquest.

As the blitz on London developed in fury and the threat of
invasion became more menacing, we crowded into our minuscule
editions all the excitement, all the challenge, all the cheerfulness
that we could muster. ROLL OUT THE BARRAGE! punned the
Page One streamer. NO INVASION TO-DAY! said a headline on
the weather forecast from Dover (we had difficulty with the censors
over this daily feature until we convinced them that the Germans
knew as much about the weather in the English Channel as we did).
'If you are an air-raid victim and gaze at your ruined home to-day,'
said a leading article, 'remember that it is better that your home
should go than an arms factory or an airfield. Every bomb which
misses a vital objective is for Hitler so much waste.'

Somebody on the staff interviewed a Boer War veteran whose son
had been awarded the V.C. for bombing the Dortmund-Ems canal.
'I am not surprised,' said his father. 'Roderick always was one for
smashing things up.'

'Live upside-down,' we advised our readers. 'Eat in the bedroom.
Sleep in the dining-room.' And for good measure we warned
Hartley Shawcross and Company, the Regional Commissioners
who were set up by the Government, not to behave like gauleiters
just because they had been given unlimited powers over the lives
and property of the entire nation.

I reckoned that by producing this kind of newspaper I was doing
a better job than I could have achieved in the Ministry of Information, even when the War Cabinet ticked me off for making William
Joyce's English broadcasts from Germany too popular. Jonah
Barrington, our radio reporter, christened Joyce 'Lord Haw-Haw'
and the temptation to report this fantastic traitor in derisive terms
day by day was overwhelming. Finally, Lord Beaverbrook telephoned to ask me to lay off.

Then I upset Churchill by calling in a leading article for the more
vigorous bombing of Berlin. 'You ought to know perfectly well,'
said a letter from 10 Downing Street, 'that the work of building up
a great bomber force takes a long time, maybe years.'

About a year later, John Strachey, then an R.A.F. public relations officer (and Socialist Minister for War) invited me to watch

the first-ever raid by the great Lancasters; it was a 'piece of
cake' target on the Renault island factory in the Seine near undefended Paris. Meantime there was some consolation to offset
Churchill's rebuke in an issue of the *Chicago Daily News*, whose
London correspondent, Robert M. Yoder, wrote:

'When the war news gives you a bad case of the gallops, it is
refreshing to look at the London *Express*. Bombs may be scream-
ing into Fleet Street, and the desks may be quivering like jelly,
but the *Express* hasn't turned a hair.

'It's the same neat, workmanlike job, with all the copy clean,
without so much as a typographical error to indicate any feeling
of haste or alarm, and the same tricky inlaid English make-up,
which always suggests that the stories are planted in the page like
flower-beds in a garden, or put together by marquetry lovers.'

Were we as cool as all that? Were we so very optimistic? Herbert
Gunn bought a revolver on the black market and kept it locked in
his desk with two bullets in the loading chamber, 'one for the first
German to get into the building and the other for myself'. Dick
Plummer and I discussed Maquis tactics for when invasion came.
And one day when the streets of London were covered with broken
glass and I was lunching off Spam in the Cock Tavern, my stomach
nearly gave out. It was not the Spam; it was the news brought to me
by Lindon Laing, the News Editor who succeeded J. B. Wilson.
This ginger-headed eccentric had run from one end of Fleet Street
to the other – the telephones had been blitzed – to whisper breath-
lessly in my ear: 'The invasion's started. The Germans have landed
in the Tyne not far from Newcastle.'
The London correspondent of the *Chicago Daily News* would not
have admired the Editor of the London *Express* so much if he had
seen him pay his bill and rush back to the office in what can only
reasonably be described as a muck-sweat.

That night, when the flap was over and my courage had returned,
Tom Driberg came to my room to tell me of a conversation he had
overheard between two soldiers in the refreshment bar at Liverpool
Street station.

'I heard on the German wireless,' said one, 'that the Editor of the *Daily Express*, a Jew named Rosenbloom, is on Hitler's Death List for after the invasion.'

Driberg interrupted the soldiers to tell them that the name of the Editor of the *Daily Express* was Christiansen.

'Is he a Jew?' asked the second soldier.

'How can a man be a Jew – if it matters – with a name like Christiansen?' Driberg had said. 'It means "son of a Christian".'

'Print that in the William Hickey column,' I said to Driberg, 'It's fun to be on Hitler's Death List.'

24 . . . Blitz – and Black-out

'The greatest newspaper story the world has ever known' was how the *Express* described the bombing of London in 1940. Maybe I took this view because I was personally involved. Editors usually order their reporters to rush to the hot spots of the world while remaining icily calm in the safety of their sanctuaries; but in the blitz the editors had to be as brave and as resourceful as the rest of their staffs. They had, in fact, to demonstrate the truth of the hoary Fleet Street legend of the Editor who said, 'Tell Peter the Painter that I am not afraid of him,' as he sent his chief reporter to try to get an interview during the siege of Sidney Street.

HITLER TOOK LONDON IN SEPTEMBER – AND DIDN'T KNOW IT! announced the headline to an article I bought from Ralph Ingersoll, Editor of the American *PM* (a newspaper that tried vainly, but bravely and idealistically, to exist in New York without carrying any advertisements). It was fine stuff, and better told in an English newspaper by an American, once the censorship on the night-by-night, bomb-by-bomb account was lifted. 'On the eighth day of this ordeal – during the afternoon of Sunday, 15 September, Adolf Hitler met his first defeat in eight years,' wrote Ingersoll, as he reported that although the R.A.F. had only claimed that 185 Luftwaffe planes had been brought down, it was certain that well over 200 had been

destroyed. 'Responsible British officers believe that if Hitler and
Goering had had the courage to lose 200 planes a day for the next
five days nothing could have saved London.'

That Sunday, close on midnight, Lord Beaverbrook telephoned
me. 'How are you treating the news?' he asked. It was a surprising
question because I had not heard from him for weeks.

I told him that the R.A.F. victory had been so tremendous that
I had had to abandon reproducing on Page One the miniature
silhouettes of the exact number of Heinkels brought down. At
twelve Heinkel silhouettes to the width of the page, up to four rows
in depth were accommodated without wasting too much space, but
186 just could not be done.

'Well, you can print in your leader column if you like,' replied
the Beaver, 'that the Battle of Waterloo took place to-day. We have
won the war.' I wish now that I had done so, but at that time even
the optimism of the *Express* would not have supported such bold
prophecy.

By their accounts of London's torment, the American correspondents in London were preparing public opinion in their own
land to support intervention in the war. When eventually the U.S.A.
came in after Pearl Harbour, I used to squabble with many of them
over the merits of Monty and Bradley and 'Blood and Guts' Patton,
and the conduct of the war, but in 1940 these correspondents were
on our side to a man. Men like Bill Stoneman, Ed Beatty, Drew
Middleton, Merrill Mueller and Virgil Pinkley, went out on
bomb stories day in, day out. Ed Murrow lay in a gutter with his
microphone so that New York could hear the crump of the bombs
at street level.

My greatest buddy was Quentin Reynolds, the husky New York
Irishman, whose gravel-voice is remembered still by millions for
his Sunday night postscripts to the nine o'clock news.

To one of these broadcasts I made a contribution. It was a
Saturday morning and Quent's manuscript had to be with the
B.B.C. for censorship by 6 p.m. The night before had been heavy
in every sense of the word. Quent's suite at the Savoy had been
crowded with newspapermen and R.A.F. fighter pilots on leave,
and as he kept open house till the last guest had gone, both the
bombs and the bottles had given all present a bit of a 'shellacking'.

'Come round and help me, old bean,' growled the host, who liked to imitate the London slang of thirty years back. 'I am short of ideas, old bean.'

When I arrived at the Savoy, Quent was propped up in bed with a portable typewriter that rocked from side to side on his knees.

'Order me a gin and lime, with lots of lime,' he groaned. 'Let's see if that will help.' But the gin and lime took so long to arrive that we batted out a couple of thousand words and reached the peroration without it.

Quent was orating from his bed and I was typing on a dressing-table as he reached the climax.

'Come on, Hitler!' he croaked derisively.

'Alter that to his real name, "Schickelgruber",' I suggested. 'Nobody in England could take a man with a name like Schickel-gruber seriously.'

'You're darn right, old bean,' said Quent. And Schickelgruber it became on Sunday night. The name was hurled like the blast of a Sahara sandstorm into the microphone, and it bounced out of five million radio sets. People laughed that night as the bombs fell. Britain's contempt for Hitler became as valuable as several squadrons of bombers in prosecuting the war.

Quentin Reynolds did everything with the extravagance of a generous nature. After the blitz he returned to New York for a spell and did a cinema tour of the big cities, telling them the story of how London had taken it. It was a spectacular show with a mighty Wurlitzer softening up the audience with 'A Nightingale sang in Berkeley Square' before Quent's speech. He also commented a film called 'London Can Take it', made by a young documentary director named Harry Watt, for the Ministry of Information. Gramophone records of his broadcasts sold by their thousands, and Quent gave the proceeds to the R.A.F. Benevolent Fund. His friends during the Battle of Britain ranged from Air Marshals to unknown young pilot officers qualifying for their first 'gong'.

'It's the least we Americans can do until we get into the war ourselves,' he growled as his hotel bills mounted into the £200-a-week range for hospitality to all and sundry in uniform.

I repaid him in small measure with an idea. It was Christmas time, and he was going home to Ginny, his bride. He wanted to take her a present that typified Britain's struggle. I suggested buying a handsome cigarette case and inscribing it with the words '*To Ginny, from* –' and then adding the signatures of Churchill, Beaverbrook, Attlee, 'Archie' Sinclair, Ernest Bevin, Herbert Morrison and the rest of the War Cabinet, the Service Chiefs and other bigwigs. 'How do we do that?' asked Quent. 'Nothing simpler,' I answered. 'We'll get them from my correspondence files, and those I haven't got, you will have.' Thus Virginia Reynolds possesses a souvenir of 1940 London so rare that she keeps it in a safe deposit box at her bank.

We lived it up quite a bit during the blitz. We slept where we dined most nights. When I was detained in Fleet Street, there were dormitories for the staff specially built on the ground floor, but Quent's apartment was usually crowded with bodies in sleeping bags. It was a relief to be invited occasionally to Lord Beaverbrook's country house near Leatherhead for the week-end.

We stood, Lord Beaverbrook and I, on the terrace of Cherkley Court one Saturday night in September, and it seemed that we could hear the whistling banshee wail of the bombs dropping even though we were twenty miles away. The horizon glowed a deep pink as helpless London burned.

'I am a foreigner,' said the Minister of Aircraft Production, his arm around my shoulder. 'And you're a foreigner too. By that I mean that I am a Canadian and you are a Dane on your father's side. Therefore, we can both look at London to-night with a degree of detachment.

'Did you ever – did you ever know such a magnificent people as the English? Did you ever know such courage and bravery? Night after night they've stood up to this dreadful ordeal.'

Having adopted London since I arrived there in 1925, I interjected, 'You mean the Londoners, the Cockneys?'

'No, I don't. I mean the English. They're all the same. They're the greatest race on earth. There's no one to touch them. And you, as a foreigner like me, ought to know it.'

This was no affectation. In fact, it was a recurring theme. In the peace and sunshine of the Bahamas years later, when his motor-boat had broken down because of a defect in some machinery manufactured in the U.S.A., I heard him say to the two Bahamians who were the crew: 'Now, you boys, let me tell you that this shaft would not have broken if it had come from a British engineering shop. The British are the most thorough-going, reliable, painstaking nation in the world. There is nothing shoddy in their work or their characters. You should be proud to be of British stock.'

Cherkley was a fascinating place at the week-end. It was here that I first met Lord Louis Mountbatten, who had just returned from the Crete evacuation. He took me on one side and demanded to know why the R.A.F. was hogging all the publicity while the Navy and the Army got little or none. I told him about Jimmy Robertson, a clever old P.R.O. at the Air Ministry, who had recruited the best Fleet Street men available when war broke out, people like Stanley Bishop and L. M. McBride of the *Daily Herald*. It was these trained newspapermen who fed the correspondents with news they were glad to print instead of providing the stereotyped hand-outs that the retired admirals and generals of the other Services relied on.

Mountbatten was angry. Not, he said, because his own Service was out of the headlines, but because the R.A.F. publicity was causing bad feeling among all the fighting men. 'Where's the Navy? Why can't they give us support like the R.A.F.?' summed up the attitude of the soldiers. As for the sailors, they resented the R.A.F. publicity to such an extent, said Mountbatten, that the smallest incident in a bar in Alexandria touched off a near-riot.

I could see Mountbatten's point. I could offer no cure except to get better Press departments for the Navy and the Army. But Mountbatten had another idea: he wanted to amalgamate the publicity machines of all three services into one. Later Mountbatten became head of Combined Operations and organised the Dieppe raid about which Beaverbrook alleged that too many Canadians lost their lives or were taken prisoner. But the Combined Press Department idea never came to anything; inter-Service jealousy was probably too great even for Mountbatten's strong personality.

The criticism which Lord Beaverbrook's newspapers make of

o

Mountbatten is severe, but my encounters with him have always been agreeable. When Jim Thomas, later Lord Cilcennin, was First Lord of the Admiralty, I was invited to a cocktail party at Admiralty House. It was alive with Sea Lords. They were all good companions; even the Admiral in charge of the Royal yacht, expenditure on which has frequently been criticised by the *Daily Express*, argued with me in the nicest possible way. But it was clear that I was being steered away from Mountbatten. In fact, it became too obvious and I was asked somewhat nervously if I would like to meet him. 'Sure,' I said. 'Why on earth not?'

We had a most helpful twenty minutes' discussion about the future of the Navy. Mountbatten is a good publicist.

But it was a different story when I was presented to the Countess after the war. We met at a reception given by the late Fred Doidge, at that time High Commissioner for New Zealand in London. Doidge, who was general manager of the *Sunday Express* when I first came to Fleet Street, was a jovial glad-hander. He rushed across and practically dragged Lady Mountbatten and me together. 'Have you met Christiansen? He's the Editor of the *Daily Express*, you know,' he said enthusiastically. I put on my best smile but the Countess's smile suggested she was sucking alum. 'We have met,' she said and turned her back. 'You should have spared your guest, Fred,' I said, for I had long since learned to be brassy and thick-skinned towards people who did not admire the Beaver and his newspapers.

One war-time week-end at Cherkley the guests included Lord Castlerosse; Lord Ashfield, a boyhood friend and chairman of London Transport; Mr A. V. Alexander, the Co-op boss who was Churchill's First Lord of the Admiralty; and Sir Edward Bridges, Permanent Secretary to the Treasury.

Bridges was pulling my leg about the *Express* anti-black-out campaign when Lord Beaverbrook joined us. He had changed into a dinner jacket that night, a habit he had abandoned since the outbreak of war. Castlerosse in brown pin-stripe, Ashfield and Bridges in Civil Service drab, Alexander in his double-breasted navy-blue serge, and I in I-forget-what, looked at him in surprise. But within minutes the explanation came, as the butler announced a visitor who was dressed, not in a dinner jacket and black tie, but in white tie and tails – the full canonicals, so to speak.

Lord Beaverbrook effects his introductions in his own highly individualistic way. He assumes that all his guests know the name of the latest arrival, maybe to suggest to the latest arrival that he is so important as not to need to be named. 'This is Lord Castlerosse,' he said to the white-tied figure. 'This is Lord Ashfield, this is Mr Albert Alexander, this is Sir Edward Bridges. And this is Mr Christiansen.'

We all shook hands. Our visitor seemed shyly impressed by the company. Lord Beaverbrook escorted him into the dining-room and placed him on his right at the table. The usual war-time meal was served – clear soup, roast chicken, sweet and coffee, and for a change, champagne was drunk; but somehow or other even the chortlings of Castlerosse did not get the party going. Lord Beaverbrook was courtesy itself to his visitor, but seemed to be as monosyllabic in mood as was his chief guest. It was a relief when he rose from the table and suggested that we should all attend a film show in the private cinema.

At the time the cinema was the pride and joy of Lord Beaverbrook's life at Cherkley. Every Sunday a new film was hired from one of the big companies – and there was in emergency also a personally owned copy of Marlene Dietrich in *Destry Rides Again* shown a score of times, principally for the purpose of hearing Marlene sing 'See what the Boys in the Back Room will Have'.

Our white-tied visitor was escorted to one of the deep arm-chairs in the slightly-raised balcony; the staff streamed in to occupy seats on the ground floor; the film began. It was a bore. Our visitor watched; Lord Beaverbrook dozed; Castlerosse tiptoed out; I wanted to do likewise, but dared not. When the lights went up at last Lord Beaverbrook again became all animation. He took his visitor's arm and led him to the sitting-room, where whiskies and sodas were produced. Conversation was spasmodic, however, and a quarter of an hour later everyone was relieved, including the unknown visitor, when Lord Beaverbrook asked, 'Have you a motor-car?' as he led the stranger to the door. 'No? Well, I will get one for you.' The pair disappeared.

Five minutes later, Lord Beaverbrook returned. 'Well, boys?' he

said, 'do any of you know who that was?' Silence. 'Neither do I,'
he continued. 'Of all the curious things that have happened at
Cherkley in twenty-one years here, nothing like this has happened
before.'

His voice rose to gale force. 'GODESON!'

Lord Beaverbrook has no use for bells for the purpose of calling
his manservants. They are expected to hear his voice in the remotest parts of the house. The butler heard. 'Yes, my lord?'

'D'ye know who that was?'

'Yes, my lord. It was Dr Bennett.'

'And who is Dr Bennett?'

'He's the A.R.P. warden for Leatherhead, my lord.'

'And did I invite him to dinner?'

'Yes, my lord. He rang up on Thursday and said he wanted to
talk to you about our black-out curtains not being good enough.'

'Wasn't that the day you came to me to say that Dr Benes, the
Prime Minister of Czecho-Slovakia, was on the telephone?'

'No, my lord. I said Dr Bennett was on the telephone.'

'I see. Thank you very much, Godeson.' (Exit the butler.)

'There y'a, boys,' grinned the master. 'I thought you were going
to meet Dr Benes and you met the A.R.P. warden, Dr Bennett. A
nice man. But no wonder the *Daily Express* campaigns against the
black-out!'

25 . . . Poole Harbour and All That

There are many contrasting ways of doing propaganda. One is to tell lies, and the British 'black' radio under R. H. Bruce Lockhart, Sefton Delmer, and Donald McLachlan undoubtedly invented a few good ones for the Nazis. When Leslie Hore-Belisha lost his job as War Minister, he set up a rival show consisting of editors and left-wing writers to discuss war-winning propaganda – I suppose on the off-chance of his regaining office. Another method was the Government's decision to let the facts speak for themselves in its handling of the Americans, droves of whom were invited to England to see our war effort and our bomb damage.

Lord Beaverbrook seemed to combine the duties of Minister of Hospitality with his other work, and as a result played host to many of the American newspaper proprietors and editors. They ranged, geographically, from Norman Chandler, the owner of the West Coast *Los Angeles Times*, a handsome man who could easily have played Cary Grant parts in next-door Hollywood, and John S. Knight, an equally handsome but tougher-looking character who owned the Middle West *Chicago Daily News*, to old London hands from New York like the dapper little giant Roy Howard of the *World Telegram*, and Colonel Joseph Patterson, the hard-drinking, lanky publisher of anti-British (peace-time) *New York Daily News*.

On the political side, there were Roosevelt's top men such as Averill Harriman, the pale, almost languid railroad millionaire with whom Beaverbrook eventually went to Russia on a mission to provide Stalin with airplanes and tanks; Robert Sherwood, author and playwright; and Harry Hopkins, F.D.R.'s painfully shy personal assistant. The Beaver introduced them all to us editors.

Said the Beaver one day: 'I've laid on a motor-car for you and Percy Cudlipp tomorrow morning, so that you can act as guides round the bomb damage for General Wesson.'

General Wesson, of the American Ordnance Department, had the power of disposal of millions of rifles that we badly needed under lease-lend, but he did not seem to be a friendly type at all. The reverse, in fact.

Nor did it appear that Cudlipp, the editor of the *Daily Herald*, and I were making much impression on him when we drove down the comparatively unmarked Strand and Fleet Street the following morning. Cities hide their wounds well. The outer shells of buildings remain intact, and by the time the blown-out window-frames have been boarded up and the rubble removed from the highway, the effects of bombing are not always impressive to look at.

Cudlipp and I showed General Wesson what we could. He was more impressed by the fact that St Paul's Cathedral was intact than by the direct hit on St Clement Danes Church, and he said so.

We just had to get those rifles – but how? We stopped outside the post-office in St Martins-le-Grand, which had been hit the previous night. 'Millions of pounds of damage here, General,' I said.

'Looks O.K. to me,' grunted the General.

'Let's see if we can get inside' – and inside we went to gaze on an indescribable confusion of wrecked switchboards, with every single telephone line in the entire City of London mutely minding its own business, as G.P.O. engineers scratched their heads and wondered how the mess would ever be unscrambled.

Perhaps General Wesson was impressed at last, for Britain got the rifles.

Life inside the *Express* building during the Blitz was a strange affair. Work went on as usual within our bricked-up windows, whatever fire and destruction might be raging outside, and dormitories had been built to house those either unable to get home or working on a fire-watch rota. The dormitory at the back of the front entrance hall of the building was for executives and senior staff; Lord Beaverbrook and members of his Ministry of Aircraft Production occasionally spent a night there. Strube also used it sometimes; he snored so loudly that we could hear him above the sound of the bombs and the gunfire. In desperation we tried strapping his chin up, but it was no good; he broke the strap and snored on as shatteringly as ever.

With so many of our people away in the Forces, we used the space left vacant by their departure for a second dormitory on the editorial floor itself. We were working on a staff of less than half our pre-war strength; the stony-hearted Minister of Labour, Ernest Bevin, had little use for civilians and ordered even our seventeen-stone crime reporter, Percy Hoskins, to be called up, along with Frank Owen, by now Editor of the *Evening Standard*; but not me, although we were all in our early thirties.

Hoskins did a month's square-bashing at Aldershot, which slimmed him by thirty pounds, before he was transferred to the Royal Army Pay Corps and stationed at Bournemouth. Somehow he managed to spend most of his week-ends in London and carried his campaign to outwit the Military Police so far that he kept his civilian clothes in a shop just outside Bournemouth West Station, which he used in preference to Bournemouth Central (alive with Military Police, he said) and had his hair cut at Trumper's in order to avoid the convict-cut administered by military barbers.

Hoskins caught a late train back to Bournemouth on Sunday nights. Arriving at four o'clock one chilly Monday morning, he had no sooner changed into his uniform than the sirens started up their wailing. There was a raid and bombs had already been dropped in the Poole district. Hoskins was the first man to arrive on the scene, and was commended in that week's Battery Orders, not only for coolness in face of enemy attack but for getting so smartly out of the bed he was never in!

A week or two later, Japanese dive bombers destroyed the U.S. Pacific Fleet at anchor in Pearl Harbour, and the fury of the American people was expressed in a spontaneous slogan that swept the world – 'REMEMBER PEARL HARBOUR'. When it reached

Hoskins in his Army Pay Corps billet he sent me a telegram:
'*Remember Poole Harbour, too.*'

My staff – in and out of uniform – were a bouncy, exuberant lot,
capable of making fun out of everything that happened. Some of
the 'fun' was macabre. Paul Holt came to me during the blitz with
an idea for a short story. 'No room for fiction,' I said.

'Listen before you decide,' said Paul; 'a milkman has rustled up
a bottle of sherry and some beer for a birthday party during the
blitz. Unfortunately, the night before the party the district is
heavily bombed and he has to spend the day cleaning up the damage.
When the guests arrive, one corner of the room is cordoned off by
a screen. But it's a wonderful party, and it's not until later someone
knocks the screen over – and there is a body.'

'This isn't fiction,' I protested. 'It's Grand Guignol.'

Holt continued: 'The dead man is the milkman's father, and the
milkman is my own milkman, and he told me this morning that he
had had to explain to his guests that Dad had been killed the
previous night but would have hated it if the party had been called
off on his account. As no one will believe this is the truth, I had
better write it as a short story.'

But I said 'No'. There was enough smell of death in the air in
those days.

When Russia was forced into the war, I remembered Holt's short
story and decided that a man with such a morbid sense of 'humour'
would make a fine Moscow correspondent, which he did – and that
is how editors often play their hunches.

Another odd character was Alan Wood, an Australian leader
writer who volunteered to be dropped with the paratroopers behind
the German lines at Arnhem in 1944. Wood's name went into the
hat with men from other newspapers, and he was one of the two
'lucky' ones, if you can use the term, to have the honour to represent
the entire Allied Press on the operation.

Wood was a rangy, difficult sour-puss, a man with a permanent
load of grievances, chief of which was that I did not pay him
enough. Even so, I did not expect to get a radio message from his
fox-hole, the last he was able to send, which said: '*How about a
rise now, Mister Christiansen.*'

When he got back I gave him a rise, a long holiday, and then a four-day week; but he never recovered from the ordeal of Arnhem and many years after the war he committed suicide. He had sent another message from that Arnhem foxhole: *'If ever you meet a man who was at Arnhem buy him a drink.'* I salute the memory of this brave, awkward man, who told no one at the *Express* office of his troubles but went his own lonely way.

War had also made a deep impression on another staff man but this time it was World War I. His service as an infantryman in Flanders was never far from the thoughts of William Taylor Knott, who became Chief Sub-editor of the *Daily Express* early in 1940, and at the slightest excuse he would reminisce and sing songs like:

> 'I don't want to be a soldier,
> I don't want to go to war.'

One night during the blitz he was hurrying back from the Press Club when he espied a German paratrooper descending right into the middle of Fleet Street.

He thought his chance had come at last to do something active in World War II, to be the first civilian to capture a paratrooper barehanded. He rushed towards the shape.

As he did so he saw it was too big to be a man; it seemed more like an enormous black pig. 'God!' said Knott. 'It's a land-mine!' and dived back into the office. There, stuttering out his story, he was received with derision, accused of lowering morale and of exceeding his proper intake at the Club. However, he persisted. Some of us went down to see.

It was a land-mine all right, hanging about eight feet from the roadway, its parachute caught fast in the telegraph wires that ran from Poppin's Court on one side of Fleet Street to the Old Bell Tavern on the other, about twenty yards from the entrance to the *Daily Express* building.

That night the police stopped our presses and those of the *Daily Telegraph* almost next door because the slightest vibration set up by any movement might have sent us all to Kingdom Come. The police advised us to evacuate the building, but nobody in the editorial department obeyed. We spent the night playing poker and holding a mock trial of Knotto for trying to arouse fear and despondency. I sentenced him to make his way to his flat in Cliffords Inn, about a quarter of a mile away, to bring back a bottle of Scotch. With the cunning of a 1914–18 veteran he eluded the police and brought back the Scotch, which saw us through till the 'All Clear' at 5 a.m.

At ten o'clock that morning the land-mine was lowered gently to earth; it was a dud. Imagine a dud stopping our presses – the only time in all the war that the *Daily Express* did not reach all of its readers.

Some reporters enjoyed the blitz, but Norman Smart hated it. He claimed to be a coward, even though he did not behave like one. 'I lay terrified on the pavement outside London Hospital,' he confessed when he came back from an East End bombing. He was therefore happy to be sent to Gibraltar as an accredited naval correspondent, and no doubt dreamed that he would see the war out in the sunshine, with only the Italian Navy to bother him. But, as Bill Knott was always reminding us, if your number is on a piece of ammo it will find you; Smart was twice torpedoed.

The second time was worse than the first, for Smart was in the *Ark Royal* (the famous aircraft carrier that Lord Haw-Haw 'sank' practically every week) when she went down in the disastrous but successful relief of Malta. He was hours in the water, and afterwards wrote a brilliant account of the great ship's death-throes.

His expenses for the trip were also brilliant. They included a calf-bound edition of the complete works of Shakespeare valued at £25 or so.

'What did you take those on board for?' I demanded.

'Well,' said Smart, 'I thought that as I was leaving Gibraltar for good I'd better take them with me.'

It seemed a strange piece of reasoning, but I gave reluctant consent to the item. Then I came across this:

One Rolls Razor – 30s 0d

'Out that comes,' I said triumphantly. 'That's sheer profiteering. You know I gave you that razor as a present.'

.   .   .   .   .

O. D. Gallagher also wrote a moving story, one of the war's greatest, when the *Prince of Wales* on which he was sailing was sunk. In fact, when James Cooper, another *Express* war correspondent, was sent to Cairo as Alan Moorehead's assistant, Moorehead wrote me: 'He's as keen as mustard to be sunk in a battleship so that he can write one of the war's great stories; I've got him accredited to the Navy in Alexandria.' Cooper's wish came true and he was duly sunk. But the Censors held his copy for three weeks in order to keep the Germans ignorant of the identity of the vessel. By that time Haw-Haw had named the ship so that all poor Cooper got for his ducking was the anonymity of the spike. His message never saw the light.

In my view the war correspondents of World War II were shabbily treated. Men like Alan Wood and Alan Moorehead of the *Express*, Colin Bednall and Alexander Clifford of the *Mail*, should have been knighted, instead of being fobbed off with O.B.E.s or M.B.E.s. Unlike Sir Philip Gibbs, Sir William Beach-Thomas and Sir Percival Phillips, those fine men of the 1914 war, the reporters of World War II were not confined to Headquarters with occasional trips to the Front. They were on Active Service throughout the war. They saw action for five years. They dropped by parachute where the battle was at its hottest. They were sunk at sea. They were unarmed throughout. Some were killed, including one of my men at the hands of the Japanese. They served their country as well as their newspapers.

For me the climax of the 'domestic' side of the war came when the staff of the newspaper held a dinner to celebrate my tenth year of editorship in November, 1943. It was a robust affair and the Dorchester Hotel did us proud despite war-time restrictions. Newsprint was found for a 'skit' two-page souvenir the same size as the *Daily Express* which Hannen Swaffer said outraged everything the *Express* stood for. I was confused with General Christensen, the Nazi Commander-in-Chief in the Netherlands; accused of bigamy in that I was married to both a woman and a newspaper; mocked in a Pocket Cartoon about my thousand-word daily bulletin. The caption read: 'He says that he wants stuff short and concise, like crisp little sparkling jewels.'

Celia Dale, then my secretary (she is now a very good novelist), wrote as my 'chief wardress': 'He has the instinct of genius, even in small things. He can tell to an instant when his guards are on the point of sitting down, and, by pressing the bell, can keep them suspended more or less permanently in a half-bent position. . . . His temper is equable, although he is given to outbursts of exuberance and energy. At these times he will shout for his guards by their Christian names rather than summon them by bell. He can also be seen pacing round the limits of his room, shirt-sleeved, hands tucked in trouser-top, his footsteps loud and commanding.'

This heels-in-the-ground walk was notorious. The William Hickey column of this souvenir edition said: '. . . he adopted rubber heels. The effect on the newspaper he contrives to control was magical and mysterious. Morale went to hell. Reporters, without the thunderous tread of their dear editor coming ever louder behind their right ears, even lost all pleasure in lying to [the Night News Editor] John Young. . . .'

To quote the entire 'cod' paper would probably present a better picture of the newspaper, its staff and its spirit, than I ever could – especially the leader column parody which quipped, 'In bad times we have said, "Be of good cheer." If a cloud has no silver lining this column has no use for it.'

We enjoyed pulling our own legs. For, as the erudite James Agate was never tired of reminding me, it was Ruskin who wrote: 'I am not afraid of the word "sensation", still less of the thing. It is not less sensation than we want but more.'

26 . . . D-Notices and A-Bombs

Editors are dogged in peace and in war by people who want to interfere with the prime reason for the existence of newspapers, which is to publish news. Before the war and after, I used to get many telephone calls which started 'I am a friend of Lord Beaverbrook's –' I knew what was coming. Would I please suppress a divorce case, or a police court report? Happily I was able to reply that as I had Lord Beaverbrook's consent to publish all news about his own family I could only suggest that they telephoned Lord Beaverbrook direct, in case my proprietor had suddenly become soft-hearted. If my advice were accepted, Lord Beaverbrook passed the buck smartly back to me and said he did not interfere with the editor.

But nobbling the Press is a subtle business. I have often fallen into the trap of receiving confidences which then make it impossible to publish and be damned. At the outbreak of war I was 'wooed' by General Dallas Brooks, now Governor of Victoria, Australia, who had been seconded from the Royal Marines to do secret work on psychological warfare. We met like conspirators in an elegant flat lent to the amiable General by Noël Coward. Thereafter I received daily, by uniformed despatch rider, 'guidance' on Britain's war effort. Not to the *Daily Express* office – that would have been too obvious. The 'guidance' came to my home. It came in two envelopes. The outer envelope was innocent enough; buff-coloured, and addressed to me; but the inner envelope was marked MOST

SECRET, and for several days I opened it with feverish anxiety. I
felt that I was really 'in' on the war effort. But what was inside the
most secret envelope could have been broadcast by the B.B.C. six
o'clock news without giving anything much away, and after a week
or two I got bored with the General's game of cops and robbers.

Obviously, I was being nobbled in some way or other by this
form of flattery. 'Old chap,' said Brooks, 'we want to keep you in
touch with our efforts to maintain morale on the Home Front and
your part in this is vital to us.' But Brooks had also something to
do with Military Intelligence and was soon asking me to allow my
staff to act for him. In other words, to spy.

I refused reluctantly. It was one thing to have parted with Sefton
Delmer, so that his fantastic knowledge of the Germans could be
at the disposal of our 'black' propaganda service. It was altogether
different to expose my war correspondents to the charge of being
spies, liable to be shot if captured. Brooks admitted that one of my
men had been a British agent even before the war, and pleaded that
he should be allowed to continue his double role. I dithered for a
while, but then decided to part company with the man. If he had
been captured, his role might have prejudiced the Germans against
any of my other men who might also have fallen into their hands.
General Brooks and I remained friendly but the supply of double-
sealed, most secret communications dried up.

In their place came daily shoals of D- (or Defence) Notices, sent
direct to the office. I reckon there must have been 5,000 D-Notices
before V-Day in 1945: don't do this; no mention of that. Censorship on newspapers throughout the war was voluntary, but the
Government left the editors in no doubt whatsoever that infringe-
ment of the D-Notices would be punished by either imprisonment
or suppression of the newspaper itself.

Just the same, I had no more than a reasonable working knowledge of the Notices. I read them on the day they arrived, had them
copied for departmental heads, stuffed them into a locked drawer
like pennies into a piggy bank, and forgot all about them. It was not
until August 1945 that I unlocked the drawer, and the sight was so
dustily appalling that I made a bonfire of the lot.

Bill Crumley, the Chief Office Censor, who knew the D-Notices
like good Scotsmen know their Bible, enabled me to sleep un-

troubled at nights. Crumley was a kindly, but sometimes bad-tempered man who seemed to snort his way through the war. When he was not snorting at his own staff of Censors – older members of the staff who were posted at the Ministry of Information to keep liaison – he was snorting at Admiral Thomson's censors. On the other hand, he distressed me by assuming that I had his own seemingly comprehensive knowledge of everything that was going on inside the War Cabinet. As a result, he talked to me in sentences which were so full of hidden meanings that they seemed to lack even verbs.

On the night of 12 May 1941 – the night that the Government stopped the newspapers from printing for many hours anything but the German version of Rudolf Hess's flight to Scotland – I thought that Crumley was going to have a stroke. Only wild Celtic incoherences issued from him as he gazed at the first edition of the *Express*, with its bald streamer headline based on the German radio announcement: HESS IS DEAD.

As far as I could gather, he was saying that the delay in getting out the British version of the news was giving Hitler time to disown and discredit Hess to the German people and that the War Cabinet were a lot of bloody fools (this frequently-used phrase in Crumley's Glaswegian always reminded me of the plonk of a mooring buoy cast overboard into the sea) not to come clean and quick. (He did not know at that time that Lord Beaverbrook was on his way to interrogate Hess, but in any case, a little thing like that would not have deterred Crumley.)

With yards of copy piling up at the Censor's office his exasperation was understandable. Our Glasgow office had interviewed David McLean, the ploughboy in whose garden Hess landed by parachute. I had got Guy Eden, the Political Correspondent, to do a column of 'think-piece' speculation on Hitler's dismay. All in all, there were six columns of matter that had not been stamped with the magic words 'PASSED FOR PUBLICATION'. But by midnight Crumley got it all through, and the Page One streamer was re-written for the 1 a.m. edition:

DEPUTY-FUEHRER GIVES HIMSELF UP

Crumley was still not happy. He dug and dug, and tried to goad me into exposing the muddle.

'Hess,' he said, 'landed in Scotland on 10 May. He trumpeted his real identity soon after and showed documents and photographs to the military authorities at Maryhill Barracks and Buchanan Castle (the Duke of Montrose's home that was converted into a military hospital during the war). Why did it take so long for the British Government to make a frank disclosure about his reasons for coming here?'

Crumley never forgot this incident. Years after the war I received a letter from him which ran:

Churchill got the blame for suppressing the Hess story. But I found out soon afterwards that it was not Churchill. I have just had my knowledge confirmed by Hector McNeil (an ex-*Daily Express* reporter who rose to be Minister of State in the Socialist post-war Administration) that it was Ernie Bevin.

Bevin was positive that the landing of Hess was some tremendous deep-laid trap. But who was there in this island at that time to be afraid of? The Fascist Fifth Column were all in one small internment camp, and the peace-at-any-price faction were an insignificant minority of the people.

Crumley continued with the view that the history of our times might have been different and our relations with Russia much better if Stalin had been informed promptly of the whole Hess story as soon as it was complete ... 'Stalin remained suspicious till he died'.

After the war I was permitted by his jailers to peep through the key-hole of Hess's cell during the Nuremberg trials – and nowadays as I recall that sad demented prisoner with the eyes of a death's head, it seems odd that the political alliances he thought possible in war should have become the realities of this so-called world of peace!

The ridiculous restrictions of the Censorship sometimes led to ingenious subterfuges on the part of newspapermen maddened by frustration and determined to get their stories through by hook or by crook. So far as I know, such scheming was not carried out by our own men; we all tried, no matter with how bad a grace, to carry out the spirit if not the letter of the Security law; but Ray Daniel of the *New York Times* cheated the censor in an ingenious manner in November 1939. Admiral Thomson tells the story in his book, *Blue Pencil Admiral.*[1]

... The cruiser *Belfast* had been damaged by a torpedo from a German submarine off the Firth of Forth. Publication of this important news was banned under censorship rules. Yet two days later I was horrified to hear that the *New York Times* had published the fact which it claimed to have received from London. There was, frankly, hell to pay!

The press of this country, who knew of the torpedoing almost as soon as it occurred, insisted that the news must have got out through Eire. I felt instinctively that they were wrong, but appearances were against me.

I had given instructions for copies of all telegrams which had left this country to be carefully scrutinised, but there was no sign of the news in any of the telegrams.

The security authorities were not satisfied with the examination made by my censors, and themselves carried out a further scrutiny in case a code had been used. But they were no more successful than the censors.

Some weeks later another correspondent of the same newspaper, who knew it had been done and which correspondent had done it, felt the matter weighing on his mind so much that he decided to come and explain the mystery to me, saying he hoped that if he gave the story away his colleague would not suffer unduly thereby.

The *New York Times* had always been most co-operative in its dealings with the censorship, and I used all the influence I possessed in recommending that the whole thing should be kept quiet. I am glad to say that no harm came to the correspondent in question and he stayed in Britain to do splendid work.

The way he tricked the censor's blue pencil was this. He sent a cable to a friend in New York saying: 'If you and James will get together we may get somewhere tonight. Remember it's the last word that counts.' James was the managing editor. And

1. REAR-ADMIRAL G. P. THOMSON: *Blue Pencil Admiral* Published by Sampson, Low.

during the evening he received seven telegrams, with consecutive numbers, but sent through two different cable companies.

The telegrams were:

> '*We are sending story about submarines.*'
> '*Please tell Harvard I want my son entered.*'
> '*As ordered, am setting forth.*'
> '*Government was not attacked.*'
> '*If you persist somebody's reputation may be damaged.*'
> '*Smith covers Dublin not Belfast.*'
> '*Untrue that any prisoners escaped.*'

Put together, the last words read: '*Submarine entered Forth, attacked, damaged Belfast, escaped. . . .*'

Despite Crumley's vast knowledge of the D-Notices, I nearly gave the enemy news of the Allied atom bomb research years before the first A-bomb was dropped on Hiroshima in 1945. Edmond Demaitre, a gay monocled Frenchman who represented us in Stockholm (his name appeared in the *Express* as E. D. Masterman because I liked my correspondents at least to appear to be British) cabled an item published in a Stockholm newspaper that Allied parachutists had raided a hydro-electric plant in Norway which was making heavy water.

As the Germans had equal access to news published in neutral papers, Crumley did not need to submit the item for the censor's approval, and it was used with a footnote explaining that, according to pre-war theories, the atom could be split 'by mixing heavy water and manium'. The significance of the news had not registered with me when Admiral Thomson invited me on the following day to visit him at his University of London headquarters.

'I've had a helluva rocket from Downing Street over this heavy water story,' said Thomson in his dry, crackling voice. 'There's to be a complete Stop on all references to atomic research from now on, and it is so important that I cannot even put a D-Notice out on the subject in case it should get into the wrong hands.'

This sounded ominous indeed; but as it did not pay to give in to Downing Street too quickly, I argued that it was fatuous to prevent the British Press from publishing items that the Germans could read in the Swedish newspapers. All I agreed to do was to consult Thomson personally if any further messages on the subject were cabled by Demaitre.

There was soon to be more news, about Allied scientist-paratroops being pursued in the mountains around Rjukan where they were operating a radio transmitter. I took the message to Thomson and suppressed it at his request. A little while later, Crumley hinted darkly that the German research at Rjukan (whatever it was they were researching neither of us knew) had taken the wrong turning.

I was not to know then the significance of this news: that the Allies would be the first with the atom bomb. But on 21 May 1945 I got Demaitre to Rjukan and published a 'Now it can be told' story which began:

> It can be revealed to-day that for five years British and German scientists fought their own war-within-a-war; a war for the atom bomb – with the most explosive force in the world – which, once perfected, would have given either side walk-over superiority.

It was a fantastic tale even as war stories go. Of raids that failed; of men living through the winter snows in conditions of incredible hardship; of the shooting of twenty-five British paratroopers, all wearing uniform, who were forced to surrender; of Norwegian patrols ultimately thwarting Germany's plan to remove twelve tons of heavy water, manufactured at a cost of £2,000 a lb., to Austria (where the A-bombs were to be made) by attaching a magnetic demolition charge to the ferry which was to transport the cargo across Lake Tinn. And of the heroism of the Norwegian chemistry professor, Major Lief Tronstad, who, just a month before the German surrender, was killed trying to prevent the Germans from sabotaging his vital hydro-electric plant.

The explosion of this news shook not only our rivals in Fleet Street that morning; it reverberated via Downing Street and the American Embassy in London as far as the White House in Washington. Once again I was invited to call on Admiral Thomson. I do not suppose he knew any more than I did that soon President Truman would authorise the dropping of an A-bomb to finish off the Japanese; but this time he did warn me that atom bomb research was going on in America, by arrangement between the two countries, and that it was vital that the tens of thousands of people engaged in the work should not know the real nature of what they were doing.

The world was not allowed to know anything about the atom bomb – until one was dropped on Hiroshima. The first war correspondent to arrive in Hiroshima, thirty days after the bomb had been dropped, was a *Daily Express* man – Peter Burchett, an Australian who had been through the Pacific War for me from the word go.

Peter was so overwhelmed by what he saw that he muddled things, and I sat down at a sub-editor's desk to re-write and re-organise his despatch. But these extracted sentences needed none of my re-writing skill:

> In Hiroshima, thirty days after the first atomic bomb destroyed the city and shook the world, people are still dying, mysteriously and horribly – people who were uninjured in the cataclysm – from an unknown something which I can only describe as the atomic plague. . . .
>
> I have seen the most terrible and frightening desolation in four years of war that makes a blitzed Pacific Island look like an Eden. . . .
>
> I found people who, when the bomb fell, suffered absolutely no injuries but now are dying from the uncanny after-effects . . . the counted dead number 53,000 . . . hundreds upon hundreds were so badly burned in the terrific heat generated by the bomb that it was not even possible to tell whether they were men or women, old or young. . . .
>
> The doctors gave their patients Vitamin A injections. The results were horrible. The flesh started rotting away from the hole caused by the injection of the needle. . . .

Lord Beaverbrook telephoned me about this appalling news. He postulated a question that will never be satisfactorily answered: Should the bomb ever have been dropped? What would have been the effect on the pursuit of peace if it had been undertaken without the Great Deterrent ever having been demonstrated? The world may come to realise that it was the worst decision of the war, said Lord Beaverbrook.

27 . . . Churchill and the Beaver

Through all the years I have only once seen Lord Beaverbrook beaten by his emotions. He seemed as hard as a piece of Land's End rock when he telephoned for news of Max, his fighter pilot son, during the Battle of Britain. The passing of friends and companions he has outlived must move him and leave him lonely – he wrote to me recently: 'There are so many friends departing that I feel like a lone tree in a clear-felled forest' – yet during the war he shrugged off his feelings with what appeared to be almost callous haste.

'What else is going on?' he asked over and over again when I told him bad tidings. The only clue to his feelings on these occasions was that he was not interested in the answer to his question and it did not spark off the usual flood of ideas and opinions which the smallest crumb of gossip usually aroused. It is one of the dangers of newspaper life that men become insensitive to the poignancy of events, and Beaverbrook's surface reactions were harder and harsher even than mine.

But one day in 1954 when we were sitting in the sunshine on the patio of his London penthouse, Churchill's name cropped up. We were discussing the bad habit of smoking to excess. 'A man who smokes too much,' said the Beaver, 'destroys his capacity for coherent, clear thought.'

'Oh, come, sir,' I said, conscious of the fact that I was a forty-a-day cigarette man, 'what about Churchill?'

'It will surprise you to know,' said the Beaver, 'that Churchill does not smoke anything like the number of cigars that you would imagine. They're nearly always out. He will stick one in his mouth when the photographers are around, but he won't be smoking it.'

'But I am a heavy smoker,' I said.

'Are you, now? I didn't know that. If I had known I would not have raised the subject,' he replied, for he was always sensitive about criticising either my journalism or my personal habits. At that point a note handed to him by a servant took him from the patio; when he returned five minutes later, the tough hard-hitting demagogue had clearly received news that had shaken him.

When he managed to speak, there were tears in his eyes which he did not bother to hide. His old friend Churchill had had another stroke and this time it looked as though it would be fatal. I was to prepare the paper for the end straight away and leave space on the front page for a document which he himself would provide. It would be in the form of correspondence that had passed between the two old warriors; but precisely what I was never to learn, because the Beaver's grief made him for once unable to continue. And, of course, Churchill survived.

Lord Beaverbrook is constantly attacked for feuding against people like the Mountbattens, Nehru, the side of the Astor family which owns *The Observer*, and not a few politicians, but his unshakable affection and loyalty to men like Winston Churchill and much smaller fry, is, like virtue, not interesting news and goes largely unrecorded.

'Max is a foul-weather friend' was Churchill's own summing up of Beaverbrook, that weather-vane of a man. Yet the two were never on the same side of the fence; they were not even born alike, for Churchill was an English aristocrat with a silver spoon in his mouth, while the only spoon that ever played a part in Beaverbrook's early life was the porridge ladle at a New Brunswick manse. Beaverbrook's dislike of the English aristocracy and their dislike of him are well known, but Churchill is the exception. When Churchill is ill, Beaverbrook fusses like a grandmother. When Churchill is attacked, the resources of Beaverbrook's newspapers are flung into the battle – witness the abuse heaped on Lord Alan-brooke's head for his criticisms of Churchill's conduct of the war. In sickness and in health, Beaverbrook is Churchill's jealous, fanatical ally.

Politically they are poles apart. Churchill has never believed in the Beaverbrook conception of the British Empire, and has never lifted a finger to help. Churchill was utterly opposed to the pre-war appeasement policy in Europe while Beaverbrook lined himself up behind Neville Chamberlain. During the war Beaverbrook stumped the country demanding a Second Front in Western Europe, while Churchill's strategy was to strike at the Germans through 'the soft underbelly', as he called it. Yet it was axiomatic that if you wished to remain a Beaverbrook editor you did not permit any word of criticism of Churchill to creep into the leading articles. The historical researcher will find much criticism of Churchill's colleagues in his war-time and peace-time Administrations, but none of Churchill.

This, of course, led to some odd situations. In 1940, when Frank Owen was mercilessly criticising the conduct of the war in the *Evening Standard*, Ernest Bevin, the Minister of Labour, got his own back, so it was said, by personally ordering Owen to be called up; not Churchill, not Beaverbrook, could do anything about it. And in the post-war years, when the only aspect of Churchill's government that the *Daily Express* in its frustration against post-war controls could find to praise was its house-building record, Harold Macmillan, the responsible Minister, whom I met at a big fight at the White City, dryly drawled: 'You praise me only because I worked for Max during the war' (Macmillan was Parliamentary Secretary to Beaverbrook's Ministry of Supply in 1942).

The warmth of Beaverbrook's affection glowed vividly when Churchill was returned to power in the 1951 election. 'He won the war as Prime Minister elected by the will of Parliament,' he said, 'but the British people rejected him at the polls in 1945. Now he has submitted himself to their will once more and has been *elected* by them as their Prime Minister. It is his proudest moment in sixty years of public life. It is the one coveted honour that has hitherto evaded him.'

The bond between the two men is more than just a long-standing

friendship – as I write they are the last surviving Cabinet Ministers
of the 1914 War; it seems to me to be based on a respect for each
other's abilities, and a love of each other's idiosyncrasies, weak-
nesses, loyalties and, above all, zest for living. They belong to a
different generation from to-day's: a generation in which no quarter
was asked, and none given. Churchill and Beaverbrook provide a
wonderful example of the harmony and vitality that can be
generated by two personalities who are poles apart from each
other.

The first time I met Winston Churchill was on the eve of the
Italian rape of Albania, as I have related. The second time was at
Lord Beaverbrook's country home just before the war, when he
defended his conduct as Home Secretary in 1910 in calling out the
military to deal with the mining riots at Tonypandy. The third
occasion was in 1941, when he kept a promise to attend a patriotic
festival which the *Express* had organised at the Albert Hall. The
festival coincided with the day the battleships *Prince of Wales* and
Repulse had been sunk by Japanese dive-bombers off Singapore,
and the Prime Minister's eyelids were pink with fatigue. 'It is a
grievous blow and it is hard to foresee the consequences of such a
disaster,' he spluttered, picking his words slowly. He was like a man
who had been felled by a blow from behind. Yet with all those
troubles on his shoulders, he watched the pageant as he had
promised to do, and consoled himself with a whisky and soda with
me before returning to Downing Street.

Even at that time Churchill was an omnivorous reader of newspapers. A motor-cycle despatch rider called at the *Express* office
every night to collect the first edition for him as soon as it came off
the presses. Often Beaverbrook used to call me long after midnight
to say that the P.M. had been on the telephone complaining about
some tiny item in the early edition.

After the war when Churchill was once again in the political
wilderness, we sent the paper to his house in Kensington by our
own despatch riders. 'Came to the door himself, he did. Had a
dressing-gown and a cigar on,' I used to hear from our riders, who
looked like Outer Space men in their crash helmets and black water-
proof over-garments.

If Churchill had been speaking in the House or in his constituency at this time I invariably heard from him.

'What was your reaction to my speech?' he would ask. He was a powerful psychologist. He knew that if I had put the speech in an obscure place and given it only an inch or two, I would most likely improve its position in the paper, or give it extra length, if he discussed with me the importance of a particular passage. Far into the night I would then listen to his views on the issues of peace and war. He was gloomy indeed in the year of the Berlin air-lift, and could see no hope of averting a new war.

Lord Beaverbrook sensed the many occasions when Churchill got more space in the paper than his speeches justified. 'Did Winston call you last night?' he would inquire. 'Be careful now. Be careful of his propaganda!'

Thanks to Lord Beaverbrook's efforts, Churchill occasionally saw the editors at 10 Downing Street during the war. There was a technique for arranging these affairs. The Beaver got in touch with one of his favourite editors with a message that if we pressed hard enough the P.M. would see us, and even suggested the subjects on which he thought the P.M. ought to give us his views. The plot invariably worked and about twenty of us from the national Press and the chief provincial newspapers would troop in to the Cabinet Room, a pleasant rectangular room overlooking the garden of No. 10, (although in war-time the view was blocked up). An enormous mahogany table laid out with blotting paper, pens, paper and ink for at least three dozen people dominated the room and at this table we doodled and waited.

A flurry of secretaries, Parliamentary and private, preceded the arrival of the master, who always struck me as being in a thoroughly bad humour on these occasions. Sitting in a bigger padded chair than the rest of us, a cigar firmly clenched between his lips, he looked smaller than any of us but twice as ferocious.

The cigar would be laid aside and in his sibilant stammer he would demand, 'Pray, gentlemen, what can I say to you?' His eyes would wander among us, settling nowhere, until he spoke again. 'Who is your leader? Will he speak?' The tones were positively menacing and I always felt grateful that Lord Beaverbrook never used me to lead the band. Even Percy Cudlipp, the Editor of the Socialist *Daily Herald*, whose leader-column struggle with Ernest

Bevin, the Minister of Labour, represented an act of courage, quailed at such times. His naturally high and musical Welsh tenor voice would rise to alto as he squeaked 'I am', and ask, perhaps, if we could have the facts on the U-boat campaign.

My proprietor eventually gave up arranging these conferences, and our later meetings were with less fearsome Ministers. Herbert Morrison, the Home Secretary, was the easiest to get on with. He liked talking about everything; he liked to 'schoolmaster' Fleet Street; he loved to tell us we were being 'naughty' (his favourite word) but that he would defend our freedom to be so; he even seemed to like to make our flesh creep, as when he gave us advance warning of the strain Londoners would have to bear when the pilotless planes known as V1s started to pour in.

A. V. Alexander, the First Lord, had the best news sense, and even got some of us to watch the death-throes of the German pocket-battleship *Bismarck* from the maps in his study at the Admiralty – a doubly thrilling and momentous occasion for me, since my wife was in a convoy returning from the U.S.A. at that time.

Clement Attlee was the most difficult, because his dry deceptive manner made him seem indifferent and tongue-tied.

Ernest Bevin was the most garrulous and often went off at odd tangents, ranging from personal hostilities to trade union diatribes. 'Never negotiate with bus drivers after they've finished their working day,' I heard him once say. 'Their nerves are frayed and you'll never make a settlement with them. And that's why you'll always have trouble in the pits – it ain't natural for men to work underground and you've got to remember that when you talk wages to a miner.' These were just the sort of remarks, perhaps preceded by 'Look 'ere, Christiansen', or 'Look 'ere, Cudlipp', which he would drop into a conference about far removed subjects, such as the call-up.

I liked Ernie Bevin and he liked me. How happy I would have been if I could have effected a reconciliation between him and Lord Beaverbrook after their war-time feuding. But they were both Old Testament-tough and yielded nothing. One of the last messages I got from Lord Beaverbrook before my editorship ended, said 'I see in the *Daily Express* an article about Ernest Bevin's broken heart. I am bound to tell you that Ernie has broken more hearts than the many occasions he claims that his own was broken.'

I was deeply moved by my last meeting with Churchill at a public dinner in his honour at the Drapers' Hall in the City of London. The occasion was the presentation, in December 1955, of the Williamsburg Award, the first of its kind, in recognition of Churchill's services on behalf of Anglo-American relations.

Colonial Williamsburg is the township near Washington, D.C., which has been rebuilt and restored to its appearance before the American Civil War; and the Award to Churchill was to take the shape of a bell used to sound the alert during that war – all of which was explained in a lavish brochure handed to each guest as he sat down to the traditional City turtle-soup dinner. The occasion was so exhilarating that I put my impressions into writing to Lord Beaverbrook, who was away in the Bahamas. In reply Lord Beaverbrook sent this message on his Soundscriber: 'What an admirable description of Churchill. I hope you will save it up for one day after Churchill goes to Heaven – which I hope is not for many, many years – so that you can pay your tribute in the obituary notices.'

But maybe it will not displease Churchill in his lifetime if I quote from my letter:

Winston entered the dining-hall after we had assembled, looking tired and old and limping badly. But the power and the grandeur of the man were never better demonstrated than in his speech. It was not what he said, but the way that he said it. In fact – to the disappointment of some of the Americans who had expected another Fulton Declaration – he said little of significance. But having accepted the Town Crier's Bell from Winthrop Rockefeller, his peroration was practically immortal. Taking the bell in his right hand, Churchill stammered:

'I shall ring it – *pause* – and I can assure you I shall – *longer pause* – whenever – *pause* – I feel – *pause* – there is duty to be done.'

With that he caused the bell to utter an enormous clang, and resumed his seat.

The cheering for this gesture went on and on. Until then we had all been muttering how ill the poor old boy looked. But now we were carried away by his sense of occasion, and by pride in his sense of duty, and by the impish way in which he had pledged it.

Ten minutes later the dinner was over, and leading the way with the American Ambassador and Rockefeller following, Churchill left the dining-hall ringing his Town Crier's bell with all the delight of a child on Christmas Day. The audience rose to him and he beamed with gratification and good humour. In fact, he was so delighted with the occasion that he brushed off Soames, his son-in-law, and Brendan Bracken, who had rushed to escort him to his car, and stayed in the ante-room for at least half an hour, receiving a host of people. Some of those present cheated by sitting in the next chair to his and having their photographs taken. He did not seem to mind the popping of the flashlights or the impertinence of using him as a vehicle for basking in reflected glory.

A little while later he decided to go. He became old again and his bad leg did not seem to belong to him. But he spurned helping hands and got down the staircase on his own. Then when he was being helped on with his overcoat he had to part with his bell. Rockefeller put it into a rich red leather case. But Churchill scowled and said: 'Give me my bell.'

He then transferred his top hat to his left hand, seized the bell once more, and tottered off in the direction of the main door in Throgmorton Street. Outside there were about a score of people – where do they come from in the City of London at this time of night? – and two enormous City policemen. They all started to clap, including the policemen. So Churchill gave them a ring on his bell once more.

He was eased into his car. Sitting there in his top hat and almost covered by a rug, he looked like a pink-faced teddy bear. We all started to clap yet again – and as the car took away the Man of the Century we could hear above the noise we were making that he was still ringing his bell.

The day after the dinner Churchill was in his seat at the House of

Commons. William Barkley telephoned from the Gallery to tell me that Churchill bounced about like a schoolboy when he saw for the first time the beard that had grown massively on the face of Sydney Silverman, the Socialist M.P. Soon he had the House rocking with laughter by pulling at an imaginary beard on his own face and clapping his hands with delight as he pointed at Silverman.

What a man! Bells, beards, bombs – they all come the same to him, making his smallest action an anecdote, and his great decisions world history.

28 . . . Monty Asks for Help

Like editors, warriors do not conform to any pattern, but it would be difficult to find two more violently contrasted men in any profession than Lord Dowding, the winner of the Battle of Britain in 1940, and Lord Montgomery, the man who accepted the surrender of the German Armies at Lüneburg Heath in 1945. I first met Dowding, a sad-faced, broken man, a few months after his decisive contribution to victory had been made. I first met Montgomery when he was poised for final victory after sweeping through France, Belgium and Holland, a cocky, self-confident figure, sure of his destiny.

Through the years I have retained the liking and respect I originally felt for both men, and it grieves me that this is apparently not the case with the *Express* newspaper group. Never an anniversary, personal or battlewise, goes by but the public is reminded of Dowding's war-time contribution; but Monty's lines of communication must have got fouled up somewhere, for when his reminiscences were published, they got such a roasting from the Beaverbrook critics that I was relieved not to be in charge. Having been educated journalistically not to criticise Lloyd George, the World War I winner, and Churchill, the World War II winner, I had set up Monty as one of my own Untouchables and was shocked by the violence of such critics as Milton Shulman, a shrewd Canadian who served in Intelligence during the war, and who is now Lord Beaverbrook's favourite hatchet-man on both military affairs and the London theatre.

Monty, of course, asks for it. He is in the Beaverbrook-Churchill mould of not expecting any quarter, or giving it. Dowding, on the other hand, seemed to me to need a lot more of the 'ask-for-it' temperament, and was in consequence trampled on and dismissed from his job when the only fitting reward should have been promotion to the highest office in his Service.

I met Air-Chief-Marshal Lord Dowding, Sir Hugh as he then was, soon after Sir Charles Portal, newly appointed to the rank of Chief of Air Staff, had retired him in November 1940. At Lord Beaverbrook's request I called on this grey and gloomy figure at his equally grey and gloomy house in Wimbledon. The Beaver was infuriated by the cavalier treatment of the man who had been, with himself, the architect of the Battle of Britain victories, the man who, by refusing to commit the forces under his command to the battle to save France, had enabled Britain to survive the German invasion threat. 'Portal's a trade unionist,' Beaverbrook rasped darkly to me. 'You go and meet Dowding – it'll do you both good.'

Whether Dowding was at that time a spiritualist, or whether his 'communications' with the dead Battle of Britain pilots gave him the deeply-convinced views that he came to hold, I do not know; but like many soldiers who have seen death at close range, he was a deeply religious man.

His voice and his manner were gentle. He gave no sign that he felt any sense of grievance at his treatment and our conversation was desultory until we got round to the miracle of Dunkirk. I called it a 'miracle' and Dowding asked if I believed in miracles. Not having bothered my head with much thought on this subject since I went to Sunday School as a boy, I gave a confused, non-committal answer.

'Will you please accept a copy of this book which I have had privately printed?' asked the Air-Marshal. He handed me a brown-paper-backed volume marked in thick black letters: CONFIDENTIAL. It was called *Twelve Legions of Angels*.

'I wanted to publish this,' said Dowding gently, 'but the Censorship will not give me permission. They say it contains information and views on the war that will give comfort to the enemy.[1] So I

1. The book was in fact published after the war, by Jarrolds.

decided to have a few copies printed for private circulation. You
must not quote from it, of course, or write about it in any way.'

I took *Twelve Legions of Angels* away with me and could find
little in it that the Germans could have made much of, unless an
exposure of Dowding's own alleged shortcomings when he was a
junior officer in the R.A.F. would have made propaganda for Lord
Haw-Haw. But I did find in it a deeply moving clue to the way in
which Dowding's religious convictions were taking him.

> The 'Miracle of Dunkirk' was wrought, I believe, in answer to
> the great volume of anguished prayer which went up at that time.
> . . . Neither the heroism of the sailors and longshoremen who
> manned the heterogeneous fleet of rescuing vessels, nor the
> courage and fortitude of the soldiers themselves, nor the utmost
> efforts of the fighters would have availed if the restless Straits
> had not been stilled into an unnatural calm for days on end.
>
> Well, there it is. Many believe firmly, and will continue to do
> so, that the success of the evacuation from Dunkirk was due to
> Divine intervention. . . . It is only by personal experience that
> complete conviction is possible.
>
> I had this personal experience in the 'Battle of Britain' . . . I
> say with absolute conviction that, but for God's intervention,
> the Battle of Britain would have been lost.
>
> Now, therefore, as I lay down my sword, I take up my pen,
> and testify.

As I read these words, I recalled that even I had contributed to
the great volume of prayer that had gone up at the time. I had gone
to church to pray for the few people at Dunkirk known to me
personally, men like Dennis Clarke, son of the famous Northcliffe
editor Tom Clarke, who had left my staff to join the Artillery; men
like Alfred Hollox, my chauffeur, of the Royal Army Service Corps.
They all came through safely, and when I listened to their contrasting stories – of Lord Gort's swagger cane, of shaving in champagne, of the Navy's cocoa and bully-beef sandwiches, of their own
cheerful, easy-going, modest resourcefulness – I had the itch and
the urge to give up being an editor and join up. I took my medical
and passed A1, but the management applied for my exemption

and the call-up never came. When I saw soldiers peeling spuds in seaside billets near my home, I reflected that war had its unromantic side, and that as I could not have brought myself to service in the Army as a Public Relations officer, maybe editing a newspaper as a civilian was a form of war service – and this is not intended to be in any way critical the vital job which people like Frank Owen, Hugh Cudlipp and Sean Fielding did in producing newspapers for the Services during the war.

In November 1944 I was invited to meet Monty at his head-quarters, in company with other editors.

Monty briefed us himself before we set off for the front line and found ourselves the first civilians to set foot 1,700 yards into Germany. 'There are seven rules for winning a battle,' he prismed and pruned in a high-pitched voice that in some words revealed the hint of a lisp or a cleft. 'Seven rules. The first rule is to win.' Half an hour of this fascinating stuff – overwhelming superiority, how to cross a river – was followed by: 'Would anybody like to ask a question?'

'What happens if the seven rules cannot be applied in one given circumstance?' I asked.

'Then I would not start the battle at all.'

A determined, confident, triumphant – and twinkling – smirk followed this remark.

I felt that here was an 'original', a man to be tolerated with all his faults because of his uniqueness. Yet he was the spitten image of someone less unique whom I knew well. Who could it be? Yes, yes, my own father! The slight body, the long nose, the penetrating eyes, the funny little moustache. But I reflected that my beloved parent approached life with the humility of Dowding, not the arrogance of Montgomery; the uncanny resemblance ended at the tips of their noses.

'Anybody like an autograph?' asked Monty, breaking my reverie. Christopher Chancellor of Reuters took one – for his daughter; why do people *always* get autographs for their children and never themselves! We were then escorted to the famous Mont-gomery caravan.

'Tell me,' I said, 'why is that picture of Rommel still in your

Q

caravan? You finished him off in North Africa. Surely you ought to have one of Rundstedt in its place?'

'Is there a picture of Rundstedt? I don't think there is one,' said Monty.

'I'll send you one directly I get back to London,' I answered.

'That,' said the Field-Marshal, 'would be splendid.' He told me that he had benefited much by studying Rommel far, far into the night before he fought him at Alamein. By looking at a man, or even by looking at his photograph, you could get inside his mind and calculate his reactions to most situations.

So to Monty went two pictures of Rundstedt. His acknowledgement dated 3 January 1945 says:

My dear Christiansen,

Thank you very much indeed for the two framed pictures of Runstedt [*Monty's spelling*]. I am delighted to have them and they are now hanging in the room where we had our talk; but they will go in the caravan when I take to the road again.

We have been having a pretty good 'party' here, away to my right. But I very soon became involved in it myself. All is well now. I hope we may meet again in due course.

Note the arrogance that so infuriated the Americans: 'I soon became involved in it myself. All is well now.' This referred to Rundstedt's desperate last throw at Avranches in December 1944, which caught Bradley's Army on the hop. Monty was given command over a section of the American Second Army when things looked bad, did what was required of him and then got on with the next task. 'All is well now.'[1]

On 29 March 1945, when the Allied Armies were sweeping into Germany, Monty wrote to me again from 21 Army Group H.Q.:

My dear Christiansen,

You once sent me a photo of Runstedt. By our operations we have unseated him.

1. When Monty revisited Normandy he listened to a discussion on Bradley's reminiscences and is reported to have chipped in casually, 'Of course I could have finished the war in 1944, if I'd been allowed to. No possible doubt whatever. But perhaps it's as well I wasn't; we'd have had a war with America.'

My opponents whose pictures are in my caravan have all departed, i.e. Rommel and Runstedt. The surest way to dispose of them seems to be to hang their portraits in my caravan! Could you by any chance send me a framed picture of Kesselring? Obviously he must go the same way!

I re-read that sentence: 'by *our* operations we have unseated him', and ordered the picture of Kesselring to be despatched. Then on 8 May, the day after the armistice had been declared, I received an acknowledgement of a cable I had sent to Monty – again in his own handwriting:

My dear Christiansen,

Thank you very much for your cable; it was kind of you to have sent it.

It has been a long journey and I am glad it is now over.

You may like to have the enclosed and perhaps you would publish it in your paper.

'The enclosed' was the Order of the Day bringing the European War to an end. It was printed in advance for the month of May and Monty had inscribed the figure 7, the day of the month, in red ink on the Order.

I have seen Monty only twice since the war ended. Once was at the Versailles Headquarters of S.H.A.P.E. when Eisenhower was the boss, and Monty, his Number 2, was still lecturing on the art of warfare although in somewhat disillusioned terms.

The second time was at the *Daily Express* Boat Show in 1958, which Monty opened. On this occasion we lunched together and I reminded him of our correspondence.

'Oh dear,' he said, 'those letters of mine. They'll get me into trouble one day!' After that he published his reminiscences, appeared on television, drew the Old Age Pension and got himself involved in controversy with Eisenhower. Plenty of trouble without any need for my intervention!

Those were the two warriors. The one, Dowding, sincerely believing in the supernatural and devoutly pleading his cause; the other, Montgomery, believing in himself and his own immortality. The only thing they had in common was – a belief in God.

29 . . . V1 – V2 – Victory

Before V-Day came on 8 May 1945, London had a final ordeal: the rocket bombs V1 and V2 which the Germans launched from sites on the French coast towards which the Allied forces were battling – oh so slowly it seemed to Londoners! – through the Normandy fields in the summer and autumn of 1944.

My desk, from which I could have viewed the bombed ruins of St Bride's Church if the windows had not been bricked up, was littered with 'Most Secret' memoranda sent to me by *Daily Express* men. It seemed that, far from the worst being over, it was yet to come.

Consider first this from Guy Eden, Political Correspondent, dated 28 June 1944:

> The Cabinet is greatly concerned about the 'morale' effect of the flying bomb, and there was a three-hours meeting last night.
>
> One result is that Leathers is going to provide a lot more trains, and that women and children are to be encouraged to leave for safer places. There will be no public announcement about it because this would give comfort to the enemy.
>
> They are considering making a frank announcement about the bombs, and telling about all the damage and lives lost. It is thought that this would be the best way to prevent a further

232

deterioration in morale. There has been quite a considerable fall in morale and some fall in production.

Counter measures we are taking to-day (as a result of last night's Cabinet) are: a double patrol of fighters over the Channel, 2,000 balloons in the 'Barrier' in Sussex and Kent, and a concentration of nearly all the A.A. guns we have in the same area.

28,000 special workmen are being drafted into London to help with repair and rescue work. Billetting will be used on a large scale, and big houses are to be taken over in various parts of London. Special buses will run for those who are moved.

Yesterday the Germans sent about 95 flying bombs over, of which about 90 made landfall. 48 got to London between 8 a.m. and 6 p.m.

Death roll up to the present, not including to-day's, is: about 1,100 dead, 4,600 odd badly wounded, a very large number less seriously wounded.

It is expected that the number sent over will be stepped up quite a lot, and that an attempt will be made to send them *over* the barrage balloons. This is technically possible.

From 1,500 to 1,600 a month are being made in various parts of Europe, and there was a considerable store of the bombs to start with.

The Government thinks that we must set our teeth and 'take it'. For this reason non-combatants and non-workers – women and children – are to be encouraged to go away from the danger zone, on the argument that men will bear it better if they know their dependents are safely out of the way. There is no real hope of stopping the attack until we take that part of France, or the Germans abandon it.

Next, on 5 July, Basil Cardew, at that time Air Correspondent, reported to me talks he had with General Sir Frederick Pile, C-in-C of Anti-Aircraft Command, while Cardew was visiting A.A. batteries in Kent. The official term for the V1s was 'diver':

Pile said he was rung up in the early hours of 15 June by a Captain Hamilton who said 'The diver has begun. Seven are reported to be approaching our coast'. Pile was at his flat and in the early morning he said Hamilton's words scarcely rang a

bell in his mind. A little later Hamilton rang again and reported
that 40 divers were crossing the coast.

At that time all the anti-aircraft guns had been deployed elsewhere and they had to be moved back to London at all speed.
Some had to be brought from as far as Cornwall. The military
authorities refused at first to allow the guns to pass through the
embarkation lines of the troops but within twenty-four hours all
the guns had been brought back and put into position.

The afternoon following the first launchings of the diver the
Prime Minister called a conference to consider the diver threat
and said he was going to hold a conference every day. He shook
Pile by ordering that the balloon barrage be increased to 2,000
balloons so that the guns protecting London had to be moved
forward and south of the balloon barrage in Kent. In the two
nights of operation over London the guns shot down an average
of 40 per cent of divers that got through.

It took three to four days to reconnoitre new heavy gun sites
in a belt twenty miles wide running across Tonbridge. When
they were temporarily installed they found that the radar did not
work very well and so the guns had to be moved again.

There are two types of guns, mobile and static. The mobile
guns were moved first but these are not so efficient as the static
guns as their predictors take longer to triangulate the divers. The
mobile with their equipment need forty-five seconds to get a fix
compared with eight to ten seconds for the static type of equipment.

So it has been decided to move the static guns and instal them
in the place of the mobile guns. They are usually bedded on
concrete and an anti-aircraft Command scientist was asked to
devise a new temporary emplacement for the static guns. He
managed to produce one in twenty-four hours, consisting of railway sleepers and lines. These are being installed at the rate of
120 a week and it will take three weeks from yesterday to get all
the static guns working at maximum efficiency.

In addition a new American radar equipment is being installed
which allows the guns to fire with greater accuracy and speed.

Pile says that he will have 1,500 guns against the divers, 500
heavies and the rest light.

Three weeks before the first diver was launched the Command was told that its threat no longer existed and they were unable to get anything done. They believed that the diver would fly high and at no great speed and these ideas were confounded.

The diver has been known to fly as high as 9,600 feet, but it usually crosses Southern England at 2,400 feet. Its speed varied tremendously and it has been clocked up to 410 miles an hour. Its average speed appears to be 330 miles an hour. It is launched from platforms of concrete about half the size of a tennis court. The older types of platforms have probably been scrapped and there are no underground workings in the modern types. It is unlikely that air attacks on them will knock them out entirely. If the belt were to be captured it would be simple for the Germans to draw back and lay out the concrete strips for further attacks by adding range to the divers. It is probable that the Germans were never seriously worried about the air attacks on the emplacements despite the R.A.F. claim that 90 platforms were destroyed.

Pile estimates that the Germans have plenty of divers and that about ten can be made for the cost in equipment and man hours of one fighter. The small huts seen near the launching platforms were probably assembly sheds and the enemy has probably ceased to bother about them, assembling the divers under trees and other camouflaged spots.

Up to yesterday, fighters had destroyed 450 divers and Anti-Aircraft Command about 290. Twenty per cent of those destroyed by ground gunners were blown up in the air.

The diver is far more difficult to shoot down than an aircraft. Frequently, half a dozen hits are registered on it without effect. It has to be shot up in the tail or on its war-head. Pile's research men are now seeking to produce a shell that will penetrate the diver before exploding. He emphasises that an enormous amount of re-equipment and recasting of ideas have been involved in tackling the first battle of the robot. 'We are pioneers in combating a weapon that may become supreme in the next twenty or thirty years of warfare,' he said. 'I do not claim that the battle has been nearly won. But we are making progress every day.'

When the diver was first picked up on radar it was found to

make only a small spot in the cathode tube and by flying low and fast its detection was a problem.

The best results achieved so far in one day were nearly 70 per cent of the divers destroyed. The ground gunners are unlikely ever to shoot down more than 45 per cent of the divers when their best equipment is in action.

Finally Morley Richards gave information about the V2 on 1 November:

V2 weighs 16 tons and has a war-head of 1,900 lb. of high explosives. It generates more HP than Battersea Power Station, travelling faster than sound at a height of from 60 to 70 miles.

It can be launched from any solid concrete platform and is not at all dependent on an elaborate structure. Its range makes it perfectly possible for it to be despatched from any part of western Germany.

It is radio controlled in its ascent from the launching platform but when it turns towards its objective its direction can only be determined by a pre-arranged adjustment of two fins at the tail.

Up to the beginning of this week about 100 had landed on British soil. Many have exploded in mid-air or fallen into the sea. V2 takes as many man-hours to make as a fighter aircraft, which limits the numbers the enemy possesses.

Only now have the enemy been getting the range of London. This is in large measure due to the paucity of the espionage service.

Our scientists say that its evolution is a great scientific achievement and there is at present no answer at all to it.

The Americans have been developing a similar rocket but with a cathode-ray tube in the war-head which they believe will give it complete accuracy. They plan to use it against the Japanese, both against the navy and land objectives.

The Germans have had a prototype in existence for several months of an atomic bomb of which we have some details. It is thought that three or four of them, if accurately placed, might level London. The enemy might be able to get it in production and working in another six months.

It looked like a tough winter – and it was. Herbert Morrison had warned the editors at a conference in his room at the Home Office, but when the first V1s came they were a shock. How glad we were in Fleet Street when the engines were still roaring as they swept overhead to cut out a mile or two farther on! And how helpless is a newspaper in such circumstances to do more than print as much comforting, gay news to keep up morale, despite the Dismal Jimmies who declare that this is head-in-the-sand journalism. I went to the gun sites at the invitation of General Pile and watched the battle. I wrote as optimistically as I dare – but by now it was the armies that mattered, not the newspapers. And so, within months, came the climax.

Hitler's game was up. The Allied armies swept into Germany and the armistice was signed at Lüneburg Heath. Lord Beaverbrook played me up on V-E Day. I had set the leader column over the whole of Page Two and he felt he should have been consulted about this first-time-ever lay-out trick. That was Armistice Day for me – a row with my proprietor because I had not told him what was happening in his own paper!

The Japanese war was still going on, of course, but Fleet Street seemed more excited by the prospect of the resumption of the circulation war between the newspapers. Beaverbrook entered the European peace almost as depressed as he had entered the war in 1939, for Lord Camrose had told him, 'The *Daily Mail* is going to do you in.'

These two cronies met constantly. Neither liked the other's paper, each tried to daunt the other by gloomy prognostication. However, it was not the *Mail* that beat the *Express* but the *Mirror*.

There is a belief in Fleet Street that sex is the surest recipe for circulation, and I won't deny it, for after all the *Daily Mirror* at this time swept ahead of the *Express*. But I rate a good political campaign very highly too, and so did Bartholomew of the *Mirror* and his successor, Hugh Cudlipp. Politics make a newspaper controversial, and controversy gets a newspaper talked about. If a newspaper is widely discussed, then it acquires new readers. These may frequently tear the newspaper into shreds and vow never, never to permit it to darken the door mat. But they come and they come again.

The Strange Case of Professor Harold Laski helped to arouse interest in the *Daily Express* in 1945. By the time Harmless Harold had been through the wringer, my poor paper had been accused of conducting the dirtiest election campaign of all time, Winston Churchill had been accused by Nye Bevan of making a speech which was 'Churchill at Beaverbrook's worst', and it was difficult to know whether the Tories or the Socialists hated the *Express* most.

But everything we printed was based on the news and I have never had any regrets or apologies to make when I have printed the news. In this election I even gave prominence, although not as much as some of the other papers, to the Beaver's jolly *gaffe* in a speech at Chatham that Brendan Bracken, First Lord in the post-war Caretaker Government, was the best First Lord since Nelson!

I believe that Harold Laski, who as chairman of the Labour Party ought to have known better, was baited by my old friend and skilled heckler, Jimmy Wentworth Day, into blurting out at a meeting in the market-place at Newark that 'if we cannot have them (Socialist policies) by fair means, we shall use violence to obtain them. . . .' But use these words he did; when Laski sued us for libel his Counsel failed to discredit Day's veracity.

In the context of those exciting election days the phrase in question was sensational, for Laski had been embarrassing his own leader, Clement Attlee, by laying down the conditions under which Attlee was to accompany Churchill to the Potsdam peace conference with President Truman and Stalin.

This strange story 'broke' calmly enough in an anonymous communication drawing my attention to a letter containing the controversial Laski quote signed by Councillor H. C. C. Carlton, published in the *Nottingham Guardian* two days previously. My secretary had instructions never to bother me with anonymous letters – all sorts of queer and sometimes obscene communications are addressed to the editor of a national newspaper – but on this occasion she had the news sense to see that this could be a policy matter.

I was having lunch with Lord Beaverbrook and the veteran R. D. Blumenfeld that day, and passed the news on to them. The effect of my bombshell was disappointing. Neither was inclined to believe that even Harold Laski would have been so foolish as to say such a thing, and I was advised to check and cross-check. But later in the afternoon the Beaver's sensory perceptions were hard at work and when I told him that the reporter's notebook had been inspected, we decided to let go with a tremendous splash:

LASKI UNLEASHES ANOTHER GENERAL ELECTION BROADSIDE
SOCIALISM 'EVEN IF IT MEANS VIOLENCE'

The first editions of the Fleet Street newspapers are eagerly scanned in the offices of their competitors. 'What's the enemy got?' is the cry of harassed Night Editors, as messengers run to their desks night after night with papers 'stolen' from the rival vans as they are driven to the railway depots.

The *Daily Herald* office that night might have been hit by a block-buster. Percy Cudlipp, the Editor, who was dining in the Café Royal, leaped to the telephone and gave instructions for two cars to be used on one assignment (an unheard-of extravagance in those days of petrol coupons) – one to fetch him back to his office in Long Acre and the other to get Laski there, too, from a London election meeting. The two cars returned almost simultaneously.

'Did you, or did you not, say these things?' demanded Cudlipp.

'I did not,' said Laski.

'In that case,' said Cudlipp, 'you must immediately issue a statement. You must say that you are prepared to take action for libel against anybody who reports you as having uttered this threat. We will print it in the final edition of the *Herald*, and it will appear to-morrow morning side by side with the accusation in the *Daily Express*.'

Leaving Laski to prepare a statement, Cudlipp warned his Night Editor about the front-page change for the final edition, had telephone calls put through to Nottingham, hoping to find some refutation of the story which the *Express* was publishing, and telephoned Fleet Street to arrange that copies of every edition of the *Express* should be rushed to him as soon as they could be obtained.

Meantime Laski was composing, in tiny, beautiful handwriting, not the short, sharp, statement conveying his intention to issue a writ for libel that Cudlipp wanted, but an essay on the rights of free speech. So, as with most editors when the emergency is great, Cudlipp drafted the statement himself in order to catch the edition.

I confess that at the *Express* office we were carried away by the excitement of the story. I thought we had an election weapon as good as the Zinovieff letter that the *Daily Mail* produced to unseat Ramsay MacDonald in the 'twenties.

Even the Socialists on the staff – and there were plenty – carried out their briefs with professional gusto. It was all-in wrestling, hand-to-hand fighting, commando stuff, and we were, we thought, very good at it. One night when I got back from supper, Brian Chapman, a Socialist who as Assistant Managing Editor was in charge of production that evening, handed me a headline which he had held out of the first edition for my consideration. 'This is pretty thick,' he said, 'but you can use it if you like.' The headline was:

THE NATIONAL SOCIALISTS

This, of course, was the official title of the German Nazi Party and the smearing implications of the headline were obvious. I gleefully gave the O.K. to print the headline. Weeks later Chapman resigned and joined the *Daily Herald* – but perhaps Socialist politics got him down, for he resigned from that too.

As for Lord Beaverbrook, he had the time of his life. Throughout the campaign he was in high good humour, even to the point of elevating me to the peerage: when he telephoned he invariably started with the words 'Is that Lord Christiansen?'

He quipped, 'Lord Blackout got a barony from Baldwin for supporting him over the Abdication. I can't see why the Tories should refuse you one for supporting them over Professor Laski!' (Lord Blackout was one of Lord Beaverbrook's pet names for Lord Southwood, the chairman of the *Daily Herald*.)

One night around midnight I took the first editions up to Arlington House where Lord Beaverbrook had come to live (almost alongside me) after Stornoway House was bombed. Brendan Bracken, the *éminence grise* of the Tory Party, was there; his power in bestowing patronage was great. As we left Lord Beaverbrook's apartment together at 2.30 a.m., Brendan put his arm around my shoulder and said, 'Chris, the Conservative Party will never forget what you have done for us.'

Nor did they! The Conservatives were beaten in the election by a whacking, thumping 295 seats.

The nation had to wait for the result of the election owing to the delay in counting the Forces' overseas vote. It was a period of strain and anxiety, but we were optimistic, and when Lord Beaverbrook conducted a poll of his senior executives, only Herbert Gunn, the Managing Editor, thought the Tories were out. It is a fault of newspapermen that they can be carried away by their own efforts and believe they are having the same effect on the readers as on themselves.

Brendan Bracken, who was more detached, knew that he had been beaten at North Paddington and was gloomy about the prospects generally. Yet from my Socialist contacts I heard that only Aneurin Bevan and Percy Cudlipp were really optimistic about the chances of their own Party.

When the Tory defeat had been recorded and the paper put to bed, I went home exhausted. From his penthouse Lord Beaverbrook telephoned me for the latest news. As I told him, I broke down. I was suffering from acute shock. I had believed that the *Daily Express* campaign would swing the election for the Conservatives. I had thought that my Press propaganda machine was invincible. I had been proved wrong and hurt where it hurt most – in my professional pride. It was not pity for Winston Churchill and his party that made me weep, but pity for myself at having failed to justify my faith in the power of the *Express*.

Hugh Cudlipp of the *Mirror* gave me a character analysis some time later. 'All you care about is the production of newspapers as such,' he said. ' "Causes" do not interest you or move you one scrap. When I get time to write another book I'll do a chapter about you – the production perfectionist without a political conviction!'

A political conviction has to be very deep before a newspaperman is prepared to sacrifice his bread and butter for it. Hugh Cudlipp, after years of Socialist spouting, quarrelled with the *Mirror* and walked across to the Beaverbrook outfit where he spent a couple of profitable years. Percy Cudlipp, his elder brother, left the editorship of the Conservative *Evening Standard* for the chair of the *Daily Herald* and wrote the best leading articles that paper has ever had. After the 1960 General Election the *Daily Mirror* under Hugh Cudlipp's vigorous leadership decided that it was too political and changed its slogan from 'Publish and be Damned' to 'Be damned with politics!'

Politics had never moved me deeply prior to the 1945 election, and I vowed thereafter that they would not do so again.

30 . . . A Babel of People

Daniel Longwell, one of the Henry Luce pioneers who retired from the American magazine *Life* in 1955, once asked me to explain how I 'kept that erratic bunch of "Beachcombers" and Lancasters to the daily output'. Actually Longwell had selected two of the most disciplined as well as the most talented *Express* contributors in trying to imply that I must have been either a madman or a genius to put up with the behaviour of some of my people.

'Beachcomber' – John Cameron Andrieu Bingham Michael Morton, C.B.E., – since 1924 the writer of *By The Way* in the *Daily Express*, said to me after the war that he was sick of rationing and controls and wished to live in Dublin, from whence he would no doubt write a better column. I answered: 'You can write your column in Timbuctoo for all I care, Johnny.'

Morton was delighted. He reminded me of a previous occasion when he had been *sent* to Dublin to cover, as a devout Roman Catholic, the proceedings of the Eucharistic Congress. 'For three days,' he said, 'I poured my soul out trying to capture the colour and majesty of the Congress without getting a line in the paper. And then on the fourth day I got a telegram from Beverley Baxter which read, '*Watch out for the incongruous as well as the beautiful*'.

'Well,' I said, 'you've been on the *Express* long enough to know that's the way we like it,' and packed him off to live in Dublin with

243

the promise that, as long as his column was never late, I would never ask him to waste his time writing for the spike on religious subjects.

The column was never late, but the Dublin experiment did not last long. 'I missed England. I missed the country lanes,' Johnny confessed a year later when he came to live and work at Tenterden in Kent. His output is prodigious and includes studies of the French Revolution, a biography of Hilaire Belloc, short stories about French bistro life, as well as his daily column, which he writes in handwriting in approximately two hours as his first task of the day. In my day he came to Fleet Street not more than once a month and on these occasions does his work in the Managing Editor's room for lack of anywhere else: in a well run office there should be no room for a desk that is used only once a month.

As to Osbert Lancaster, whose first Pocket Cartoons earned him a couple of guineas each in 1936 (each stroke of his pen earns him that much nowadays) the difficulty is to keep him *out* of the office. He arrives in Fleet Street soon after lunch, invariably from the St James's Club, that annex of the Foreign Office, and spends the afternoon gathering ideas by gossiping with the erudite George Malcolm Thomson, the women's page staff and Harold Keeble, the Associate Editor whose office is as crowded as the foyer of the Savoy Hotel, yet still contrives to be the source of most of the big projections that adorn the *Express*. The Pocket Cartoon – a *fait accompli* that I had either to accept or have no cartoon for the next day's front page – was ready by 6 p.m., after which he smoked an esoteric Turkish cigarette and occasionally had a dry Martini in, of all places, the four-ale bar of the Kings & Keys before setting off to his home at Henley-on-Thames.

Untemperamental as a clothes-horse, Osbert Lancaster was insistent only on his right to go for a holiday to Greece or some such place whenever he wished, and for as many as five or maybe six weeks, which is a long time for a contributor to be absent from his newspaper. I put up with managerial criticisms about Lancaster's holidays in the belief that if he had left the *Express* front page altogether it would have been a permanent, not a temporary, calamity. In cut-throat Fleet Street good men can command their own price from rival concerns. It speaks well for their loyalty that cash is rarely responsible for changes in the higher echelons.

'Offer him another two thousand a year,' said the Beaver many years ago, about one of the *Daily Mail* stars.

'But I don't want him at any price,' I said innocently.

'I know that. Nor will he come to you. But the *Mail* will have to give him a big increase just the same, and that will teach them not to try to poach *your* staff.'

Keeping his bunch of prima donnas happy is the most wearing, exhausting and exciting part of an editor's business; and the more successful his newspaper, the more prima donnas he will gather round him.

'I protest with all the force at my command,' wrote René Mac-Coll, in an airmail letter from the American Middle West, 'against the alteration of the word "rabbit" into "bunny" in my copy. I am used to the stupidity of sub-editors, but this is so intolerable that I am in despair.'

As MacColl is one of the Crown Jewels – he came to the *Express* in 1945 in preference to rejoining the *Daily Telegraph* – I swallowed hard and held an inquest; the poor sub-editor explained that Mac-Coll had used the word 'rabbit' three times already in that particular sentence and that 'bunny' seemed to him to be a warm, human alternative when 'rabbit' appeared for the fourth time.

MacColl had cooled off by the time he got back to London, and over a prodigious lunch in Soho he told me that he was not going to stay with the *Express* unless he got more work to do. This was something new, a hitherto unheard-of complaint. 'I like to see my by-line in the paper,' said MacColl. 'I'm vain. I don't want three weeks of doing nothing between assignments.' MacColl has itchy feet; he must keep moving. (Some of his best off-centre work is done in airplanes; he once bought a copy of Bram Stoker's blood-sucking *Dracula* to read in an airplane and reviewed it as though it had been published that day.) Yet give him an assignment three thousand miles away and he will immediately ask to be transferred to something more exciting that is breaking elsewhere. Sometimes I gave in, as when during Princess Margaret's tour of the West Indies in 1955 he pleaded by cable, *For pity's sake recall me, I cannot stand these dreadful women sob-sisters another minute.*

René (his father was a Scottish painter and his mother was

R

French) took some handling, just the same. Washington was the only place he did not want to come home from, but as his wife hated it so much that she refused to live there, he did a stint as Paris correspondent before the title 'Roving Reporter' was invented for him. As Roving Reporter, he lives in Sussex and travels 25,000 miles a year. I affirm that when I was his editor every mile gave me pleasure. The MacColls of journalism are worth all the headaches they engender, for the newspaper throbs with their vitality.

My methods of editing, or if you put it another way, my sense of public relations, did not always succeed.

I kept more good men than I lost, but I could not retain those fine writers, Alan Moorehead and James Cameron, because they revolted against the Beaverbrook political policies. Moorehead, an Australian, joined the *Express* as a linage 'stringer' at the time of the Spanish Civil War. He became the greatest of the war correspondents quite fortuitously; he happened to be Rome correspondent when hostilities began in 1939, and it was quicker to move him on to Cairo when we needed reinforcements in the Middle East. It was not then apparent that his literary skill even existed – it developed as he described the Rommel campaigns. My part in his career was to put up his salary so fast that by the time he was reporting the German surrender at Lüneburg Heath he was in a higher pay bracket than Field-Marshal Montgomery himself. But I lost him just the same.

As to James Cameron, on the day of his resignation he wrote a letter 'exposing' the methods of the Beaverbrook Press, which had been lambasting John Strachey, the Socialist Minister of War, and *The Times* gleefully published the letter. But I loved Cameron, a dark-mooded Scot, and mourned his departure. Maybe he too felt deeply, for when I left Beaverbrook in 1959 he wrote in the *News Chronicle*: 'Fleet Street without Chris is going to be pretty odd, like the Crazy Gang without . . . no, what I meant was, like Shakespeare without Olivier. For a quarter of a century Chris not only ran the *Express*, but in most senses WAS the *Express*, or as nearly as anybody could be who was not Max Aitken . . . I worked for Chris for ten years. Mostly it was like working for a benzedrine factory. If he didn't teach me all he knew, he taught me plenty of things I hadn't known existed. He was the only one of his kind.'

Each newspaperman and woman who is any good is a new problem to an editor. I wrote an article once about my staff, recounting that in the Fleet Street headquarters alone I employed 58 provincials, 35 Londoners, 8 Scots, 7 Welsh, 3 Irish, 3 Australians (the best newspapermen of the overseas crowd), 3 Canadians, 1 South African, 1 New Zealander, and 1 Channel Islander. Of those, 59 were Church of England, 8 Roman Catholic, 7 Presbyterian, 4 Methodist, 3 Baptist, 2 Congregationalist, 1 Quaker, 1 Jewish, 14 agnostic, 12 in genuine doubt and 5 with no religion. 'I had no other ambition', I wrote, 'than to be a journalist, and with this team I seek to be nothing else.'

But this Babel of people has no idea, or at any rate seems not to care about the cumulative load their separate problems create. If in the course of one day William Barkley threatens to go on strike because the Night Editor has spiked his best work, Trevor Evans spits Welsh blood because he is being made to seem a fool by 'crazy re-writing', Duncan Webb has been arrested for posing as a police officer, a young executive has been found unconscious in his hotel, Anne Edwards doesn't want to write a page on Monday mornings any more, the Night Editor has piled his car up so badly that he won't be out of hospital for a month, four reporters are demanding pay increases, the Political Correspondent is fed up with his job because he wants to be an executive, Lord Beaverbrook thinks the new William Hickey is no good, or for that matter the old dramatic critic – then, bless them, things are apt to get on top of one.

Here is Giles, the great Giles, in eruption on the telephone. He is the apple of Lord Beaverbrook's eye since the proprietor spotted him drawing for *Reynolds*, the Co-op Sunday paper, and persuaded John Gordon to sign him up for the *Sunday Express* at eighteen guineas a week. 'What's the matter with you, Carl? Want to come up to London to discuss things? All right, but don't be late – I'm busy.'

Giles is not late, but by the time I am ready to take him to lunch he has disappeared. He has gone to Poppin's to buy drinks for Anne Edwards, Eve Perrick and Drusilla Beyfus. When I catch up with him he is in high good humour; the girls make a great fuss of him and he is snorting incoherently to express his pleasure.

I look at this curious wisp of a man with affectionate curiosity. Unlike Osbert Lancaster, a product of the Slade School, Carl Giles has never had an art lesson in his life. He lives on a farm outside Ipswich where he has built his own studio, brick by brick, plank by plank. Hobbies: making furniture, building caravans, selling cattle, riding point-to-point, welding, knocking down walls, rebuilding them, making aquariums, drinking, playing the piano (jazz or classical), home movies, entertaining G.I.s based in East Anglia, boating, fast cars, dogs. All these things he does with as much gusto as he draws his cartoons – and he loves cartooning so much that he once drew 137 separate characters in just one of them.

My arrival in Poppin's does not dampen anyone's spirits, and I have the utmost difficulty in getting him to leave the place. The girls go reluctantly, and other customers buttonhole Giles and buy him 'just a small one for the road'. 'Now you see why I hate London,' he grins into his glass.

Amid all this good fellowship I inquire why he had wanted to see me so urgently and angrily. He says mildly that some ass had sliced half an inch of sky off the top of a cartoon. A temperamental explosion always follows this kind of desecration. Giles believes – and rightly – that if he wants a cartoon 8 inches in depth, then $7\frac{1}{2}$ inches will not do.

It is 4.30 by the time I sort this out and get back to my desk. There is a queue, controlled by Doreen Chaundy, my last secretary, waiting for the O.K. on this, for consultations on that. Will I telephone Lord Beaverbrook who has been 'on' five times since half past two? Will I see the Foreign Editor before I do anything else? Don't forget you promised to call the Home Secretary at halfpast three. All right, all right, Miss Chaundy – keep everybody out till I see what Beaverbrook wants. 'You were calling me, sir?' 'Yes, I was, but I can't remember what it was now. Good-bye to you.' Get the Home Office, Miss Chaundy. The inter-com buzzes while I am holding on: Lord Beaverbrook is on the other line, so I hang up on the Home Office and take the proprietor's call. 'I hear Giles is in London. Send him along to see me.'

Where's that fellow Giles? He's disappeared again. The pubs are closed, so try the Press Club. Not there! Comb London till he is found. Watch the Ipswich-bound trains at Liverpool Street. But

Giles is in fact in the photo-engraving department arguing with the Overseer about the making of line-blocks. He reappears in my room like a genie-out-of-a-bottle and I am so happy he is found again that I forgive all the chaos he has caused for the sake of half an inch of 'breathing space' at the top of a cartoon.

Two days later, a souvenir to commemorate this day is delivered. It is a full-size cartoon for my private collection, and it shows me sitting at my desk, my brow furrowed, my aspect grim. Around the door a tiny, shrinking, nervous figure which does not reach up to the door-knob gazes at me apprehensively. This is Giles as he sees himself and he is saying: *Tell me, Mr Christiansen, why are you not always cheerful?*

Marie Stopes, the birth-control pioneer whose books have sold by the hundred-thousand, shared with Winston Churchill a dislike of the Giles caricatures of the human race.

In 1949 she wrote cancelling her order for the paper 'so long as you poison it with Giles's productions. . . . . They denigrate humanity and are very seldom funny, and their injurious work is corrosive.'

I sent Miss Stopes a mollifying letter and published hers in the *Express*.

Next day, I received a letter from Giles, accompanied by a drawing of a father and his eleven children (one of them in his side pocket). Giles's letter read:

Very well, Marie, if you're not going to take the *Express* any more because of my cartoons, I'm not going to read any of your little books.

On the whole, women journalists are less temperamental than men although this may merely seem so because they are heavily outnumbered by men despite the amount of space they occupy in to-day's popular newspapers. My women had an irritating habit of taking a long time to answer a summons, due to nose-powdering, eye-shading and lip-sticking that went on first in the powder room. As a result they always seemed marvels of composure and beauty when they eventually appeared; but rumour came back that a summons from me struck apprehension into their bosoms.

'I hate him,' said Eve Perrick when I had criticised what she

thought to be her best work. But black-haired Mrs Perrick, who
joined the *Express* as a secretary after a career that included a spell
as a saleswoman in Fenwicks of Bond Street, was unhappy and went
to the *Daily Mail* after I left the *Express*.

A kind of chain reaction followed Mrs Perrick's departure, for
the elegant Anne Scott-James switched from the *Daily Mail* group
to the *Express*, and the icy-brained but wholly feminine Anne
Edwards switched from the *Express* to the *Sunday Dispatch*. As
each Anne is as good as the other, neither group could be said to
have gained anything from the swop, but the ladies did so well with
lush new contracts that a special investigator for *Time* magazine
published a report that Miss Edwards was getting £7,500 a year
plus the use of a pale blue chauffeur-driven limousine. She was
doing pretty well when she was under contract to the *Express*, but
not as well as that!

When all this was in negotiation, I had ceased to be the Editor
of the *Express*, but volunteered to try to keep Miss Edwards in the
Beaverbrook orbit. We lunched at the Ecu de France in Jermyn
Street and I suggested we should drink pink champagne. 'Let's,'
said Anne. 'I've never had it before. I thought only Lady Docker
could afford to drink pink champagne.' But even after we had
finished the bottle and eaten the first salmon of the season she was
still determined to leave the Beaverbrook group – which is one
reason why she can be described as icy-brained.

Between 1933 and 1957, my years in the Editor's chair, the *Daily
Express* employed twenty-three William Hickeys. Tom Driberg,
the original Hickey, set such a standard that it was a heartbreaking
job trying to find a successor for him after we had parted company
– we quarrelled over his use in a war-time political speech of a red-
hot scoop about the future of Sir Andrew Duncan, Minister of
Supply, that I had held out of the paper for further checking.

The record holder for speed in and out of the Hickey job was
Derek Tangye, husband of Jean Nichol, famous publicity girl at
the Savoy Hotel who gives me the credit for starting her career.

I came in specially on a hot Sunday afternoon to superintend
the birth pangs of Tangye's first William Hickey column and I was
confident that, with Jean's news contacts at the Savoy and Derek's

experience as a gossip writer on other Fleet Street journals, all my troubles in this direction were over. But as I read Tangye's first column, my stomach turned over. I sent for Tangye and asked him to do a complete re-write.

There was a light sweat on Derek's balding brow as I spoke, and I could sense that he was in a panic. 'It's no good, Chris,' he groaned. 'I'll never be any good as Hickey. I'd better quit now.' And I could do nothing to reassure him. He had joined the staff that day at 3 p.m.; it was only three hours later that he left my room and never came back.

When next I saw Jean and Derek Tangye, in 1947, I was recuperating in Cornwall from a breakdown in my health. They had bought a farm and were growing flowers and early vegetables and occasionally entertaining old friends like A. P. Herbert in order not to become vegetables themselves. No breakdowns in health for them. 'Come and stay with us any time,' said Jean. 'You gave me my chance in Fleet Street and you gave Derek his urge to get out of it, so we owe this lovely new life all to you!'

There were only two good William Hickeys out of the twenty-three. One was Simon Wardell (son of Brigadier Michael Wardell, once a Beaverbrook Managing Director and now a newspaper proprietor in Canada) who had the knack – and doing a passable imitation of Driberg's stylish prose was a knack – but after a while he got bored and went to live in the West Indies.

The other – and twenty-third – William Hickey was a big discovery. Donald Edgar joined the *Express* from the rival Tanfield's column in the *Daily Mail*, in the year of the Queen's coronation. But Edgar, a handsome man with a Sherlock Holmes profile, who had spent the entire war as a prisoner of the Germans, had almost as disastrous a start as Derek Tangye. Nothing went right for him at first and I was resigned to the fact that I had made another monumental error of judgement when, in marking the list for special writers to cover various aspects of the Coronation, I found I had one ticket too many. 'Put that fellow Edgar in the tent; nothing much is likely to happen there,' I said. 'The tent' was the annex to the Abbey in which V.I.P.s were allowed to wait from 6 a.m. onwards. No other newspaper bothered very much with it, but

Edgar wrote three columns of brilliant detail about the fidgets of
the mighty, about the hip-flasks that were secretly swigged for
breakfast, about the painting and the powdering and the impatient
posturings that went on as the hours dragged by. From that day on
Edgar found his confidence and conducted a new kind of William
Hickey column based on his own personality and not on the ghost
of Tom Driberg.

Edgar could make a column out of the pleasure he got from
eating half a dozen oysters in a Margate fish bar while the Labour
Party was in conference a few doors away. When he was hard up
for a subject he would make up a dream-sequence of startling
imagery. He could make the buildings in his beloved King's Road,
Chelsea, talk to him. But one day Lord Beaverbrook thought that
Edgar was stringing it out and that the Hickey column should con-
sist of short sharp paragraphs about important, glamorous people
in the news. Edgar and the *Daily Express* parted; and now I understand at least six people do a composite William Hickey column.

I guess that by now there must have been a round three dozen
William Hickeys since Tom Driberg's day.

Tom Driberg, who now writes a political column in *Reynolds
News* that cannot compare with his *Daily Express* work, came back
into my life in 1956, when he published a biography of Lord
Beaverbrook.[1] The Beaver is fascinated by Left Wingers and when
Driberg asked him for facilities to study private files in order to
write the book, it was roses all the way for him, including a four-
figure advance fee. The shrewd E. J. Robertson was against it and
so was I. I went so far as to resist a suggestion that Driberg should
return to the staff to make a trip to Red China, because I feared
that my old friend was by now more of a propagandist than a
reporter.

For a time it looked as though the combined judgement of
Robertson and myself was wrong. The first twenty-five thousand
words of the book about the Beaver's early life were couched in
warm, affectionate and scintillating terms; but then Driberg's
personal observations of the Beaver began to obtrude. Out to

---

1. DRIBERG: *Beaverbrook. A Study in Power and Frustration*. Published
by Weidenfeld & Nicolson.

Nassau went the rest of the manuscript for Lord Beaverbrook's perusal. Out to Nassau also went Tom Driberg as the Beaver's guest. And back from Nassau came Driberg very hurriedly when the nature of the book became apparent. Driberg had not only put interpretations on many aspects of Beaverbrook's public life that were outrageous, but had made offensive references to his private life.

I was not concerned in the negotiations that dragged on for almost a year before the book was eventually published. The task was nearly a whole-time one and occupied Robertson and Lord Beaverbrook's son Max for months. But eventually a version was agreed on, even though this seemed hostile enough in all conscience. 'Driberg is a funny chap,' said Kingsley Martin, Editor of the *New Statesman*, to me at the time. 'He honestly believes that he can bite the hand that feeds him and be thanked for it.'

As for the Beaver, after preparing some articles which gave Driberg 'what for', he decided to kill the lot and instead asked me to publish extracts from the book in the *Daily Express*. The articles had been a defence and explanation of Beaverbrook and were therefore alien to his technique, which is attack, always attack. That is the Beaverbrook way when he is mauled, and the Driberg serialisation was used for this purpose. Thus one instalment carried an extract from the book telling how Lord Beaverbrook once authorised a free gift of £1,000 to a member of the *Express* staff, who had asked for a loan to be repaid out of salary. The book had not revealed that Driberg was the man concerned, but a footnote to the extract did so.

I became the centre of controversy over this incident. Old friends with Left Wing views accused me of being a cad to expose Driberg. But I had no bad conscience. If a man is given access to another man's private papers and accepts a large sum of money to do a job which turns out to be something of a mud bath, then that man deserves all he gets.

When I suggested to Lord Beaverbrook that Driberg should be invited to the Fleet Street farewell dinner in my honour, we all three met again. But it was possibly only out of compliment to me that the Beaver buried the hatchet for that one night.

It is in the various pubs of Fleet Street that many of its citizens
can often be found, and many of its strains and stresses are ironed
out. Every newspaper in Fleet Street has its favourite pub, where
its staff gathers to plot and plan with all the venom and subtlety of
the revolutionaries. Interlopers from other offices are smartly
frozen out if they dare cross the threshold of a rival's pub; it is an
unwritten law of the Street that this is not done.

But there is one tavern which is in effect neutral ground; El
Vino, the wine bodega, which is crowded every day with Fleet
Street's 'intelligentsia' despite the fact that it is ruled with iron
discipline by Frank Bower, a florid vintner who is not afraid to
quarrel with his customers.

Lord Beaverbrook dislikes the place. He says it is a time-wasting
haunt of gossip and intrigue. He is reputed to have snarled at one
of his executives 'You won't find Alfred Hinds in El Vino', when
the *Express* had taken a beating from the *Mail* over news of that
celebrated jail-breaker. But if you want to patch up a quarrel, the
back room of El Vino is the place, away from the crowd in your
own office pub, away from the stink of ink.

It is here that I often came after a set-to with one of my unruly
ones.

'I can manage one of you on my staff,' I exploded to a star writer.
'But you'd have to put me in a strait-jacket if there were two of
you.'

The temperamental fellow ran his fingers through his hair and
snorted down his handsome nose. We were in my office and both
near breaking-point.

'Sometimes,' I shouted, in a rare burst of invective, 'sometimes
you wear your heart next to your heart, sometimes you wear it on
your sleeve, and sometimes you wear it on your backside. But
wherever you wear your heart it shows. Now get the hell out of
here!'

Five minutes later, I got a telephone call. 'Come to El Vino and
have a drink and let's forget it,' said the victim of my wrath. 'I'm
sorry I'm such a nuisance to you.'

Not all editors drink in the pubs with their staffs; in fact except
for the *Mirror* group's Hugh Cudlipp, I was probably the only one

in my time. There are good arguments against a boss hob-nobbing regularly with his staff, but I never found it detracted in the least from my authority. Perhaps my enjoyment of being around with my staff, outside as well as inside the office, answers to some extent Daniel Longwell's query as to how I kept 'that erratic bunch . . . to the daily output'.

31 . . . Palace and Press

E. J. Robertson, by now chairman of the *Express* organisation, came through on the inter-com one day in 1947. 'Chris,' he said, 'can you be free at five o'clock to-night to come with John Gordon and me to the Mountbattens for a drink?'

Five o'clock was news conference time, but I handed over the chair to Percy Elland, my second-in-command, and went with Robertson and Gordon to the house in Wilton Crescent which the Mountbattens had rented after the war.

We were shown into a comfortable, traditionally old-fashioned sitting-room on the first floor. Lord Mountbatten, as handsome in civilian clothes as in uniform, greeted us as though we were old friends, and Lady Mountbatten beamed graciously. But my attention went to a fair-haired young man in naval uniform in a corner of the room who was introduced by Lord Mountbatten as 'my nephew Philip.'

The conversation which followed was initiated by Lord Mountbatten, taken over by Lady Mountbatten, taken back by Lord Mountbatten and eventually continued by both simultaneously. We were being asked to advise the Mountbattens 'as the top newspapermen in Fleet Street' on the probable public reactions to their nephew taking out naturalisation papers.

At that time the possibility that Prince Philip, fifth child and only

256

son of Prince Andrew of Greece, would be engaged to Princess Elizabeth had not been discussed. Years later it was stated in *Time* magazine that the King was concerned about the effect on public opinion of an engagement between his eldest daughter and a Greek Prince. I doubt that, but certainly the Mountbattens seemed anxious that their nephew should be acceptable as a British subject.

We gave our opinion unanimously that Prince Philip's war service in the Navy entitled him to British nationality, apart altogether from his English upbringing by 'Uncle Dickie'. If he were embarrassed by the conversation, Prince Philip showed no sign; he remained in his corner, grinned cheerfully from time to time, and said nothing. He was so little part of the gathering that when whiskies and sodas were served he was not included in the round.

We left after an hour. Back at my office, I telephoned Lord Beaverbrook and told him the news. 'Well, you fellows surprise me,' said the proprietor. 'Don't you know that the oldest trick in politics is to muzzle the Press by taking it into your confidence?' He meant that if any of our reporters were to get the news that a naturalisation application had been made for Prince Philip we would have to suppress it until it became official because the Mountbattens had confided in us. That was indeed so, but I did not see how we could have avoided falling into the trap – if it were one – without giving a churlish refusal to the Mountbattens' invitation.

Prince Philip was soon to show that he had a good sense of Press technique and public relations, independent of his distinguished uncle. Soon after the announcement of his engagement to Princess Elizabeth he was involved in a slight car accident. The *Express* got the news exclusively and on this account gave it a more emphatic front-page display than the event itself perhaps justified. When the Press Association finally stuttered out the facts, I was long since home and in bed. The Night Editor telephoned me. 'Take it down to a single-column headline for the last edition,' I advised. 'It's not worth a double-column if all the papers have it.'

A few days later I met Prince Philip. He told me that when he heard that the *Daily Express* was the only paper making inquiries, he had himself telephoned the Press Association with the news of his accident so that 'you blighters on the *Express* wouldn't make too much of it.'

Prince Philip was a member of a much-discussed institution called the Thursday Club, to which I belong. It was formed by Baron, the photographer and a friend from my Manchester days, Sean Fielding, then Editor of *The Tatler*, and Frank Shaw, a West End publicist and impresario. The fact that Prince Philip and his best man, the Marquis of Milford Haven, were members, caused ridiculous legends to surround the Thursday Club's activities. All we did – and still do – was to meet for lunch in Wheeler's in Old Compton Street, Soho, every Thursday, when there is good talk and much laughter. Our guests have included officials of Buckingham Palace, Cabinet Ministers, and café society celebrities like Orson Welles, Sam Speigel and Robert Helpmann. Before his marriage Prince Philip lunched at the Club regularly when he was in London and about once a year he still climbs the three flights of stairs to our club-room.

It is a pity we do not see more of him for he used to enjoy his oysters and the atmosphere of what could well have been a naval wardroom. Just occasionally after his marriage, a few of the members of the Club dined with him at Baron's flat, but with Baron's tragic death in 1956 at the age of fifty, these intimate occasions came to an end.

An attempt to revive the circle was made in 1958, but we made the mistake of taking over a small restaurant in Knightsbridge for the night and the news got into the *Sunday Dispatch* under the headline:

THE DUKE'S STAG PARTY BOOS THE PARKER BEER

The headline was based on the fact that Commander Michael Parker, former secretary to Prince Philip, imported for the occasion some beer from Australia, his native land. The article was accurate enough, except that it said that the diners were forming a Monday Club, because the Thursday Club was attracting too much publicity. As a newspaperman I envied the *Dispatch* its story. It would have looked good in the *Express*! But this is the newspaperman's dilemma: if he mixes with people who make news he must respect their confidence; if he does not mix he cannot be a good newspaperman!

Prince Philip, who likes a game of cricket, had to give up coming
to the Thursday Club's annual match because someone tipped off
the Press. He went with Baron to Tolleshunt D'Arcy in Essex, where
Philip Youngman Carter and his wife Margery Allingham, the
novelist, got up a team of locals to play the Club. The Youngman
Carters have their own cricket pitch, but that did not stop a *News
of the World* photographer leaping out of the bushes as the Prince
went in to bat. The picture made a fine exclusive on the front page
of the *News of the World*, but it upset the day, as our hosts were on
edge for fear of further incidents.

I once heard Prince Philip say to a gathering of journalists, 'I am
a complete stoic, I now read about myself as if I were an animal in
the Zoo.'

He has a ready tongue and a capacity for calculated indiscretion
which gives much pleasure. On one occasion a young woman pre-
tended to swoon as he passed by and he grinned at her: 'Steady
now!' But newspapermen have had to bear the brunt of his temper
and tongue, both strong and rich.

I suppose he cannot be blamed for his occasional show of hostility
to the Press. He and the Queen undoubtedly had cause for complaint over the conduct of some newspapers in seeking news of the
Prince of Wales's school life at Cheam. An appeal to the Press
Council was at one time under consideration, a step that was
avoided only at the last minute by the calling of a conference of
editors at Buckingham Palace. I had left my job when this took
place, but one of the editors who was present told me it was a
spirited affair, with Commander Richard Colville, the Palace Press
Secretary, making heavy weather when it was pointed out that
public interest in Prince Charles was great and that the normal
restrictions imposed by Palace protocol on news about the boy
should be relaxed. It must, however, have been hard for the Queen,
or indeed any mother, to read that her son had carved his initials
on a pew in the parish church when it just wasn't true, and other
stories of that kind. Yet with the years the novelty has worn off
and both Press and public are behaving much more sensibly about
the education of the Heir to the Throne.

Lord Beaverbrook's newspapers are mistrusted and disliked in
Court circles. Once upon a time it was said that this dated from the

hostility of King George V to the activities of Beaverbrook during and after the First World War; then the support Beaverbrook gave to Edward VIII over Mrs. Simpson was cited; nowadays it is the Beaverbrook-Mountbatten feud. Certainly there is a continuing hostility, which goes much deeper than intrusion into the privacy with which the Queen wishes her children to be brought up – a subject on which the Beaverbrook papers have been reasonably circumspect and uncurious.

Criticism of the Royal Family is never popular. Since George V first stumbled on the secret of mass appeal by his Christmas Day fireside broadcasts, the popularity of the Royal Family has reached emotional heights which sometimes border on the hysterical. (It must have come as something of a shock to the Royal circle when newspapers ranging from the *Daily Telegraph* to the *Daily Mirror* criticised the incorporation of the name Mountbatten in the Royal Family name when the announcement was made early in 1959; and also that the Queen's pride in her German ancestry, publicly declared when the President of Western Germany was in London in 1958, should continue to be the subject of critical comment – 'Who advises the Queen? Can no one be found to explain this stark, simple, well-established fact: that Germans, whether of high or low degree, are not popular here?' said one newspaper six months later.)

The campaign which the *Express* conducted against extravagant expenditure on the Royal yacht was tremendously unpopular. I know people who would like to see John Gordon impeached for some of his writings about Prince Philip in the *Sunday Express*. And when the *Express* supported Mr Attlee in 1952 in his demand that the amount of the allowance paid to Prince Philip should be made public, my post-bag contained more than one hundred letters asking what business it was of ours or of Attlee's.

Lord Beaverbrook is blamed for everything hostile to the Royal Family that appears in his newspapers. He probably deserves it, since he lays down the broad policy that no government, no party, no institution, not even the Royal Family, shall be on an untouchable pinnacle. But sometimes the side-kicks are unfair. He was even attacked over a comparison of headlines in the *Express* and the *Mail* on the annual American election of the year's best-dressed women. The *Express* headline read: THE QUEEN CHOSEN FIFTH

FOR DRESS. The *Mail* headline read: THE QUEEN WINS FASHION
HONOUR. Typical of Beaverbrook, wrote one reader, to demote
the Queen to fifth place; why did his Lordship allow such sneering
headlines?

With public opinion like this, it is almost impossible to do right
by Royalty. In 1957, when the Queen and Prince Philip celebrated
the tenth anniversary of their marriage, I asked Anne Edwards to
write a series of articles on the changes that the decade had brought.
To meet Left Wing criticisms that newspapers were too sweetly
sentimental on such subjects I told Miss Edwards to cut out the
guff. But you cannot win.

'Miss Edwards is a mistress of the art of sowing nettles among
the hot-house plants,' commented Francis Williams in the *New
Statesman*. 'While curtseying smartly and in properly graceful
fashion at the appropriate places,' he continued, 'she contrived to
spread among the loyal readers of the *Express*, opinions about the
Queen as a confirmed chip off the Victorian block which must have
come as a slight shock to one or two of them even now. As for
instance: "It is the sentimental fashion to picture the Queen as a
gentle bird beating its wings against the bars of a golden cage. In
fact, it is she who insists that the cage is there – and strong.": Or "It
is the general idea that a set of fuddy-duddies are surrounding the
Queen and running her. Nothing could be further from the truth.
She runs them." '

I have had a look through the *Daily Express* library file on the
Royal Family, a formidable task. I find there is as much praise and
friendly comment there as there is criticism, and I am sure that
Prince Philip, who is an able, shrewd and politically-minded man,
understands that detached and candid comment sustains the
Monarchy more effectively than obsequious servility.

If the frank opinions of a free Press were not allowed, all manner
of abuse by officials of the Court and members of the Government
would be possible. A vigilant and independent Press must surely
be a help rather than a hindrance to the Queen and her husband,
even if the road seems at times to be all cobblestones.

I have never been sympathetic to the generally held view in Fleet
Street that relations between the newspapers and Buckingham
Palace should be more intimate. I believe that Commander Richard

S

Colville, the Press Secretary, does a very difficult job very well indeed and that there is no reason at all why the Palace should be represented by people whose function is to get news *into* the paper. That job in relation to the Royal Family should be left to the enterprise (and good taste) of the newspapers.

Intimate relations between the high and mighty and the newspaper can be journalistically disastrous. The function of a newspaper is to print the news, and to offer guidance, according to its beliefs, on the news in its leading articles. Social or professional relationships which prejudice the achievement of these two fundamentals are in theory always bad and in practice frequently so.

The national interest is best served by continuing the present situation between the Palace and the Press, where an arm's length distance is maintained, so that there can be no obstacle to free and constructive comment.

32 . . . Burgess and Maclean

But how did you get your news, Mr Christiansen? It is a question
that never ceases to be asked. Let me answer statistically; in 1959
the Beaverbrook organisation spent £918,197 on buying news
services such as Reuters and on maintaining 165 correspondents
throughout the world before one penny in salaries had been paid.

But figures dull the imagination. Let me put it another way.
Primroses in December are news. So is the sound of the first cuckoo
in spring. So is a rise of one-halfpenny in the price of bacon. So is
the winner of the hundred yards' sprint at your son's school sports
day. So is your wedding day. Everything is news and the getting of
it is merely a matter of training, of knowing where to look, of how
to ask the right people the right questions at the right time. Good
newspapermen can 'smell' stories a mile off, as dogs smell bones.

Here are two stories, one of a piece of news that I printed and the
other of a piece of news I suppressed. The link between the two is
that both were alleged to be concerned with 'national security', an
overworked phrase that governments frequently use in peace-time
to nobble the newspapers, usually for the purpose of concealing
departmental incompetence.

Larry Solon, chief correspondent of the *Daily Express* in Paris,
had a good nose for news, but neither he nor I realised just how big
the news was when he telephoned London on the night of 6 June

1951 with a five-line 'squib' reporting that two Foreign Office employees whose names, he believed, were Maclean and Burgess, had
disappeared from London, and that the French police had been
asked to check up on their movements.

It was ten o'clock and the front page of the first edition of the
Daily Express was just 'going under the mangle' in the printing
office. I was at my desk in the Big Room glancing through the page
proofs. It was one of those nights when we needed no more news, for
Page One was half-filled with an account of the siege of a house in
Chatham by two hundred armed police officers. A nineteen-year-
old gunman was holding out there after shooting a policeman dead
earlier in the day. But with news it is either a famine or a flood, and
when the Foreign Desk Night Editor rushed over with the Solon
message, it was 'Action Stations' again for the entire staff.

Here was a piece of news that would have to be checked and
double-checked. A mistake in publication is bad in any circumstances, but in the atmosphere of that year, when deep suspicion of
British security had been aroused in the U.S.A. by the activities of
Nunn May, Fuchs, and Pontecorvo, the three atomic scientists
who had revealed their vital know-how to the Russians, it would
have been calamitous.

I took charge of the investigation; to the chief re-write executive:
'Get the Foreign Office List from the Library and check the names
"Burgess" and "Maclean" '; to the switchboard girl: 'Get me
Percy Hoskins wherever he is, and Derek Marks at the House';
to the Foreign Desk: 'Get Paris office on the telephone.'

Hoskins is through first and is asked to check with his Special
Branch contacts. Marks, the Political Correspondent, is next and
is asked to check with his Foreign Office contacts. Now Solon is on
the line. 'Larry,' I say, 'how hard is this story?' Solon, a soft-spoken,
bulky, bespectacled American of vast experience both in his own
country and in Britain, is not too convincing. He had got the tip-
off that two British diplomats were 'on the spree' in Paris and might
no longer be there from Georges Gherra, the crime reporter of
France-Soir, the Paris evening paper in whose building the *Express*
had a couple of rooms.

'Georges wasn't certain of the names,' said Larry, 'and all I had
to go on was a phonetic rendering of them. Translating them from

his French into names that appear in the Foreign Office list hasn't been easy.'

'For Pete's sake, that's risky,' I exploded.

'Well, just a minute, Chris,' Larry replied. 'Before I put the message over I tried the names out on a contact at the British Embassy. He reacted so violently that I'm sure we're on to something. Anyway, it was getting late and I thought it best to put over as much as I know.'

He told me that, on reflection, his news contacts had been behaving mysteriously all day. A friend at the American Embassy had asked him over a pre-lunch drink if he had been following any hot clues lately, and had seemed oddly reserved thereafter. Later a French police source had gone out of his way to make it clear that he had no good stories to give to the newspapers that day, despite the fact that he had not been asked. Then when Larry had put in a routine call to the Duty Officer at the Sûreté, he had been brushed off so curtly that he had hared back to the office in the Rue Réaumur and made contact with Gherra.

On the spree? On their way to Russia perhaps? How did they get to Paris? When did they arrive? Solon could help no further, and my dilemma was acute until well after midnight, when Hoskins came on with the cross-check (you do not, by the way, embarrass your specialist reporters for their sources of information, you employ them and trust them) and with a few additional details which made me decide to take the plunge. But although we had checked that there was a DONALD DUART MACLEAN and a GUY FRANCIS DE MONCY BURGESS in the Foreign Office List, I accepted the advice of the shrewd lawyer who reads every word of the newspaper for libel and other legal pitfalls, that the story would be safer if published anonymously. Thus the first news of the Burgess and Maclean scandal appeared in its opening paragraphs as follows:

Scotland Yard officers and French detectives are hunting for two British Government employees who are believed to have left London with the intention of getting to Moscow.

According to a friend, they planned the journey to 'serve their idealistic purposes'.

One report says that the two men were employed by the Foreign

Office, and there is the possibility that they may have important papers with them.

When I got home about 2.30 a.m. I did not sleep. Panic seized me and I lay groaning with fear, convinced that I had acted precipitately and foolishly. A whole day's consideration should have been given to a story of this dimension, I thought as I lay there sweating. Why rush into print after a couple of hours' work which had produced only the flimsiest of confirmation? A copy of the 1 a.m. edition was on the floor at the side of my bed and I picked it up to read again the sensational headlines on the seven paragraphs of dynamite which would blow me out of my job if they were wrong. I looked at my watch. It was 4.30 a.m., and within five minutes the presses would have completed their task of printing four million copies, every one of which could sink me.

An editor's job is one of the loneliest in the world; when panic seizes him in the black hours before the dawn, it is also one of the cruellest. I took two sleeping pills and passed out. . . .

When, with the arrival of daylight, confidence returned, or at any rate a resigned acceptance of fate, come what may, I found myself sitting on the biggest news block-buster I had been called upon to handle since the blitz on London – what is more, a delayed-action bomb that was not to explode finally for nearly four and a half years.

My 'foolish and precipitate' conduct unearthed a situation that the British security authorities were doing their damnedest to conceal. As the days passed, one grudging admission after another (allied to fine detective work by *Express* reporters) revealed that Burgess and Maclean had been missing for three weeks when we stumbled on the news of their disappearance, that there had been pointers of all kinds to their intention to bolt, that they were Communists, that little or no attempt had been made to trace them beyond a few routine enquiries which would not have strained the imaginative resources of a cop on a country beat, and that the whole investigation had been hampered by the desire for secrecy, for fear the Americans would get to know too quickly.

But when the Establishment, or the Government, or officialdom, is caught with its trousers down, it defends itself vigorously. Herbert

Morrison, the Foreign Secretary, immediately attacked the newspaper for making the work of the Security Services more difficult; and that kind of smoke-screen was put up constantly, even until a Conservative government came in, when Anthony Nutting, the Foreign Office Under-Secretary, smeared us with an accusation of witch-hunting.

'Those masters of ours in Whitehall,' wrote John Gordon in the *Sunday Express* at the time, 'are very sensitive about their two miserable renegades . . . we have the right to know who in the Foreign Office disregarded the warnings they had concerning the dangerous character of these two men.'

Meantime a smoke-screen of another kind had developed on the flank, when George Joyce, an *Express* reporter, telephoned Mrs Melinda Maclean and in his story of their conversation used a phrase indicating that the lady had smiled at him. Ha-ha! The *Express* caught out in the act of faking the news! How could a reporter *see* Mrs Maclean smiling down the mouth-piece of a telephone? Convinced of the rightness of her cause and of the innocence of Melinda (who was to know that she was even then making plans to join her husband in Russia?) Lady Violet Bonham Carter wrote to *The Times* about the way in which *Express* reporters were behaving. Jo Grimond, her son-in-law and a Liberal M.P., asked questions in Parliament. The *Observer* and *The Spectator* combined in a personal attack on my editorship of such violence that Lord Beaverbrook sent me a note saying:

The attack on you by David Astor could not be couched in more bitter and hostile terms – he even suggests that your reporter was an innocent party to the whole thing and was instructed by you as Editor of the *Daily Express* to get up to some rascality.

Lord Beaverbrook loved every moment of this aspect of the story, and while I directed news operations I was also writing at his instigation columns of pro-*Express* propaganda which appeared on our own front page as well as going out through the Press Association for publication in other newspapers. There were moments when the half-world of homosexuality and drunken

parties that my reporters were unearthing in their inquiries from
Kensington Gore to the Isle of Capri took a back-seat to the war of
words over the honour of the newspaper.

The interview with Mrs Maclean is a bad case on which to argue
on either side about the ethics of newspaper reporting. The howls
of protest that went up at the 'persecution' and the 'hounding' of an
innocent wife and mother were seen to be misplaced when the lady
vanished with her children to join her husband behind the Iron
Curtain. This was not a forsaken, defenceless heroine battling alone
against the hordes of the Yellow Press. This was a resourceful,
efficient woman who, if she was not privy to her husband's plans
before he carried them out, was able to conceal both the receipt of
his instructions to follow him and her methods of doing so.

The *Express* was not wrong in seeking to keep contact with
Melinda Maclean. Our news-hunch told us that there was something fishy about her, something that did not smell quite right; and
with just a shade more determination and drive we might have been
able to follow the story through to the point where we uncovered
the underground route by which she – and who knows who else ? –
reached Moscow.

On the other hand, the fact that Mrs Maclean was not an innocent
victim of both her husband and the Press cannot justify the falsification of news, even by implication. What the reporter did is easy
to do; the telephone 'smile' makes a story more 'human', more
vivid, and also more authentic. But with the best intentions in the
world, newspaper executives cannot check on everything that goes
into the paper, and it must be a reportorial responsibility to write
the *exact* truth, not an approximation of the truth.

Melinda Maclean was a case where vigilance was justified; but
what about all the other intrusions into private life which Fleet
Street practises to-day ? As I have said elsewhere, people who court
publicity must take the rough with the smooth; Royalty cannot
help but receive publicity and have learned to accept most of it
with good grace; but the pestering by reporters of people who are
unfortunate or unhappy and who do not wish any part of it is not
what I had in mind when as a young man I tried to open out the
'human angle'.

When a murderer was hanged I wanted to know how his children

were faring; when a girl rocketed to stardom I wanted to know
what her parents had contributed. I wanted to know about people
– humble, unimportant people as well as those who were established.

But the idea got out of hand. The human story, like the size of
headline type, seems often nowadays to be sought ruthlessly at
the sacrifice of taste, sense and decent feeling.

I record it; and I deplore it; but in the case of Mrs Melinda
Maclean I am unrepentant.

The final proof that Burgess and Maclean were in Moscow kept
eluding us. One day the Beaver telephoned, very hot on the trail.
'Maclean has sent his wife the sum of £1,000 through a Swiss Bank,'
he said. 'If you can check it you've got what you want.' It took a
fortnight to check and I cannot reveal even now either where Lord
Beaverbrook got the tip or how its accuracy was established; I was
just delighted to pay his informant £250 and forget her name.

But even this revelation failed to force any admissions out of the
British Government; nor did the news that Guy Burgess had written
a Christmas letter to his mother. (We got a scoop on that too, for a
friend of the family sold us the information.)

The letter was posted in London and we deduced that it had been
brought here by a member of the crew of a Russian ship that had
arrived in London Docks a few days previously. Next, when René
MacColl was in Belgrade he picked up the news that the diplomats
were living just outside Moscow. Still officialdom stonewalled.
Sighed one weary M.P. in Parliament, 'If I put down a question in
three years' time could you give a better answer?'

Then, in September 1955, came the official revelations of
Vladimir Petrov, the Soviet spy who sought asylum in Australia.

Authority could stall no more. Mr Eden had by this time become
Prime Minister, and in Parliament announced the formation of a
committee of privy councillors to examine Britain's security
arrangements. That night I found myself whistling the tune 'Eleven
more months and ten more days –'. What a time it had taken to
crack the Burgess and Maclean nut!

Afterwards Larry Solon, the originator of the Burgess and
Maclean story, wrote to me:

> Editors like H. L. Mencken, Harold Ross of *The New Yorker*

and yourself might have made successful gamblers, because intuition – a sense of the right moment and the outsider who will come out in front – also creates an *ambiance* of good luck. I have been in journalism since I was a kid and I've always felt this *ambiance* when it existed. When it didn't I got myself another job. Working with you I had a strong sense of this intangible. With another editor at the helm, the few sparse clues that turned into the Burgess and Maclean story might easily have been ignored by the reporter.

I wouldn't have laid six to four on my *ambiance*, or even on the certainty of keeping my job, as I lay tossing and turning in bed on the night I first printed the news!

Later on the *Express* organisation decided to publish a book[1] on the case. It was assembled by John Mather, who master-minded the presentation of the story in the paper, and Donald Seaman, a brilliant reporter who had covered the escape route of the diplomats almost yard by yard. I wrote a short preface, only one sentence of which needs to be quoted: 'this book is a story of pressure by newspapers to get the news and of determination in high places to conceal the news.'

That is a recurring theme in the long struggle between journalism and authority. In that statement is the entire case for a free, unfettered, uncontrolled Press.

Now let me tell of an occasion when I came to the aid of the Security Services by suppressing news of an incredible piece of official bungling and incompetence. I did so because at the time delicate negotiations were reaching their climax between Britain and America for the exchange of atomic information. The Atomic Energy Act is now through Congress, so there can no longer be any purpose in suppression.

Mr Eric Tannock, a London businessman who reads the *Daily Express* (readers of newspapers are a valuable source of information; many make quite a tidy amount of pin-money in this fashion) telephoned Morley Richards, the News Editor of the *Express* one night in the autumn of 1955 in a high state of indignation. His story

1. *The Great Spy Scandal:* A *Daily Express* publication.

was so extraordinary that two reporters and a photographer were dispatched to Mr Tannock's flat forthwith, for the entirely respectable and innocent Mr Tannock had been accused of kidnapping a man.

The Tannock Tangle is best begun at its fantastic beginning, by explaining that the British Secret Service has a number of trainees, part of whose job is to interrogate and also to know how to resist interrogation if captured by a hostile Power.

On the day Mr Tannock's affairs and those of the Secret Service became mixed up, two Secret Service trainees had been detailed for a training exercise. They were told to interrogate a man of a certain description who would follow Sir David Maxwell Fyfe, the Home Secretary, out of a building near the Thames Embankment at a certain time. They had never met this man, although they knew he was another trainee being tested in the art of resisting interrogation.

A flat near Old Brompton Road owned by a Foreign Office official associated with the Secret Service was placed at their disposal for the exercise. So was a fawn car.

At the appointed time Sir David, who did not know he was being used in the exercise, left the building followed by a man who seemed to answer to the description given to the trainees. They pounced on him, bundled him into the car, and drove him to the flat despite his protests. There they gave the terrified man the works. They even removed his trousers to search for hidden messages and administered other forms of Third Degree.

But the nut failed to crack, and after quite a time the wretched fellow was still sticking to his story that he was a low-level Civil Servant on his way home. It then dawned on the two interrogators that they had picked up the wrong man. All they could do was to release him with the warning that he had better keep his mouth shut. But the terrified man, thinking that he had narrowly escaped being murdered by lunatics or Russian agents, went to the police. The police, of course, could hardly be blamed for being incredulous, but took him back to the block of flats in Old Brompton Road to check up.

Now although the innocent man had not been blindfolded, his confusion was understandable and he took the police to the wrong flat – the flat occupied by Mr Tannock. The fact that Mr Tannock owned a foreign-made car, which was parked outside, did not help, and pretty soon he was being grilled by the police. Mrs Tannock was almost in hysterics as accusations that her husband was a kidnapper were aggressively pursued, and by the time the police decided that Mr Tannock was innocent, he also was more than worked up. The moment the police left, he telephoned the *Daily Express*.

However, while our reporters and photographer were on their way, the police found the right flat, one floor above. The tenant, a Foreign Office official, who had rushed home on being told the sad tale of the bungle, explained the situation to the police and asked if they could silence Mr Tannock by telling him that what had happened was all a horrible mistake which could not be explained because it was 'top secret, a vital matter of security'.

Mr Tannock was given this message and also warned to keep quiet. But it was too late. The *Express* reporters had arrived on the scene. The anxious Foreign Office man realised that something was going on in the flat downstairs, checked up, and then telephoned the Deputy Director of M.I.6. I should explain that officially the department known as M.I.6 does not exist, so that it was impossible for it to enlist my co-operation; therefore M.I.6 asked M.I.5 (which as Military Intelligence does exist) if it could help to call the *Express* off – National security and all that, old boy – and what a mess!

Admiral George Thomson, the war-time Chief Censor, was still the go-between on such matters. He telephoned Harry Chapman Pincher, our Science and Services man, and then I was consulted. To give myself time to ponder the facts, which seemed to out-cloak and out-dagger even the climax of the Burgess and Maclean case, I agreed to hold up the story, at any rate for the night.

Meantime, the Foreign Office man, no doubt thinking that the *Express* reporters had left the premises, called on Mr Tannock, and in order to impress on him the need for complete secrecy, made a clean breast of the affair. But one *Express* reporter was still there and, through an open door, heard Mr Tannock being told that the *Express* was being 'taken care of'.

This was reported to me. I do not like being 'taken care of' at all, but just the same I decided to honour my promise not to publish the story that night. 'But you can tell Admiral Thomson,' I said, 'that we will be going full steam ahead to-morrow.'

Then the real pressure started. It was represented to me by Admiral Thomson with considerable skill and much persuasion that to expose the stupidity of our Security men would prejudice and maybe destroy the negotiations with America on the exchange of missile secrets.

The arguments were overwhelming, but before I gave in I said to Thomson, 'Tell me, what happened to the stooge who should have been following the Home Secretary?'

'Oh,' said Tommy, 'it was really most unfortunate. He missed his train!'

33 . . . End Message – and Beginning

'I am sick of editors,' the second Lord Rothermere is reported to have said when during the war he decided to appoint a new one to the *Daily Mail* and to call him 'Acting' Editor in case he did not fill the bill. Lord Rothermere could hardly be blamed for his sentiments, as the *Mail* has had a dozen editors since the great Tom Marlowe's partnership with Northcliffe ended, whereas the *Daily Express* has had only four in its sixty years, R. D. Blumenfeld, Beverley Baxter, myself and now Edward Pickering.

The *Express* form of wastage was in Assistant Editors, or Managing Editors as they are now called, American style. 'A Managing Editor is a man who just manages to edit,' sneered old Swaffer, who loathes any American influence on British journalism. But the only merit of Swaff's crack is that it is slick. Three of my seven Managing Editors became Editors, and one, Herbert Gunn, is now editing his third paper since he left the *Daily Express*.

The Editor is Captain of the ship; the Managing Editor is Chief Engineer. It is his job to get the paper out, to interpret policy, and put it into practice. He sometimes comes down to Fleet Street before lunch, but his busiest time is between 3 p.m. and 3 a.m. the following morning. As the day of talk translates itself into deeds, the job calls for increasing concentration, a cool head, rapid judgement, and an infinite capacity for improvisation. The lawyer may 'kill' his best Page One story on the grounds of libel fifteen minutes before press time. What to do?

'Boy,' calls the Managing Editor, 'send for the Page One make-up' (the drawn plan of the page like a fitted jig-saw puzzle from which the printer assembles the type). The air is blue with cigarette smoke and bad language as a piece of news that was scheduled to appear on Page Two is elevated in place of the legal 'kill' to Page One, or a snippet at the foot of Page One is promoted to a position it hardly deserves.

A couple of minutes later, with one little crisis settled, the Reuter tape machine may spluttered the words CANCEL LEBANON SHOOTING – SUBSTITUTE STORY FOLLOWS. Another hole in Page One. Get on to Reuters, says the Managing Editor, ask them what the hell they're playing at and how long the 'substitute' story will be in coming.

'Boy,' he calls, 'get me the Page One make-up again.' This time a sweating Head Printer personally brings the make-up to the editorial floor. He is nearly hysterical. 'Do you know we're five pages behind schedule already?' he shouts, regardless of anyone's dignity. 'If this goes on, we'll never get to press even by next week.' To which the Managing Editor says he can't print what he hasn't got, so what?

And yet, fifteen minutes later it is all over. The printers, at last allowed to have a cigarette, stand round in the Composing Room exhausted by the strain, wondering for the thousandth time why editorial men are such incompetents. And the editorial men, half of whom have been down in the printing office cutting stories to fit space, sneak out to the pubs to revive their energies before the next edition.

This is not a description of an exceptional night in the daily birth of a newspaper; it is the rule, not the exception. Short of turning our newspapers into shabby, out-of-date imitations of *Pravda*, there seems no way around it, for news takes no account of time, trains or edition schedules. The job of Managing Editor is an exacting and exhausting one, and many cannot stand the pace.

Where is the Editor while all this is happening? If the news is big, he will be there, mucking in with the rest of the staff; but if things look peaceful, which earlier in the night they usually do, he is at

home or in a restaurant enjoying a brief hour with his wife, or talking to-morrow's business with a politician or an author. Wherever
he is, the Managing Editor has the Editor's telephone number so
that he can be consulted immediately.

For instance: Franklin Roosevelt died suddenly at four minutes
past midnight when the war was reaching its climax. I was having
an early night and was asleep when the telephone called me. I was
back in the office by 12.30. Herbert Gunn took over the news; I
took over the Features. A new leading article was written. A re-
write man compiled from library cuttings a selection of Roosevelt's
famous sayings. Another told the story of his illnesses. Another
swept through the records of 'My Day', Mrs Roosevelt's newspaper
column. Pictures were selected. Tape machines fumed with the news
from Washington. The Press Association poured out tributes from
the Churchills, the Beaverbrooks, and any other famous men who
could be contacted at that hour of night.

By 4.30 a.m. we were all sitting around exhausted but gazing with
pride on a newspaper transformed, a newspaper that we knew would
not be bettered that day. On nights like this newspapermen do not
go home; they stand around smoking their fiftieth cigarette, dry-
tongued and excited. The let-down must come slowly. The younger
ones go to Covent Garden market, where the pubs are open for the
greengrocery men. Only ultimate wisdom drives the older men
eventually to catch their all-night trains to Beckenham and
Bromley and Orpington.

On this night I offered a lift to anyone going my way home and
when we got there invited them in as usual for 'one for the road'.
But by now the cool early-morning air had brought us back to
reality, and no one accepted. It was long after 5 a.m. and to-
morrow was just another day that had already dawned.

There are said to be thirty-three basic rules to be observed before
a golf ball can be struck successfully. There are probably as many
rules for the production of a successful newspaper, except that no
one has ever analysed them; and I do not propose to undertake the
task, in this book at any rate. But one of the rules must surely be to
encourage your staff to keep its tail up and to have fun. A modest
staff will produce a modest newspaper. A depressed staff will produce a depressed newspaper. A high-spirited staff will produce a

high-spirited newspaper – and a high-spirited newspaper will radiate its confidence to an ever-widening band of readers.

I took immense pains to keep my staff high-spirited. The process began at morning conference, which everybody who was anybody on the staff was allowed to attend. It was 'Standing Room only' most days and what happened there led William Barkley in his book *Reporter's Notebook* to comment: 'for a quarter of a century the best variety show in London or out of it was Chris's morning conference . . . a tape recording of them would have sold the paper.'

I tried to make even my sternest rebukes seem to be all part of the joke. I noticed, for example, that some of my Top Twelve were drinking too steadily, and sometimes in office hours at that. Their capacity was immense and their capabilities undiminished, but drinking is a habit that grows quickly and it had to be halted. So I formed the Waggoners' Club. The aim of the club: one month's teetotalism. The subscription: five guineas. The rules: no drinking in Fleet Street whatsoever; no drinking outside Fleet Street unless the 'offence' was reported to my secretary, who would record in the Club register two black marks per drink of spirits, one black mark for wine or beer. The reward: the member with the fewest marks should be awarded the entire subscription.

The struggle was even for a few days. Then a big story broke in the early hours and a weary executive had to admit to three double Scotches (six points) in the Press Club.

Next, as good as a bottle of gin had been consumed by a senior reporter on an exhausting and difficult out-of-town assignment where the facts could be gathered only in saloon bars.

As the month wore on, one or two of the dozen members fell so far behind that they gave up altogether, but the rest of us stuck it doggedly and the results were splendid.

I won by several points, because I have a Northern Nonconformist conscience which tells me that drinking is evil; I would need little incentive, despite a good capacity, to become a complete teetotaller. The other members of the Waggoners' Club, however, alleged that I had won by 'squaring' my secretary. Therefore, I hired a room in a Piccadilly restaurant and blued in the sixty guineas (plus a bit more) on a gargantuan meal that included such post-war rarities as caviare, vodka and out-of-season asparagus.

T

Conversely, the staff of the newspaper took immense pains to keep me happy too. In 1947, when I had been twenty-one years with the Beaverbrook organisation, they celebrated by forming a dining club named the 1933 Club, after the year of my appointment to the editorial chair.

Eligible for membership were those who had either joined the paper in 1933 or, having joined before that date, were promoted in my first year as boss. It was a shock to realise that, such is the wastage of talent in Fleet Street, there were only ten others entitled to membership: Morley Richards, the News Editor; Guy Eden, the teetotal Political Correspondent; John Young, a sixteen-stone Scot who after many years as a theatre gossip writer had become Night News Editor; Paul Holt, the Entertainment Page columnist and critic; Norman Smart, by then Foreign Editor; Basil Cardew, the Motoring Correspondent; Montague Lacey, who has surmounted painful physical handicaps to become the doyen of Fleet Street shipping reporters; Kenneth Pipe, who was discovered by Lord Beaverbrook in Norfolk and remained Agricultural Correspondent for thirty years; Frank Butler, the sports writer now with the *News of the World*; and Trevor Evans, who came to London with me from Manchester and is now a director of Beaverbrook newspapers.

The 1933 Club's generosity to me was unbounded, for not only was there an annual dinner but an annual presentation, which ranged from a specially commissioned scale-model cargo-boat (to commemorate my other love, the sea) to a number plate for my car, AC 30 (it originally belonged to a pre-war motor coach) to commemorate my thirtieth year in Fleet Street in 1956.

I tried to give as good as I got; I booked a couple of boxes each winter for the Crazy Gang Show, back-stage afterwards to see Bud Flanagan and the Gang, followed by an oysters and cold beef supper at my flat; I designed a Club tie, with the *Daily Express* Crusader as the motif; Club braces, ditto; a club money wallet, ditto; and if the club had not come to an end with my departure from the organisation, maybe by now we would have had Club socks, ditto, too!

To celebrate Lord Beaverbrook's seventy-fifth birthday in 1955, the 1933 Club sent John Young and Sandy Trotter, Editor of the

Scottish *Daily Express* and by then a co-opted member, to Edinburgh on a special mission. It was to buy a Readers' Bible of the size and dignity associated with the pulpit of the Presbyterian Church. Lord Beaverbrook acknowledged it by saying that he was tempted to break his custom of adding gifts of books to the Library at New Brunswick University, of which he is Chancellor and patron.

'The good book,' he wrote, 'tells us we should not be covetous. There are occasions when we should yield to temptation, even if it is so that grace may be abounding.'

The Beaver, of course, took part in the general hubbub by keeping us both anxious and happy. Little escaped him – he had news on every part of the paper. Thus:

'It is nonsense to say that there is controversy about television announcers. They don't produce anything. They don't deliver anything, except other men's work. And they don't deliver that with any emphasis. If they did give it emphasis they would find themselves in difficulty, because it would be said that they were emphasising the news to the detriment of one political party or the other.'

And by contrast: in the days soon after the war when snook and whalemeat were the common fare, some of the senior American correspondents invited Aneurin Bevan to dine with them at an expensive Soho restaurant. Bevan was constantly denigrating the newspapers so I could not resist reproducing the mouth-watering menu on Page One. Said Lord Beaverbrook:

'I thought you gave too much space to Aneurin Bevan on 23 November. He thrives on that sort of thing. Remember he is pulling your leg. He does not really mean the things he says. He is just acting out a part and that part is to attack the Press, to exasperate you if he can, and to exaggerate your faults and persuade you to give much of your space to his activities.'

Conversation at Arlington House in August 1957:

Beaverbrook: 'Vivien Leigh will be damaged by going abroad with her ex-husband on holiday.'

T*

Myself: 'I don't think so. Nothing damages actors and actresses. Indiscretions merely attract the public in a greater degree to the box-office.'

Beaverbrook (*to a guest*)*:* 'There you have the whole of the *Daily Express* in one sentence.'

When I had been Editor of the *Express* for twenty-one years I received a cardboard box with an inscription in Lord Beaverbrook's handwriting saying: 'Send this to Mr Christiansen.' The box contained a three-and-sixpenny toy, which when wound up played 'Happy Birthday to You'.

A month or two later, and for no reason, he sent me £1,000. I replied that I would willingly work for him for nothing. 'That may be,' he replied, 'but we've all got to live.'

If the morning was bright and the telephone rang at ten minutes to nine in the post-war years, it was sure to be Lord Beaverbrook – no one else I knew was conscious at such an ungodly hour. Our conversation never varied:

'Where are you?'

'In bed, sir.'

'How long will it take you to call for me here to go walking?'

'Be there at 9.30, sir.'

'Good-bye to you,' the brisk, bad-tempered early-morningish 'good-bye to you' (that mellowed during the day) of a man who did not like to be kept hanging around.

An-apple-a-cup-of-tea-a-three-minute-bath-a-two-minute-shave-and-a-seven-minute-taxicab-ride later, there I was pink and smiling on the threshold of the Beaverbrook flat in Arlington House, while the proprietor was being bullied into wearing an extra woolly by his man Charles because the early sun is deceptive. Beaverbrook's menservants all have their characteristics. Charles, with the Irish accent, was the kindest. Knockles was the lordliest; he had a bedside manner and used the royal 'we' to indicate his master and himself; e.g. 'We haven't seen much of you lately, sir.' Mead was the most traditional. Raymond was the most temperamental, even to the point of being quarrelsome if things did not please him. But all shared one thing in common – they gave orders to their master as well as received them. 'Put your nasal spray in that pocket or you'll think you've forgotten it.' 'You'd better wear a scarf and your heavy coat this morning.' 'Here is some loose change; put it in your pocket now – you forgot it yesterday.'

It is like getting a boy off to school, but eventually we are ready and set off past the Ritz Hotel at a good pace. The *Evening Standard* news-seller on the corner gives us a cheerful 'Good morning, milord' and has his palm surreptitiously crossed with silver.

Some days we go up Bond Street to call in at Agnews and other art dealers to inspect a Gainsborough or a Constable. Some days we head towards Piccadilly Circus and pull up at a second-hand silversmiths where some pretty hard bargaining goes on (maybe, I reflect, millionaires become millionaires because they insist on 'discounts for cash', whereas you and I don't even think of it).

Other days we go straight to the open spaces and walk the Green Park down to Buckingham Palace, up the side of Constitution Hill, across into Hyde Park and on to Kensington Gardens before turning homeward again. But whichever way we go the walks turn into editorial conferences. Beaverbrook's firecracker delivery is always so phrase-worthy as to merit a verbatim, but all I can do is to scribble an odd word or two on a sheet of paper as we stride along.

This is spring in the year of Suez, my last in active journalism. It is clear to me that the Beaver has been seeing Anthony Eden, the Prime Minister, for out of his pocket he produces a series of pencilled notes on which he has scrawled figures relating to Britain's financial extravagance, mostly military. 'I am giving you these figures in the confidence with which we can speak,' he says in his favourite phrase for such moments. In turn I produce a notebook and try as we stride along to jot down the figures. But I am sharply reproved. I will have to carry the facts in my head, and in any case communicate them to no one; they are for my background guidance only.

We pause at a shrubbery where this time one of the gardeners has his palm crossed with silver, says that his wife is getting better slowly, thank you, milord, and would have written about the letter and the present herself if she had been well enough.

On we go: 'You know where I got these figures from?' I reply laconically that I do, but the name Eden is not mentioned by either

of us. I am pleased for the Beaver's sake that the new Prime
Minister and he are on friendly terms; Churchill seems to have been
his only post-war friend in political high places and there have been
times when I felt, rightly or wrongly, that Lord Beaverbrook has
been left out of the political hurly-burly in which he has spent so
much of his life, and in consequence is a frustrated, angry man.

The conversation drifts. I have been having a medical check-up.
Why, he asks? Because, I answer, I am a heavy smoker and I want
to satisfy myself that the pains I am getting in my chest are not
cancer of the lung. Would you want to know if you had it? he asks.
Yes, I reply.

He cannot understand my point of view; it is difficult for me to
find the right words to indicate that editing the *Daily Express* is
becoming so arduous that, much as I like the job, it is not the way
I would wish to spend my days if I had only another six months or
so to live.

'We must support Eden in all our newspapers,' he says, changing
the subject abruptly. 'Give him our strongest support. We can start
to-night by taking a line on the incompetence of the Service departments; that will help him in his fight.' With the Suez adventure still
so far away, this was prophetic stuff.

But Beaverbrook's desire to support Churchill's successor
through thick and thin came crashing down in June when the
Government gave permission to the Trinidad Oil Company, bossed
by Mr Simon Vos, to sell out to the Texas Oil Company of America.

This was something Beaverbrook could not bear. He had been
violently hostile to the Abadan oil settlement by which the
Americans got a grip on Persian oil supplies which had hitherto
been exclusively British. And now, with Middle East oil falling
more and more under American control, it seemed to him ruinous
folly to sell out our oil interests in the Caribbean. Just as we had
not attacked Churchill while we were assailing many of his
Ministers, so now we laid off Eden and gave his responsible
Minister, Harold Macmillan, the big stick.

Macmillan was Chancellor of the Exchequer, and needed all the
dollars he could get, but even he admitted that he first heard the
news of the sell-out 'with dismay'. Before long, however, he had
veered round and was jibing in Parliament that the *Daily Express*

and the Communist *Daily Worker* made strange bed-fellows. The Socialists and the *Daily Herald* were on our side too.

At first it looked as though the violence of the *Express* campaign would stop the sale, especially as the powerful Tory 1922 Committee was against the deal also. But when it came to the vote, Harold Wilson proved to be correct when he had forecast that 'Lord Beaverbrook's Chocolate Soldiers' (the 1922 Committee) would meekly march through the Government Division lobby.

In the excitement of this flaming political June, I had forgotten my chest pains, and had worked a sixteen-hour day, six-day week, throughout the campaign, sub-editing news stories, laying-out pages, writing headlines, directing leading articles, conferring with Lord Beaverbrook, staying up late with my friends, snatching a game of golf at week-ends, driving up to London against the coastal traffic stream to take afternoon news conference on Sunday afternoons while my deputy was on holiday – having, in fact, the usual wonderful time.

Then came Nasser's seizure of Suez. I spent the afternoon of my fifty-second birthday in the Cabinet Room alone with Mr Eden while he explained the situation to me. He indicated that he had been in previous communication with Lord Beaverbrook, but that as he was in the South of France, he would like me to get the facts of the situation to him.

In the past my visits to 10 Downing Street had been mostly with colleagues; this was only my second private audience with a Prime Minister. Eden sat in the Prime Minister's large arm-chair and of the other two dozen or so chairs around the long Cabinet Room table I had my choice. I took the chair on the Prime Minister's immediate right and waited until he spoke. I formed the view that Britain was going to fight. He seemed calm and resolute (some time later Lord Rothermere told me that his calmness and resolution varied according to the fever that wracked his health-sapped body) and I went away impressed with his firmness of purpose.

That July night I wrote to Lord Beaverbrook in the South of France as follows:

Here is my appraisal of the Suez situation.[1]

1. This 'personal' approach was to conceal from prying eyes that I had been talking to the Prime Minister.

All the evidence shows that we are preparing on a big scale to stand up to Nasser. The operation is so big that it will take some time to mount, and will play havoc with the programme of economies which was under active preparation.

It has been intended to devote all this week to Defence Committee meetings for the purpose of driving the economies through, but that has all gone by the board.

One of the biggest problems will, of course, be the hiring of merchant ships, as our troop-ships are scattered over the seven seas.

Cyprus will have to be reinforced, and Malta too.

The French are enthusiastic in their support, and have promised us military aid. But, of course, no one knows just how much the French have got to offer, and we must, on that account, make preparations on such a scale as to secure success if we have to go it alone.

The Americans are not being at all helpful. They pay their canal dues in Cairo, unlike the French and the British, who pay them in Paris and in London, and are not prepared to upset these arrangements.

If Nasser should demand cash down for passage through the Canal, it would not necessarily lead to an 'incident'. To drive a ship through the Canal, escorted by a gun-boat, is out of the question. The Egyptian shore batteries would open fire on the merchant shipping, and by sinking our ships would, of course, block the Canal for a considerable time.

If, therefore, Nasser forces cash payments, ships at the entrance of the Canal or in the Canal would at first pay their dues in order to get clearance, for it would be ridiculous to have ships lying idle around the Canal area. Thereafter all ships would be re-routed to avoid the Canal, and this of course would bring economic consequences to Egypt of an acute nature.

I assume at this point we would go in and re-open the Canal by occupying the whole of the area and not just taking over the old Army base once more. There is, of course, nothing left in the base, and it is to be hoped that the Egyptians will seize it, as this would be an illegal act under the terms of our departure, and would give us a legal right to take military action.

I gather that the one direction in which the Americans have been most helpful is in relation to the Israelis. I do not believe that the Israelis will take advantage of the situation in all the circumstances.

Some destroyers in British waters are to be handed over to Egypt – they have already been paid for and we have no right to detain them. But if and when they sail, they will carry no ammunition. We have satisfied ourselves that there is no source of supply anywhere in the world for this type of ammunition. It would be an easy matter for the British Navy to sink them. It could be, of course, that there will be all sorts of delays in getting them into a seaworthy condition to make the journey to Alexandria.

Less than a week after this letter, I was back in Downing Street with the rest of the editors – so many of them, when the London editors of the leading provincial dailies were included, that there was no room for us all at the Cabinet table. I sat in an arm-chair buried away behind the Prime Minister, and reflected, I fear, that the Big Brass present might not frighten the Egyptians but they put the fear of God into me!

The whole affair seemed an awful muddle. The purpose of the conference was to ask newspapers not to be too specific about Britain's military preparations, not to reveal, for example, that troops were being despatched to Malta and to Cyprus. The editors grumbled so much about the vagueness of this proposal that Sir Walter Monckton, Minister of Defence, offered to set up a Committee to which messages could be submitted.

'Hey, that's censorship in peace-time,' I expostulated, speaking for the first time. And so it went on. Nothing was decided, and I came away very depressed. Eden's grip on the conference was as unsure and uncertain as his private talk with me had been convincing.

But the big news when it broke was not for me. I had handled my last story. A couple of weeks later, while at Lord Beaverbrook's villa at Cap D'Ail for a week-end, I had a heart attack. I was flown back to London and to hospital. While I was there Britain and France invaded Egypt – and I was not allowed to see a single newspaper, or talk to a single newspaperman.

For a year or two thereafter I had time to contemplate. I was invited to set down my story – and this is it – from one angle anyway.

The end of one story; the beginning of a new one. Thirty pounds lighter in weight, better in health than I have been since I was twenty-nine, with a grown-up family standing on its own feet, I came increasingly to the view that my contribution to national journalism had been made. The role of Elder Statesman ill fitted my direct-action disposition and the moment to quit Fleet Street seemed to have arrived.

With no plans in mind, I made my farewell. It was grievous saying farewell to the Beaver, but I felt that it had to be, and that our friendship would in consequence develop rather than wither.

Then the unexpected happened, and I entered the new world of television.

Will television be to the next generation what newspapers were to mine – the means of projecting the news and the personalities of the day in terms that the ordinary folk of places like Derby and Rhyl can understand and enjoy? It seems to me that they are similar mediums, differing only in that television animates the scene while the printed word 'freezes' it. Both have the same possibilities for educating, encouraging and entertaining – and both the same possibilities for falsification, intrusion and lack of proportion.

One medium of communication is new; the other is old. Both have an immense future. It will be fun to have straddled the twin giants in one lifetime, and, I hope, to have made a good effort on behalf of both.

Index

References to Lord Beaverbrook and the *Daily Express* are so frequent that they are not listed.